Introducing Microsoft® Windows Vista™

William R. Stanek

FEB 0 8 2007   351664

PUBLISHED BY
Microsoft Press
A Division of Microsoft Corporation
One Microsoft Way
Redmond, Washington 98052-6399

ISBN-13: 978-0-7356-2284-5
ISBN-10: 0-7356-2284-1
Library of Congress Control Number 2006924470

Printed and bound in the United States of America.

3 4 5 6 7 8 9   QWE   1 0 9 8 7 6

Distributed in Canada by H.B. Fenn and Company Ltd.

A CIP catalogue record for this book is available from the British Library.

Microsoft Press books are available through booksellers and distributors worldwide. For further information about international editions, contact your local Microsoft Corporation office or contact Microsoft Press International directly at fax (425) 936-7329. Visit our Web site at www.microsoft.com/mspress. Send comments to mspinput@microsoft.com.

Acquisitions Editor: Martin DelRe
Project Editor: Karen Szall
Technical Editor: L. J. Zacker
Copy Editor: Jennifer Harris
Indexer: Patricia Masserman

Body Part No. X12-41775

Contents at a Glance

Table of Contents

Part I   Getting to Know Windows Vista

Part II   Essential Features in Windows Vista

What do you think of this book? We want to hear from you!	Microsoft is interested in hearing your feedback about this publication so we can continually improve our books and learning resources for you. To participate in a brief online survey, please visit: *www.microsoft.com/learning/booksurvey/*

Acknowledgments

Introducing Microsoft Windows Vista provides a first look at the latest desktop version of Microsoft Windows. Writing this book based on the beta product was challenging because there wasn't any documentation for anything. I had to dig deep into the operating system to understand how everything works and then document what I found in this book. I hope you find the resulting book a good start for learning about the new features of Windows Vista.

I'd like to thank everyone from Microsoft who contributed to this project. Karen Szall, as the project editor for Microsoft, did a great job and I couldn't have completed this project without her help. I'd also like to thank Martin DelRe, Heather Stafford, and Sandra Haynes, who provided help at critical points of the project. Jennifer Harris and Linda Zacker provided content and technical review of the project. Thank you, Jennifer and Linda, for all your hard work.

Throughout this book, you'll find a new sidebar feature called "From the experts." This sidebar is meant to provide additional details and pointers about topics of discussion, and you'll find contributions from myself and various other Microsoft experts, including: Jerry Honeycutt, Tony Northrup, and Mitch Tulloch. Thank you Jerry, Tony, and Mitch for your contributions to the experts' sidebars. I need more good friends like you guys.

Introduction

Introducing Microsoft Windows Vista presents Microsoft Windows Vista, the latest version of the Windows operating system, and provides a comprehensive overview of the new Windows features for power users, administrators, and developers. This book has been written using the Windows Vista Beta to provide an early introduction to this powerful operating system.

Writing a book to a beta product has many benefits but also some drawbacks. Microsoft is able to publish the first edition of this book prior to the official release date of Windows Vista, which allows you to get advance information about the operating system. This will not only help you get a head start on learning the new Windows features, but it should also help you install, work with, and manage Windows Vista in the future.

Because I am writing this book based on a beta product, features are subject to change, especially with regard to the user interface and screens. For example, I might discuss the Network Center, Network List, and Network Map tools as separate features, while in the final product these features might be combined into a single tool with multiple views named Network Center, Network List, and Network Map. Or I might show a screen that has a Make Fonts Large Or Smaller option, and in the final product this option might be renamed Adjust Font Size.

Who Is This Book For?

Introducing Microsoft Windows Vista discusses both the home and business versions of Windows Vista, and where possible, points out the differences between the two versions. The primary focus of this book is on productivity and business, including the related reliability, security, usability, and mobility features. The book doesn't go into depth on home entertainment features, such as Media Center, Windows Media Player, Windows Movie Maker, or Windows Photo Gallery. This book is designed for

- Current users of Windows operating systems.
- Current administrators of Windows operating systems.
- Current developers of Windows operating systems.

The focus of the book is on new features. As a result, I discuss previously implemented Windows features primarily with regard to how they relate to new features. After reading this book, you should be ready to get started with Windows Vista. For detailed information about Windows Vista administration, I recommend *Microsoft Windows Vista Administrator's Pocket Consultant* (Microsoft Press, 2006).

How Is This Book Organized?

Introducing Microsoft Windows Vista is designed to help you learn about and get started with Windows Vista by providing an early introduction. The book consists of 15 chapters, divided into four parts. Each part provides an opening paragraph or two about the chapters contained in that part.

Part 1, "Getting to Know Windows Vista," provides an overview of Windows Vista. Chapter 1, "Introducing Windows Vista," presents the features you'll need to know about to get started using Windows Vista and to navigate the interface. The chapter also provides an overview of how Windows Vista works from startup to power down.

Part 2, "Essential Features in Windows Vista," discusses the fundamental features of Windows Vista. Chapter 2, "Working with Windows Vista," introduces some of the new menu and interface features. The chapter starts with a look at taskbar changes and enhancements, including live thumbnails, Windows Flip, and Windows Flip 3D. Then discusses changes to the Start menu, All Programs menu, and Control Panel. Chapter 3, "Managing Information," examines features you can use to manage information stored on a computer. You'll learn about new ways of using Windows Explorer to work with files and folders; how to add keywords to files and tags to pictures; and how to use virtual folders to save search results. You'll also learn about new desktop features, such as the Windows Sidebar. Chapter 4, "Using Internet Explorer 7," explores Internet Explorer 7, the newest version of Internet Explorer. You'll learn about improvements for navigation as well as new safety and security features. Chapter 5, "Collaborating, Connecting, and Sharing," looks at the new tools and features you can use for collaborating with others, connecting to networks, and sharing data. Chapter 6, "Managing Programs and Multimedia," discusses new features to help you better manage installed programs, file associations, and AutoPlay options. The chapter also discusses enhanced tools for managing your multimedia, including Windows Media Player for playing digital media including music and videos; Windows Movie Maker for creating movies using pictures, videos, and music; and Windows Photo Gallery for viewing, editing, organizing, and sharing pictures and videos. Chapter 7, "Working with Laptops and Tablet PCs," examines supported features and enhancements for laptops and tablet PCs. Chapter 8, "Improving Accessibility," examines the accessibility enhancements included in Windows Vista. You'll learn about improvements to standard features and the new speech recognition technology.

In Part 3, "Securing Windows Vista," you'll learn about the security features of Windows Vista. Chapter 9, "Protecting User Accounts and Using Parental Controls," discusses new features for protecting user accounts, including parental controls and user account controls. Chapter 10, "Protecting Your Computer," discusses architecture changes in Windows Vista that are designed to provide multiple layers of protection for computers. The chapter introduces the new boot environment and new security features, such as Windows Service Hardening and Network Access Protection. Chapter 11, "Protecting Your Data," introduces data protection and encryption. The chapter discusses trusted platforms, Trusted Platform Modules (TPMs) and BitLocker Drive Encryption. Chapter 12, "Networking Your Computer," examines enhancements for networking and restricting access to Windows Vista systems. Chapter 13,

"Securing Your Network Connection," discusses security tools, including Windows Security Center, Windows Firewall, and Windows Defender.

Part 4, "Supporting and Deploying Windows Vista," details the support and deployment features of Windows Vista. Chapter 14, "Supporting Windows Vista," introduces tools and techniques for supporting Windows Vista. Chapter 15, "Deploying Windows Vista," examines features and techniques for deploying Windows Vista in an enterprise.

Conventions Used in This Book

I've used a variety of elements to help keep the text clear and easy to follow. You'll find code terms and listings in monospace type, but when I tell you to actually type something, the text to be typed appears in **bold**. When I introduce and define a new term, the term appears in *italic*.

Other elements include

- **Note** To provide details on a point that needs emphasis
- **Caution** To warn you when there are potential problems you should look out for
- **Tip** To offer helpful hints or additional information

I truly hope you find that *Introducing Microsoft Windows Vista* provides everything you need to get an early start with Windows Vista. You're welcome to send your thoughts to me at williamstanek@aol.com. Thank you.

Support

This book is written to the Windows Vista Beta and is meant to provide an early introduction. The interface and features discussed are subject to change in the final product. If you have comments, questions, or ideas about this book, please send them to Microsoft Press using either of the following methods:

Postal mail:

Microsoft Press
Attn: Editor, *Introducing Microsoft Windows Vista*
One Microsoft Way
Redmond, WA 98052-6399

E-mail:

mspinput@microsoft.com

Please note that product support isn't offered through the mail addresses above. For support information, visit Microsoft's Web site at *http://www.microsoft.com/support.*

Part I
Getting to Know Windows Vista

Introducing Microsoft Windows Vista introduces Windows Vista and provides a comprehensive overview of the new features in Windows. This book is written using the Windows Vista beta to provide an early introduction to this powerful and versatile operating system. The interface and features discussed throughout this book are subject to change in the final product. Chapter 1, "Introducing Windows Vista," describes the different versions of Windows Vista and their features. This chapter is designed to help you get started with Windows Vista.

Chapter 1
Introducing Windows Vista

Microsoft Windows Vista is the latest workstation version of the Windows operating system and is designed for both home and business users. MSN Encarta describes a *vista* as a scenic or panoramic view, and that's exactly what Windows Vista provides. Not only does Windows Vista have an all-new look, complete with stylish graphical visualizations, easier-to-navigate menus, and enhanced personalization capabilities, but the operating system is also the first version of Windows in which the user experience scales to the hardware capabilities of the computer on which Windows Vista is installed. Although the graphical bells and whistles are excellent, many of the most powerful features in Windows Vista are those that you won't see at first glance, including the many enhancements for reliability, security, usability, and mobility.

In this chapter, we'll look at the issues and features you'll need to know about to start using Windows Vista effectively. The chapter begins with a look at the versions of Windows Vista that are available and then continues with a discussion of getting started using Windows Vista. Next, the chapter discusses using Windows Vista in workgroup and domain configurations, focusing on the differences between these environments and how permissions for user accounts have changed between this and previous versions of Windows. Last, the chapter discusses the important procedure changes for turning off and shutting down computers running Windows Vista.

Note   This book was written using the Windows Vista Beta to provide an early introduction to the operating system. More so than any other area of Windows Vista, the security features discussed in this book are subject to change. Some of the features might not be included in the final product, and some of the features might be changed substantially.

Introducing the Windows Vista Versions

Microsoft provides multiple versions of Windows Vista. There are two versions for home users and two versions for business users as well as an all-encompassing version for users who want all available features. Unlike its predecessors, Windows Vista allows you to upgrade between versions.

 Note   Regardless of which Windows Vista version you are using, the core features and the way you work with the operating system are the same. Because of this consistency, this book points out the differences between Windows Vista versions only where necessary.

Overview of the Windows Vista Versions

The five versions of Microsoft Windows Vista are:

- Windows Vista Home Basic
- Windows Vista Home Premium
- Windows Vista Business
- Windows Vista Enterprise
- Windows Vista Ultimate

The home versions of Windows Vista include entertainment features that aren't found in the business versions. The business versions include management features that aren't found in the home versions.

Windows Vista Ultimate combines the best of all the available features, giving you a complete package for home and business use. When you use Windows Vista Ultimate, you can get additional programs and services as well as tips and tricks documentation from the Windows Download Center by using the Windows Ultimate Extras utility in Control Panel.

Upgrading the Windows Vista Versions

Unlike its predecessors, you can easily upgrade Windows Vista versions by using the Windows Anytime Upgrade utility or a Windows Anytime Upgrade disc. You can:

- Upgrade from Windows Vista Home Basic to Windows Vista Home Premium or Windows Vista Ultimate.
- Upgrade from Windows Vista Home Premium to Windows Vista Ultimate.
- Upgrade from Windows Vista Business to Windows Vista Enterprise or Windows Vista Ultimate.
- Upgrade from Windows Vista Enterprise to Windows Vista Ultimate.

Windows Anytime Upgrade (WindowsAnytimeUpgrade.exe) is stored in the %SystemRoot%\System32 folder. You can start an upgrade by selecting Windows Anytime Upgrade on the Start menu and then following the prompts. When the upgrade is complete, you can search for "**What's New**" in Windows Help And Support to learn about additional features and enhancements that have been installed. You can access Windows Help And Support by clicking Start and then clicking Help And Support.

Getting Started with Windows Vista

From the moment you start Windows Vista, you'll know it's a different kind of operating system from its predecessors. During the installation of Windows Vista (described in the appendix), Setup prompts you to create a local machine account. This account is created as a computer administrator account. When the operating system starts, you can log on using the account and password you specified during setup.

Working with the Welcome Center

By default, the operating system displays the Welcome Center at startup. You can access the Welcome Center console, shown in Figure 1-1, from Control Panel.

Figure 1-1   The Welcome Center

The Welcome Center provides an overview of the system and quick access to perform tasks that help you get started using Windows Vista. To display all the available options, click Show All 12 Items. The available options include the following tasks:

- **Add New Users**   Configure user accounts for each person who will log on locally to the computer. You can manage account settings and parental controls for accounts, as discussed in Chapter 9, "Protecting User Accounts and Using Parental Controls." This option isn't available when you log on to a domain.

- **Personalize Windows**   Control the appearance and sound effects used by Windows Vista. You can manage settings for the display, visual appearance, desktop background, screen saver, sound effects, mouse pointers, and themes.

- **Set Up Devices**   Check for devices that Setup did not install as part of the upgrade or installation. If you elect to set up devices and new hardware is found, you'll be guided through the process of installing the device.

- **Windows Easy Transfer**   Run the Windows Easy Transfer Wizard, which can be used to transfer user accounts, files and folders, program settings, Internet settings (including favorites), and e-mail settings (including contacts and messages) from your old computer. For the transfer, you can use CDs, DVDs, a universal serial bus (USB) flash drive, or external hard drives, as well as network folders and a USB cable that connects to both computers. To transfer settings, the old computer must be running Windows 2000, Windows XP, or Windows Vista.

- **View Your Computer Details**   Display the default view for the Welcome Center, which provides an overview of the system configuration. Use the More Details link to access the System console and view additional information about the computer.

By default, the Welcome Center displays each time you start the computer. If you don't want the Welcome Center to be displayed the next time you start the computer, clear the Run At Startup check box.

Getting Basic System Information

In the Welcome Center, you can click More Details to access the System console and view additional information about the computer, as shown in Figure 1-2.

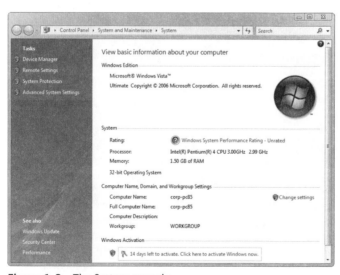

Figure 1-2   The System console

The System console is divided into four basic areas that provide links for performing common tasks and a system overview:

- **Windows Edition** Displays the operating system edition and version.

- **System** Shows the processor, memory, and performance rating of the computer. If the computer has not yet been rated for performance, you can click Performance under See Also to access the Performance Rating And Tools console. In this console, click Rate This Computer to start the performance rating process and then follow the prompts.

- **Computer Name, Domain, And Workgroup Settings** Lists the computer name, description, domain, and workgroup details. If you want to change the computer's name, domain, or workgroup, click Change Settings, and then make changes in the Computer Name Changes dialog box. In the System Properties dialog box, click the Network ID button, and then make the necessary changes.

- **Windows Activation** Shows whether you have activated the operating system and the product key. If Windows Vista isn't activated yet, click the link provided to start the activation process and then follow the prompts.

When you're working in the System console, links in the left pane provide quick access to key settings, including the following:

- Device Manager

- Remote Settings

- System Protection

- Advanced System Settings

If you prefer, you can view the classic-style System Properties dialog box at any time by clicking Change Settings under Computer Name, Domain, And Workgroup Settings.

Activating Windows Vista and Changing Product Keys

Volume-licensed versions of Windows Vista might not require activation or product keys. For retail versions of Windows Vista, however, Windows Activation and product keys are just as important as they are in Microsoft Windows XP. Retail versions of Windows Vista are validated by using Windows Activation and product keys. In the Welcome Center, the Activation Status entry specifies whether you have activated the operating system. If Windows Vista has not been activated, you can activate the operating system by clicking More Details to access the System console and then selecting Click Here To Activate Windows Now under Windows Activation.

Unlike in Windows XP, you can easily change the product key used by the operating system. In the System console, click Change Product Key under Windows Activation. In the Windows Activation window, shown in Figure 1-3, type the product key, and then click Next. As in Setup, you do not need to type the dashes in the product key.

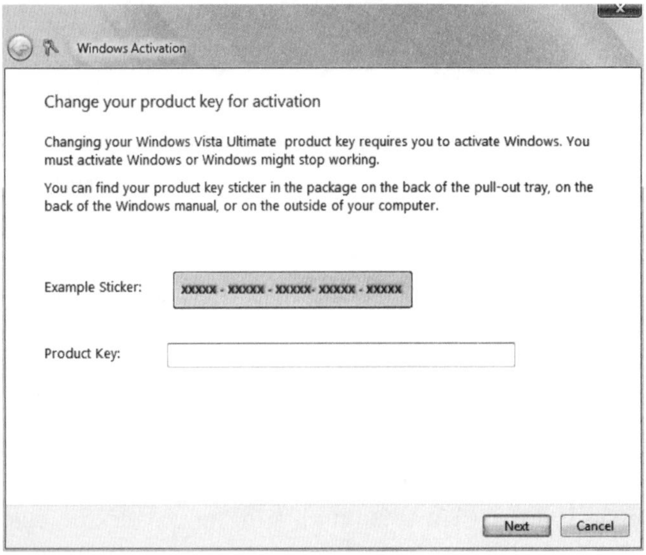

Figure 1-3   Changing the product key

Using Windows Vista in Workgroups and Domains

You can use Windows Vista in workgroup configurations and domain configurations. *Workgroups* are loose associations of computers in which each computer is managed separately. *Domains* are collections of computers that you can manage collectively by means of domain controllers, which are servers running Windows that manage access to the network, to the directory database, and to shared resources. Typically, home users will use Windows Vista in workgroup configurations and businesses will use Windows Vista in domain configurations. Although all versions can be used in workgroup configurations, you cannot use the home versions in domain configurations.

Understanding Log On, User Switching, Locking, and Log Off in Windows Vista

In a workgroup configuration, Windows Vista displays the Log On screen at startup. All standard user and administrator accounts that you've created on the computer are listed on the Log On screen. To log on, you click the account name. If the account is password protected, you must click the account name, type the account password, and then click the arrow button.

In a domain configuration, Windows Vista displays a blank startup screen after initializing the operating system. You must press Ctrl+Alt+Del to display the Log On screen. By default, the last account to log on to the computer is listed in *computer\username* or *domain\username* format. To log on to this account, you type the account password and then click the arrow button. To log on to a different account, click the Switch User button, and then click Log On As

Another User. Type the user name and password, and then click the arrow button. Keep the following in mind:

- If the account is in the default domain, you don't have to specify the domain name.

- If the account is in another domain, you can specify the domain and the account name using the format *domain\username*, such as cpandl\williams.

- If you want to log on to the local machine, type **.\username** where *username* is the name of the local account, such as .\williams.

Both the workgroup and the domain configurations of Windows Vista allow fast user switching. You can easily change passwords, lock a computer, and log off as well.

Switching Users

You can switch users by following these steps:

1. Press Ctrl+Alt+Del, and then click the Switch User button.

    ❑ In a workgroup configuration, the Log On screen is displayed as at startup.

    ❑ In a domain configuration, a screen appears with the message "Press Ctrl+Alt+Del To Log On". To display the Log On screen, you must press Ctrl+Alt+Del again.

2. Once the Log On screen appears, you can log on to another account using a technique similar to logging on at startup.

Note   You can also initiate the switch-user process by clicking Start, clicking the Options button to the right of the Power and Lock buttons, and then clicking Switch User.

Changing Passwords

You can change passwords by following these steps:

1. Press Ctrl+Alt+Del, and then click the Change Password option.

    The account name for the current user is listed on the change password screen. In a domain configuration, the user account name is listed in *domain\username* format. In a workgroup configuration, the local user account name is listed.

Tip   By clicking in the User Name text box, you can change the account name. Specify the domain and the account name using the format *domain\username*, such as cpandl\williams. Type **.\username** where *username* is the name of the local account, such as .\williams.

2. Type the current password for the account in the Old Password text box.

3. Type and confirm the new password for the account in the New Password and the Confirm Password text boxes.

4. Click the arrow button to confirm the change.

Locking and Unlocking a Computer

You can lock and unlock the computer by following these steps:

1. Press Ctrl+Alt+Del, and then click the Lock This Computer option.

2. In a workgroup configuration, a lock screen is displayed with the name of the user who is logged on. Clicking the account name or picture allows you to log on again as that user. If a password is required for the account, you'll need to enter the password before logging on.

3. In a domain configuration, a lock screen is displayed with the name of the user who is logged on. If you want to log on again as the user, you must press Ctrl+Alt+Del and then type the user's password.

4. You can click the Switch User button to log on as a different user.

> **Note**   You can also lock the computer by clicking Start and then clicking the Lock button. The Lock button is a blue button with a picture of a lock on it.

Logging Off a Computer

You can log off by pressing Ctrl+Alt+Del and then clicking the Log Off option. If there is a problem logging off, the Log Off dialog box appears. This dialog box shows the programs currently running on the computer.

If one of the currently running programs is causing a problem with logoff, an explanation of the problem is displayed below the program name. You can then cancel the logoff or continue:

■ If you cancel the logoff, you can resolve the issue with the problem program—for example, by saving your work and exiting the program.

■ If you continue logging off by clicking Log Off Now, Windows Vista will force the program causing problems to close, and you might lose work as a result.

> **Note**   You can also log off by clicking Start, clicking the Options button to the right of the Power and Lock buttons, and then clicking Log Off.

Understanding Windows Vista User Accounts and Windows Security Permissions

Windows Vista has two primary types of local user accounts:

- **Standard user** Standard user accounts can use most software and can change system settings that do not affect other users or the security of the computer.

- **Administrator** Administrator accounts have complete access to the computer and can make any desired changes.

In Windows Vista, all applications run using either standard user or administrator permissions. As discussed in Chapter 9 under "Introducing User Account Control," this change has far-reaching effects on the operating system as well as how you work with user accounts and manage applications. Because of User Account Control, whether a user logs on as an administrator or a standard user, the user sees a User Account Control dialog box containing a warning prompt stating, "Windows needs your permission to continue." This dialog box is shown in Figure 1-4.

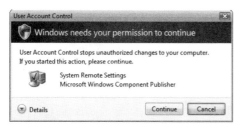

Figure 1-4   The User Account Control dialog box

The way the prompt works depends on whether the user is logged on with an administrator account or a standard user account. Users with administrator permissions are asked for confirmation. The user can click Allow to allow the task to be performed or Cancel to stop the task from being performed. Clicking Details shows the full path to the program being executed.

Users with standard accounts are asked to provide a password for an administrator account. In a workgroup configuration, each local computer administrator account is listed by name. To allow the task to be performed, you must click an account, type the account's password, and then click Submit.

In a domain configuration, administrator accounts for users who have logged on to the computer are listed. These accounts can be both domain administrator accounts and local computer administrator accounts. You also have the option of choosing a different account. To run the task using a different user's permissions, click Use Another Account, type the user account, and then type the account's password. If the account is in the default domain, you don't have to specify the domain name. If the account is in another domain, you can specify the domain and the account name using the format *domain\username*, such as cpandl\williams.

> **From the experts**
> ### Security must be easy to be effective
>
> User Account Control is as much about usability as it is about security. Unlike earlier versions of Windows, any user account can be used to run administrator programs. You don't need to know which programs require administrator permissions beforehand; you simply run the program and respond as appropriate if you are prompted. This makes it much easier to use a standard user account as your everyday user account—and it is why Microsoft recommends this as a best practice as well.
>
> **Tony Northrup**
> *Author, MCSE, and MVP–For more information, see http://www.northrup.org.*

Turning Off and Shutting Down Computers Running Windows Vista

When it comes to turning off and shutting down, Windows Vista isn't like earlier versions of Windows. In Windows Vista, turning off a computer and shutting down a computer are completely different operations. Turning off a computer doesn't power it down; only shutting down the computer powers it down completely.

Turning Off Computers: What's Changed

By default, when you turn off a computer running Windows Vista, the computer enters the sleep state. When entering the sleep state, the operating system:

- Automatically saves all work.
- Turns off the display.
- Puts the computer in sleep mode.

In sleep mode, the computer's fan stops, the computer's hard disks stop, and the computer enters a low-power consumption mode in which the state of the computer is maintained in the computer's memory. The next time you turn on the computer, the computer's state will be exactly as it was when you turned off the computer.

> **Note**   Because the operating system saves your work, you don't need to save documents and exit programs before turning off the computer. Because the computer is in a low-power consumption state, the computer uses very little energy. For mobile computers, the sleep state will use very little battery power. If, while in the sleep state, the mobile computer's battery runs low on power, the state of the computer is saved to the hard disk and then the computer is shut down completely—this state is similar to the hibernate state used in Windows XP.

You can turn off a computer and make it enter the sleep state by following these steps:

1. Click the Start button.

2. Click the Power button.

To wake the computer from the sleep state, you can do either of the following:

- Press the power button on the computer's case.

- Press a key on the computer's keyboard.

You can turn off and turn on mobile computers by closing or opening their lid. When you close the lid, the laptop enters the sleep state. When you open the lid, the laptop wakes up from the sleep state.

Using the Power Button: What's Changed

Regardless of whether you are using a desktop computer or a mobile computer, the way the Power button works depends on the system hardware, the system state, and the system configuration:

- If the computer hardware doesn't support the sleep state, the computer can't use the sleep state, and turning off the computer powers it down completely.

- If the computer has updates installed that require a restart or you've installed programs that require a restart, the computer can't use the sleep state, and turning off the computer powers it down completely.

- If you or an administrator has reconfigured the power options on the computer and set the Power button to the Shut Down action, the computer can't use the sleep state, and turning off the computer powers it down completely. See Chapter 7, "Working with Laptops and Tablet PCs," for more details on configuring power options.

To help differentiate between turning off and shutting down a computer, Windows Vista displays two different views for the Power button:

- An amber Power button, depicting a shield with a line through the top of it, indicates that the computer will turn off and enter the low-power sleep state.

- A red Power button, depicting a shield with a line through the middle of it, indicates that the computer will shut down and completely power off.

Because the computer is still drawing power in the sleep state, you should never install hardware inside the computer or connect devices to the computer when it is in the sleep state. The only exception is for external devices that use USB or IEEE 1394 (FireWire) ports. You can connect USB and FireWire devices without shutting down the computer.

Shutting Down and Restarting Computers: What's Changed

As mentioned earlier, turning off a computer running Windows Vista puts the computer in a low-power sleep state instead of completely powering down the computer. To completely power down the computer, you must shut it down. Shutting down the computer ensures that the power to the computer is turned off.

Because of possible confusion regarding the sleep state and the power-down state, be sure to unplug a computer running Windows Vista before installing or connecting devices. To shut down a computer running Windows Vista, use one of the following techniques:

- Click Start, click the Options button to the right of the Power and Lock buttons, and then click Shut Down.

- Press Ctrl+Alt+Del. The red (Shut Down) Power button should be displayed in the lower-right corner of the window. Click the Power button.

Caution   Do not install hardware inside a computer running Windows Vista or connect non-USB/non-FireWire devices without first ensuring that the computer is completely powered down. If the computer's Power button is red and shows a shield with a line through the middle of it, the Power button shuts the computer off and completely powers it down. If the computer's Power button is amber and shows a shield with a line through the top of it, the Power button turns off the computer and puts it in the low-power sleep state.

To shut down and then restart a computer running Windows Visa, you can use either of the following techniques:

- Click Start, click the Options button to the right of the Power and Lock buttons, and then click Restart.

- Press Ctrl+Alt+Del. Click the Options button to the right of the Power button, and then click Restart.

A restart is sometimes required to complete the installation of programs and automatic updates. A restart might also be required to finalize a system configuration change.

Part II
Essential Features in Windows Vista

Part 2 of this book discusses the fundamental features of Microsoft Windows Vista. Chapter 2, "Working with Windows Vista," introduces some of the new menu and interface features. The chapter starts with a look at taskbar changes and enhancements, including live thumbnails, Windows Flip, and Windows Flip 3D. The chapter then discusses changes to the Start menu, All Programs menu, and Control Panel. Chapter 3, "Managing Information," examines features you can use to manage information stored on a computer. You'll learn about new ways of using Windows Explorer to work with files and folders; how to add keywords to files and tags to pictures; and how to use virtual folders to save search results. You'll also learn about new desktop features, such as the Windows Sidebar.

Chapter 4, "Using Internet Explorer 7," explores Internet Explorer 7, the newest version of Internet Explorer. You'll learn about improvements for navigation as well as new safety and security features. Chapter 5, "Collaborating, Connecting, and Sharing," looks at the new tools and features you can use for collaborating with others, connecting to networks, and sharing data. Chapter 6, "Managing Programs and Multimedia," discusses new features to help you better manage installed programs, file associations, and AutoPlay options. The chapter also discusses enhanced tools for managing your multimedia. Chapter 7, "Working with Laptops and Tablet PCs," examines supported features and enhancements for laptops and tablet PCs. Chapter 8, "Improving Accessibility," examines the accessibility enhancements included in Windows Vista. You'll learn about improvements to standard features and the new speech recognition technology.

Chapter 2
Working with Windows Vista

As you learned in Chapter 1, "Introducing Windows Vista," Microsoft Windows Vista is different from earlier versions of Windows, especially when it comes to user accounts and shutdown procedures. Prior to performing tasks that require administrator privileges, users are prompted for a password if they are using a standard user account or confirmation if they are using a computer administrator account. When you turn off a computer running Windows Vista, the computer typically enters a sleep state instead of completely powering down. You must, in fact, shut down the computer to power down completely. Beyond these important differences, you'll find many other interface differences between Windows Vista and earlier versions of Windows, and examining these differences so that you can effectively work with Windows Vista is the subject of this chapter.

The primary means of getting around in Windows Vista are the taskbar and the menu system. The entryway to the menu system is the Start button on the taskbar. You use the Start button to display the Start menu, which in turn allows you to run programs, open folders, get help, and find the items you want to work with. From the Start menu, you can access the All Programs menu, which provides access to all the programs and tools on the computer and to Control Panel, which provides access to utilities for working with system settings.

With all the new taskbar and menu features, you might want to finally stop using Classic View for Control Panel, Classic Start menu, and double-click to open an item. Why? The answer is twofold. First, it's so much easier to get around in Windows Vista using the standard configuration, and going back to the classic configuration means losing some of the most powerful features in Windows Vista. Second, it's so much more intuitive to use single-clicking to open items because Windows Vista makes extensive use of links in its consoles and dialog boxes, and these links open items with single clicks.

> **Note** This book was written using the Windows Vista Beta to provide an early introduction to the operating system. More so than any other area of Windows Vista, the security features discussed in this book are subject to change. Some of the features might not be included in the final product, and some of the features might be changed substantially.

Getting Around in the Windows Vista Taskbar

In Windows Vista, by default, the taskbar is locked so that it is always displayed, as shown in Figure 2-1. The Start button, shown on the far left, is one of the key features on the taskbar. Quick Launch items are displayed to the right of the Start button, followed by buttons for running programs, and then the notification area. Each of these areas has feature enhancements, which are discussed in the sections that follow.

Figure 2-1   The taskbar in Windows Vista

Working with the Quick Launch Toolbar

By default, the Quick Launch toolbar displays a quick access button for the desktop. A new feature in Windows Vista is the ability to add any program directly to the Quick Launch toolbar from the Start menu. To do this, click the Start button, navigate to the program on the Start menu that you want to be able to access quickly, and then right-click the program name. Last, select Add To Quick Launch to add the program to the Quick Launch toolbar.

The Quick Launch toolbar is displayed by default. If the Quick Launch toolbar isn't displayed and you want to display it, right-click the Start button, and then select Properties. In the Taskbar And Start Menu Properties dialog box, click the Taskbar tab, and then select the Show Quick Launch check box.

Using Taskbar Thumbnails, Windows Flip, and Windows Flip 3D

In earlier versions of Windows, the taskbar displayed a button for each running program. Clicking the button allowed you to display the program window in front of all other windows. Windows XP included an enhancement that grouped similar taskbar buttons. For example, if you opened eight folders in Windows Explorer, these items would be grouped together under one taskbar button. Clicking the taskbar button would then display a dialog box with an entry for each folder window, allowing you to select which folder window to display.

Windows Vista significantly enhances the taskbar by modifying taskbar grouping and also providing the following taskbar improvements:

- Live taskbar thumbnails
- Windows Flip
- Windows Flip 3D

Using Live Taskbar Thumbnails

When you move the mouse pointer over a taskbar button, Windows Vista displays a live thumbnail of the window, showing the content of that window. The thumbnail is displayed regardless of whether the window is minimized and regardless of the type of content. If the content in the window is being updated, such as with a running process or a video, the thumbnail continuously updates to reflect the live state of the window. For grouped taskbar buttons, Windows displays a thumbnail of the most recently opened window and makes the thumbnail appear to include a group of windows.

Using Windows Flip

When you press Alt+Tab, Windows Vista displays a flip view containing live thumbnails of all open windows, as shown in Figure 2-2. Holding down the Alt key keeps the flip view open. Pressing Tab while holding down the Alt key allows you to cycle through the windows. Because the thumbnails are live views, the thumbnails continuously update to reflect their current state regardless of the type of content. When you release the Alt key, the currently selected window is brought to the front. You can also select a window and bring it to the front by clicking the thumbnail.

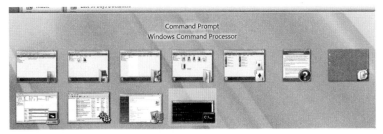

Figure 2-2   Working with Windows Flip view

Using Windows Flip 3D

When you press the Windows logo key and Tab, Windows Vista displays a 3D flip view. As Figure 2-3 shows, the Flip 3D view provides a skewed 3D view of all open windows. Holding down the Windows logo key keeps the Flip 3D view open. Pressing the Tab key while holding down the Windows logo key allows you to cycle through the windows. Because the 3D window views are live, the windows continuously update to reflect their current state regardless of the type of content. When you release the Windows logo key, the currently selected window is brought to the front. You can also select a window and bring it to the front by clicking the 3D window view.

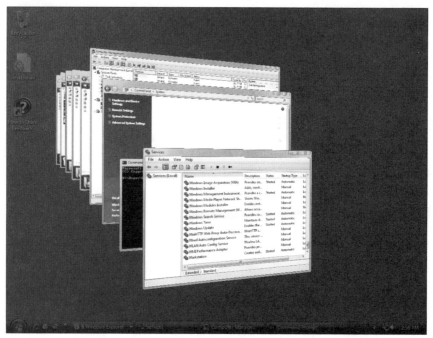

Figure 2-3   Working with Windows Flip 3D view

Working with the Notification Area

The notification area is on the far right on the taskbar. By default, the notification area is divided into two areas:

- An area for standard notification icons, such as those used by programs you've installed

- An area for system notification icons, such as those for the clock, volume, network, and power

Unlike earlier versions of Windows, notification area configuration in Windows Vista is controlled on a separate tab in the Taskbar And Start Menu Properties dialog box. To modify the default settings, right-click the Start button, and then select Properties. In the Taskbar And Start Menu Properties dialog box, click the Notification Area tab. You can then manage how notification icons are used.

You can display the date and time by clicking the clock in the notification area. As Figure 2-4 shows, the system clock is significantly different from earlier versions of Windows. You can use the date and time to view the current month's calendar and browse a month-to-month calendar. Time can be shown with a traditional clock or a digital clock, and if you click the Date And Time Settings link, you can add up to two additional clocks for other time zones.

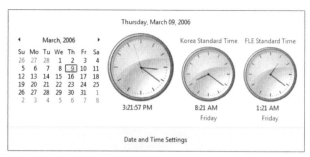

Figure 2-4 The system clock

From the experts

New ways to change the system time

Getting multiple clocks to display different time zones simultaneously is definitely pretty cool, and definitely something a lot of people have asked me about. If you use the time display as a cheap calendar—like I often do—you'll be happy to know that Windows Vista includes a full-blown calendaring program called Windows Calendar, which you can start by clicking Start, pointing to All Programs, and clicking Windows Calendar. Changing the system time is more involved than it used to be, however, and you still need to have administrator privileges.

To change the time, you must click the clock in the notification area on the taskbar and then click the Date And Time Settings link. In the Date And Time Properties dialog box, click the Change Date And Time button to change the date and time, or click Change Time Zone to change the time zone. After you change the date and time or the time zone and click OK twice, the time is updated to reflect your changes.

By default, Windows Vista automatically synchronizes system time with an Internet time server once a week. The goal of synchronization is to ensure that system time is as accurate as possible. By default, the time server used for synchronization is time.windows.com. Although other time servers can be selected, businesses with networks might prefer to have computers synchronize with internal time servers. For more information about configuring time and using Internet time servers, refer to *Microsoft Windows Vista Administrator's Pocket Consultant* (Microsoft Press, 2006).

William Stanek
Author, MVP, and series editor for the Microsoft Press Administrator's Pocket Consultants

Navigating the Start Menu: What's Changed

Clicking the Start button on the taskbar displays the Start menu. You can also display the Start menu by pressing the Windows logo key. As with Windows XP, the Start menu in Windows Vista has two views:

- The Start menu (or Simple Start menu, as it is sometimes referred to) is the default view which provides easy access to programs, folders, and search.

- The Classic Start menu is an alternative view which provides the look and functionality of the Start menu in Windows 2000 and earlier versions of Windows.

The Start menu, shown in Figure 2-5, has three key areas:

- **Programs list**   Displays recently used programs and programs that have been pinned to the Start menu. By default, Internet Explorer and Windows Mail (previously called Microsoft Outlook Express) are pinned to the Start menu, and up to eight recent programs are displayed as well.

- **Search box**   Allows you to search your entire computer for files, folders, or programs. To use the Search box, open the Start menu, type your search text, and then press Enter. The Clear button appears when you type your search text. Click the Clear button to clear the search results and return to the normal view.

- **Right pane**   Provides access to commonly used folders and features. The right pane also provides the Power button (puts the computer in sleep mode or shuts it down, depending on the system configuration), the Lock button (locks the computer), and the Options button (displays the following options: Switch User, Log Off, Lock, Shut Down, and Restart).

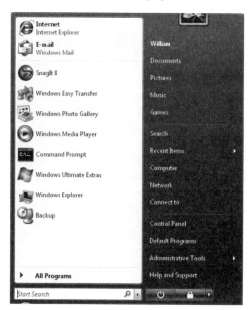

Figure 2-5   The Start menu

Managing Programs List on the Start Menu

The left pane on the Start menu displays recently used programs and programs that have been pinned to the Start menu. By default, Internet Explorer and Windows Mail (previously called Outlook Express) are pinned to the Start menu, and up to eight recent programs are displayed as well.

When you are working with the standard Start menu, you can modify the programs list in several ways. To modify the default settings, right-click the Start button, and then select Properties. In the Taskbar And Start Menu Properties dialog box, the Start Menu tab is selected by default. Click Customize, and then set the Number Of Recent Programs To Display option as appropriate. By configuring the Show On Start Menu options, you can stop displaying links for the Web browser and mail program or configure a different browser and mail program to which you want to link.

Tip   If you want to provide quick access to programs, you can pin those programs to the Start menu. To do this, click the Start button, navigate to the program you want to be able to quickly access, and then right-click the program name. Select Pin To Start Menu to add the program to the Start Menu.

Using the Right Pane on the Start Menu

The right pane on the Start menu provides access to commonly used folders and features. The right pane also provides the Power button (puts the computer in sleep mode or shuts it down, depending on the system configuration), the Lock button (locks the computer), and the Options button (displays the following options: Switch User, Log Off, Lock, Restart, Sleep, and Shut Down).

Important but subtle interface changes are reflected in the right pane of the Start menu. By default, Windows XP and Windows Vista store user documents in different ways:

- In Windows XP, user documents are stored by default in personal folders under %SystemDrive%\Documents and Settings\%UserName%. A user's personal folder contains a My Documents folder, which in turn contains other folders, such as My Pictures and My Music. Windows XP also has folders named My Computer and My Recent Documents.

- In Windows Vista, user documents are stored by default in personal folders under %SystemDrive%\Users\%UserName%. A user's personal folder contains separate Contacts, Desktop, Documents, Pictures, Links, Downloads, and Favorites folders. Windows Vista also has folders named Computer and Recent Documents.

Because of the different way that Windows Vista stores user documents, the My, My, My is gone, gone, gone from the interface, which might be just as well. C:\Users\William\Documents is much easier to use and reference than C:\Documents and Settings\William\My Documents. That said, however, Windows XP and Windows Vista both track the location of the currently logged on user's profile folder by using the %UserProfile% environment variable.

From the experts
Using the command line

The Windows Vista changes to where documents, pictures, and user profiles are located also make it easier to navigate the file system from the command line. For example, when you open a command prompt in Windows XP, your current directory is your user profile directory %UserProfile%, which is C:\Documents and Settings\Mitch Tulloch on my computer. If I want to change my current directory to where my pictures are located, I have to type the following:

```
cd "My Documents\My Pictures"
```

Note the need to enclose the path in quotes—these are needed because of the spaces present. In Vista however, I need to type only this:

```
cd Pictures
```

Less typing means more productivity. In fact, I might need to type only **cd p** and press TAB a few times until **cd Pictures** appears, and then press Enter. You can do the same for the Windows XP example, but you'd have to do it in two steps. That is, type **cd m** (TAB, TAB, TAB... and press Enter) followed by **cd m** (TAB... and press Enter). The bottom line, though, is that the fewer times you need to enclose paths in quotes, the easier it becomes to navigate from the command line. Now if only they had changed the Program Files directory into just Programs!

Mitch Tulloch
Author and MVP—For more information, see http://www.mtit.com.

Within the newly reorganized structure of personal folders, a user's document and data folders are stored as top-level folders within a personal folder. Thus rather than the Documents folder containing a number of subfolders for pictures, music, and so on, the Documents folder is meant to contain only documents. Reorganizing the structure of personal folders should make it easier to manage and back up a user's personal data.

Other important changes are reflected in the right pane as well. To understand these changes, let's review the option buttons provided in the right pane. From top to bottom, the option buttons are as follows:

- **Current user**   The name of the currently logged on user. Clicking this option opens the user's personal folder in Windows Explorer.

- **Documents**   Opens the %UserProfile%\Documents folder in Windows Explorer.

- **Pictures**   Opens the %UserProfile%\Pictures folder in Windows Explorer.

- **Music**   Opens the %UserProfile%\Music folder in Windows Explorer.

- **Games**   Opens the %ProgramFiles\Microsoft Games folder in Windows Explorer. The Games item is not listed in the Start menu for business editions of Windows Vista.

> **Tip**   In Windows Vista Home Premium, games available include Chess Titans, Hearts, Minesweeper, Solitaire, FreeCell, Mahjong Titans, Purble Place, and Spider Solitaire. Windows Vista Home Basic has all the games except Chess Titans and Mahjong Titans. Saved data for games is stored in the %UserProfile%\Saved Games folder. Click the Options menu to configure the Set Up Game Updates And Options dialog box options to keep games up to date automatically, clear history details on the most recently played games, and unhide games. Group Policy can be used to control the availability of the Games option.

- **Search**   Opens a local computer search in Windows Explorer. Use the Search In list to select or specify an alternative search location.

- **Recent Items**   A menu view that lists recently opened files.

- **Computer**   Opens a window where you can access hard disk drives and devices with removable storage.

> **Tip**   The Computer window is the fastest way to open Windows Explorer and access a computer's disks. In the Computer window, double-click a disk to browse its contents. By default, the Search box in Windows Explorer performs localized searches of the currently open folder and its subfolders.

- **Network**   Opens a window where you can access the computers and devices on your network. Also provides quick access to Network Center and the Connect To A Network wizard.

- **Connect To**   Displays the Connect To A Network dialog box for connecting to wireless networks.

- **Control Panel**   Opens Control Panel, which provides access to system configuration and management tools.

- **Default Programs**   Displays the Default Programs window, which lets you choose the programs that Windows Vista uses by default for documents, pictures, and more. You can also associate file types with programs and configure AutoPlay settings.

- **Help And Support**   Displays the Windows Help And Support console, which you can use to browse or search help topics.

Several additional options can be added to the right pane, including:

- **Administrative Tools**   Clicking this option displays a list of system administration tools. To display the Administrative Tools option on the Start menu, right-click the Start button, and then select Properties. In the Taskbar And Start Menu Properties dialog box, click the Customize button on the Start Menu tab. In the Customize Start Menu dialog box, scroll to the end of the available options. For System Administration Tools, select Display On The All Programs Menu And The Start Menu.

■ **Printers**   Opens a Printers window, which lists and provides access to currently configured printers.

■ **Run**   Displays the Run dialog box, which can be used to run commands. To display the Run option, right-click the Start button, and then select Properties. In the Taskbar And Start Menu Properties dialog box, click the Customize button on the Start Menu tab. In the Customize Start Menu dialog box, scroll down and then select the Run Command check box.

> **Note**   Because the Search box can be used to open and run commands, you might not need to use the Run option. For example, to open a Microsoft Management Console, you can click the Start button, type **MMC**, and then press Enter. You don't need to click in the Search box before you begin typing. Pressing Enter opens the first item in the results list. If for some reason MMC isn't the first item, you would need to click MMC in the results list rather than pressing Enter.

Using the Search Box on the Start Menu

The Search box on the Start menu allows you to search your entire computer for files, folders, or programs. To use the Search box, open the Start menu, type your search text. Search results are displayed in the left pane of the Start menu. Clicking an item in the results list opens that item. To clear the search results and return to normal view, click the Clear button to the right of the Search box or press the Esc key.

> **Note**   Because the Search box is the only text entry field on the Start menu, you don't need to click in the Search box before you begin typing. Just type your search text.

Computer searches are performed by Windows Search Service. Windows Search Service searches the entire computer using the search text you've specified. The search proceeds on several levels. Windows Search Service:

■ Matches the search text to words that appear in the title of any program, file, or folder and then returns any matches found.

■ Matches the properties of programs, files, and folders as well as the contents of text-based documents.

■ Looks in the Favorites and History folders for matches.

Because Windows Search Service indexes content and caches properties as part of its normal processes, results typically are returned quickly. You can configure the types of items searched in the Start Menu Properties dialog box.

Tip   Windows Search Service is the next generation of the Indexing Service included in earlier versions of Windows. By default, the service indexes the documents contained in the %SystemDrive%\Users folders. The Indexing And Search Options utility in Control Panel can be used to view indexing status and to configure indexing options. By default, index data is stored in the %SystemRoot%\ProgramData\Microsoft\USearch folder.

Windows Vista can perform several other types of searches as well:

- **Local Folder Search**   When you open a folder, you'll find a Search text box in the upper-right corner of the Windows Explorer window. By default, typing search text in this text box and pressing Enter performs localized searches of the currently open folder and its subfolders. Unlike the Search box on the Start menu, you must click in this Search text box prior to entering your search text. You can use the Search In list to specify alternative search locations.

- **Internet Search**   Click the Options button to the right of the Search text box, and then select the Search The Internet option. Search The Internet uses the computer's default search provider to search the Internet using the search text you've provided. The default search provider is MSN Search. You can set the default search provider using the Internet Options utility in Control Panel.

Using the All Programs Menu: What's Changed

As with earlier versions of Windows, when you want to work with programs installed on a computer running Windows Vista, you'll use the All Programs menu. Like many aspects of Windows Vista, the All Programs menu has changed as well. When you click the Start button and then point to All Programs, you'll see a list of programs installed on the computer, followed by a list of folders.

Depending on the system configuration, the programs you'll see include:

- **Contacts**   Allows you to manage personal and professional contacts.

- **Media Center**   Allows you to manage home entertainment options for pictures, videos, movies, TV, and music.

- **Program Defaults**   Allows you to choose default programs for certain activities.

- **Windows Calendar**   Allows you to manage appointments and tasks by using a calendar. You can publish your calendar to the Internet or to an organization's intranet, and you can subscribe to other people's calendars as well.

- **Windows Collaboration**   Allows you to set up or join a Windows Collaboration session for sharing ideas, presentations, and documents. Windows Collaboration uses the People Near Me feature for sharing information. Windows Collaboration also requires that you enable file synchronization and configure a Windows Firewall exception. You will be prompted to automatically configure these options the first time you run Windows Collaboration.

- **Windows Defender**   Allows you to protect the computer from malicious software (also known as *malware*) by automatically blocking and locating spyware and other types of malicious programs.

- **Windows Fax and Scan**   Allows you to manage incoming faxes and to send faxes. Faxes can be received and sent over TCP/IP as well.

- **Windows Mail**   Allows you to send and manage e-mail. Windows Mail is the replacement for Outlook Express.

- **Windows Media Player**   Allows you to play and manage music.

- **Windows Movie Maker**   Allows you to create and manage movies using still images and videos.

- **Windows Photo Gallery**   Allows you to view and manage pictures and videos. You can organize your media using folders, create slideshows, and add tags for quick searching.

- **Windows Update**   Allows you to manage the Windows Update feature.

The folders on the All Programs menu also have changed. The top-level folders are:

- **All Programs, Accessories**   Includes the most commonly used accessories, including Calculator, Command Prompt, Connect To A Network Projector, Run, Sync Center, Windows Explorer, and Windows Sidebar.

- **All Programs, Accessories, Ease Of Access**   Includes the accessibility tools, such as Magnifier, Narrator, On-Screen Keyboard, and Speech Recognition.

- **All Programs, Accessories, System Tools**   Includes commonly used system tools, such as Backup, Disk Cleanup, System Restore, and Windows Easy Transfer. Windows Easy Transfer replaces the Files And Settings Transfer Wizard in Windows XP. This folder also includes Internet Explorer (No Add-ons), which is a version of Internet Explorer without browser extensions or other add-ons.

- **All Programs, Games**   Includes games that might be available, depending on the system configuration.

- **All Programs, Maintenance**   Includes maintenance tools, such as Backup And Restore Center, Problem Reports And Solutions, and Windows Remote Assistance.

- **All Programs, Startup**   Lists programs that are set to start up automatically.

It might take you a while to get used to the changes to the All Programs menu. But once you get used to the changes, navigating the menus will seem like second nature.

Navigating Control Panel: What's Changed

Clicking the Start button on the taskbar and then clicking Control Panel displays Control Panel. You can also display Control Panel in any Windows Explorer view by clicking the leftmost option button in the Address bar and then selecting Control Panel. As with

Windows XP, Control Panel in Windows Vista has two views:

■ Category Control Panel, or simply Control Panel, is the default view and provides access to system utilities by category and task.

■ Classic Control Panel is an alternative view that provides the look and functionality of Control Panel in Windows 2000 and earlier versions of Windows.

With Windows Vista, Microsoft finally got the marriage of category, task, and utility access right in the default Control Panel view—so much so, in fact, that you might want to say good-bye to Classic Control Panel forever. Here's how the Category Control Panel works now:

■ Control Panel opens as a console in which 10 categories of utilities are listed. Each category includes a top-level link, and under this link are several of the most frequently performed tasks for the category.

■ Clicking a category link provides a list of utilities in that category. Each utility listed within a category includes a link to open the utility, and under this link are several of the most frequently performed tasks for the utility.

■ In Category Control Panel view, all utilities and tasks run with a single click. When you're browsing a category, the left pane of the console includes a link to take you to the Control Panel Home page, links for each category, and links for recently performed tasks. It's all very efficient, and very easy to use.

Figure 2-6 shows the Control Panel Home page. From any category page, you can access the home page by clicking the Control Panel Home link in the upper-left corner of the Control Panel console.

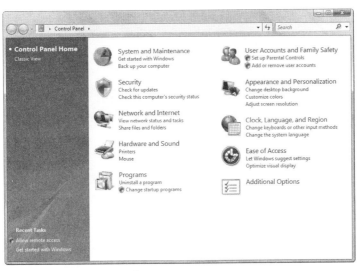

Figure 2-6   Control Panel

Because menu options and Control Panel options open with a single click by default, you might want to change the computer to use single-click to open items. This should avoid confusion over when you need to single-click or double-click.

To configure single-clicking for opening items, follow these steps:

1. Click the Start button, and then click Control Panel.

2. In Control Panel, click Appearance And Personalization.

3. Under Folder Options, click Specify Single- Or Double-Click To Open.

4. In the Folder Options dialog box, select Single-Click To Open An Item (Point To Select), and then click OK.

Once you have everything set to open with a single click, you'll find that working with Control Panel and Windows Explorer is much more intuitive.

Chapter 3
Managing Information

Microsoft Windows Vista includes many new features to help you manage information, whether that information resides on your computer, the company's network, or the Internet. In this chapter, we'll look at managing information on your computer. You'll learn new ways of using Microsoft Windows Explorer to work with files and folders, adding keywords to files and tags to pictures and using virtual folders to save search results. You'll also learn about the new desktop features, such as Windows Sidebar. In the next chapter, we'll explore features for sharing documents with others through collaboration, sharing files and folders, and connecting to shared resources.

The primary means of working with files and folders in Windows Vista are the desktop and Windows Explorer. As in earlier versions of Windows, the desktop continues to be the main screen area and the place where you perform your work, and Windows Explorer continues to be the tool of choice for working with files and folders. What's changed is that many new features have been introduced, and some previous features have been modified to work in different ways than they have in the past.

Note   This book was written using the Windows Vista Beta to provide an early introduction to the operating system. More so than any other area of Windows Vista, the security features discussed in this book are subject to change. Some of the features might not be included in the final product, and some of the features might be changed substantially.

Getting Around the Windows Vista Desktop

At first glance, the Windows Vista desktop is similar to the Windows XP desktop. The core aspects of the desktop haven't changed much, but there are a few changes that should be noted. Beyond this, the primary new features for the desktop are Windows Sidebar and the mini-applications (called *gadgets*) that you can add to the sidebar or to the desktop itself. Figure 3-1 shows the Windows Vista desktop with the sidebar.

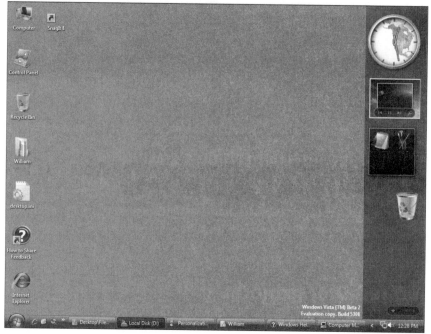

Figure 3-1   The desktop, with Windows Sidebar and gadgets

Working with the Desktop

When you open programs or folders, they appear on the desktop. You can arrange open programs and folders on the desktop by right-clicking an empty area of the taskbar and then selecting an appropriate option. Options available include Cascade Windows, Show Windows Stacked, and Show Windows Side By Side. If you click Show The Desktop, Windows minimizes all open windows and displays the desktop. Clicking Show Open Windows restores the minimized windows to their previous states.

You can put files, folders, and shortcuts on the desktop. Any file or folder you save on the desktop appears on the desktop. Any file or folder you drag from a Windows Explorer window to the desktop stays on the desktop. You can add a shortcut to a file or folder to the desktop by right-clicking the file or folder, pointing to Send To, and then selecting Desktop (Create Shortcut).

By default, the only item on the desktop is the Recycle Bin. You can add or remove common desktop icons by right-clicking an empty area of the desktop and then selecting Personalize. In the Desktop Icon Settings dialog box, you can then add or remove Computer, Control Panel, Internet Explorer, Network, Recycle Bin, and User's Files icons by selecting or clearing the related option. You can use these icons as follows:

- **Computer**   Double-clicking the Computer icon opens a window where you can access hard disk drives and devices with removable storage. Right-clicking the Computer icon and selecting Manage opens the Computer Management console. Right-clicking the Computer icon and selecting Map Network Drive allows you to connect to shared network folders.

- **Control Panel**   Double-clicking the Control Panel icon opens Control Panel, which provides access to system configuration and management tools.

- **Internet Explorer**   Double-clicking the Internet Explorer icon opens the Internet Explorer window with your default home page. Right-clicking the Internet Explorer icon and then selecting Start Without Add-Ons starts Internet Explorer without using browser extensions or other add-ons.

- **Network**   Double-clicking the Network icon opens a window where you can access the computers and devices on your network.

- **Recycle Bin**   Double-clicking the Recycle Bin icon opens a window where you can view files and folders you've marked for deletion. By selecting Empty The Recycle Bin, you can permanently delete all the items in the Recycle Bin.

- **User's Files**   Double-clicking the User's Files folder opens your personal folder.

 Tip   If you no longer want an icon or a shortcut on the desktop, right-click it, and then select Delete. When prompted, confirm the action by clicking Yes.

Working with Windows Sidebar

Windows Sidebar is a view pane that you can add to the left or right side of the Windows Vista desktop. The sidebar is used to display and work with gadgets that are installed on the computer. Windows Sidebar and gadgets are not displayed by default on the desktop. You manage the sidebar's basic configuration through the Sidebar Properties utility in Control Panel. To display and configure Windows Sidebar, follow these steps:

1. Click Start, click Control Panel, click Appearance And Personalization, and then click Windows Sidebar.

2. In the Windows Sidebar Properties dialog box, shown in Figure 3-2, select Start Sidebar When Windows Starts.

Figure 3-2   The Sidebar Properties dialog box

3. Optionally specify whether the sidebar appears on top of other windows, whether the sidebar should start when Windows starts, and whether the sidebar appears on the left or right side of the desktop.

4. Click OK. The sidebar appears the next time you log on.

Working with Windows Gadgets

Windows Vista comes with several basic sidebar gadgets, including:

- **Calculator**   Displays a calculator with standard arithmetic functions. By default, the calculator's background color is gray. If you right-click the Calculator gadget and select Settings, you can use the buttons provided to change the color, and then click OK to save the changes.

- **Clock**   Displays an analog clock with hour and minute hands. Moving the mouse pointer over the clock shows the digital time, date, and time zone. The time zone used can be different from that used by the computer clock. Based on the time zone used, the background for the analog clock shows a map of the continent or region on the world map. By default, the analog clock shows a bright gray background during the day and a dark gray background at night. To change the time zone or modify other options, right-click the Clock gadget, and then select Settings.

- **CPU Meter**   Displays the current percentage utilization of the computer's CPU and memory. Similar to a tachometer in a car, the CPU and memory gauges show high utilization in yellow and red.

- **Feed Viewer**   Displays the data from a selected Really Simple Syndication (RSS) feed that has been configured in Internet Explorer. RSS feeds can contain news headlines, lists, and other information. After you add an RSS feed to Internet Explorer, you can begin viewing the feed in the Feed Viewer gadget. Right-click the gadget, and then select Settings. Select the feed in the RSS feed list, and then click OK.

- **Recycle Bin**   Displays the Recycle Bin. If you right-click the Recycle Bin gadget and select Settings, you can choose a different icon, such as a plastic cup, an aluminum trashcan, a tin cup, or a wooden cup.

- **Slide Show**   Displays pictures from a selected folder as a continuous slide show where pictures rotate at a specified interval. Moving the mouse pointer over a picture in the slide show causes the navigation buttons to appear. You can navigate through the pictures using the Previous, Pause and Next buttons. By default, pictures in the %UserProfile%\Pictures folder are used for the slide show. By right-clicking the Slide Show gadget and selecting Settings, you can modify the Directory setting to use any preferred folder. You can also modify the transition and slide show speed settings.

- **Weather**   Displays a window pane with a background image that depicts the local weather and shows the current temperature. The weather data is from MSN.com and is based on the location you've entered in the location settings. To configure the location, right-click the Weather gadget and then select Settings. In the Location field, enter your current location, click Search, and then select the closest match for your location. Click OK to save the changes.

To add gadgets to Windows Sidebar, follow these steps:

1. Click the + button at the top of the sidebar.

2. In the Add Gadgets dialog box, shown in Figure 3-3, double-click each of the gadgets you want to add to the sidebar. To find additional gadgets, click Get More Gadgets Online. The sidebar launches the Microsoft Gadgets site (*http://microsoftgadgets.com/*), where you can download custom gadgets or find instruction on how to build your own gadgets.

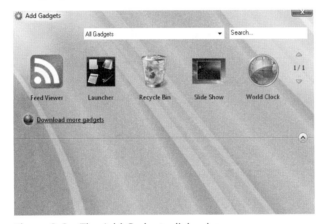

Figure 3-3   The Add Gadgets dialog box

When you have finished adding gadgets, click the Close button.

You can work with gadgets in a variety of ways:

■ Gadgets can be detached from the sidebar and moved around the desktop by right-click-ing the gadget and selecting Detach From Sidebar. Once you've detached the gadget, you can click and drag to move it to different locations on the desktop. To put the gadget back on the sidebar, right-click the gadget and select Attach To Sidebar.

■ When gadgets are detached, they can be displayed on top of all other windows by right-clicking the gadget and selecting Always On Top. Once you've moved the gadget to the top, right-clicking the gadget and selecting Always On Top a second time clears the setting and makes the gadget work like any other window that can be brought to the front when in use or moved to the back when not in use.

Using Windows Explorer: What's Changed

In earlier versions of Windows, the many different faces of Windows Explorer from Control Panel to My Computer to My Network Places weren't tightly integrated and seemed more like different tools than different faces of the same tool. In Windows Vista, Windows Explorer behaves more like a console or browser shell, and the many "faces" Windows Explorer has to offer are all tightly integrated.

When you start working with the new Windows Explorer, shown in Figure 3-4, you'll notice many important changes, including:

- A new Address bar to replace the old Address bar.

- A Quick Search box.

- New view panes to replace the Explorer bars.

- The addition of virtual folders to save search results.

- More options for working with file properties and the addition of metadata for indexing and search.

Figure 3-4   Using Windows Explorer

These new aspects of Windows Explorer are examined in the sections that follow.

Navigating the Windows Explorer Address Bar

The Address bar, shown in Figure 3-5, appears at the top of Windows Explorer and displays your current location as a series of links separated by arrows. This allows you to see your current location on the computer, on the network or on the Internet in relation to the locations you've navigated.

Figure 3-5   The Address bar in Windows Explorer

Note   The term *location* is used rather than *folder* because folders aren't the only types of resources you can navigate in Windows Explorer. For example, you can navigate virtual folders in addition to standard folders. You can also navigate Control Panel categories and network devices.

In the example shown in Figure 3-5, the folder path is:

Computer, Local Disk (D:), Users, William

From left to right, the Address bar has these key features:

- Forward/Back buttons
- Recent Pages button
- Location History drop-down button
- Address path
- Refresh button

The Forward and Back buttons on the far left of the Address bar allow you to navigate locations you've already visited. Similar to when you are browsing the Web, the locations you've visited are stored in a history, and you can browse the history using the Forward and Back buttons.

The Recent Pages button is located to the immediate right of the Forward and Back buttons. When you click this button, a drop-down list of recently accessed pages is displayed, allowing you to quickly access a recent page.

To the right of the Forward and Back buttons is a down arrow; this is the Location History button. Clicking this button shows a drop-down list containing a history of the locations you've visited; you can select any entry to access that location. Pressing Ctrl+H allows you to display a history of resources you've accessed. By default, Windows organizes the history by day of the week, allowing you, for example, to quickly locate a file or system tool page that you accessed on a particular day of the week.

Like the Address bar, the Address path has several key components:

- Location Indicator icon

- Location path
- Path Selection list button

On the far left of the Address path is the Location Indicator icon. The Location Indicator icon depicts the type of resource you are currently accessing. You'll see different icons for disk drives, folders, virtual folders, and so on. Clicking the Location Indicator icon shows the actual path or location, such as D:\Users. If you click the Refresh button to the right of the Address path, Windows Explorer shows the link path again.

You can navigate each link in the location path in several different ways:

- You can access a folder anywhere along the path that is displayed in the Address bar by clicking the link for that folder. Following this example, you could open the Users folder by clicking the Users link.
- You can access a subfolder of any folder displayed in the Address bar by clicking the arrow to the right of the folder. This displays a list of all folders in the selected folder. To access one of these folders, you click the desired folder in the list.

At the far right of the Address path is the Path Selection button. Clicking this button shows the base locations available (such as Desktop and Control Panel) as well as recent paths that you've accessed, listed according to their actual path or location.

The base locations are important because they allow you to access quickly key locations and management areas on the computer. Clicking the arrow to the right of the Location Indicator icon is the easiest way to access and navigate base locations. This icon and its related arrow button are on the far left of the Address path. The base locations available are as follows:

- **Current User**   Accesses the currently logged on user's personal folder in Windows Explorer. Based on your selection, the taskbar is updated to include additional tasks, such as: Share, which allows you to share the personal folder or a selected item, and Previous Versions, which allows you to browse previous versions of files stored in the personal folder or a selected folder.
- **Computer**   Accesses the base page for the computer in Windows Explorer. This page lists the hard disk drives and devices with removable storage on the computer. The taskbar is updated to include two tasks: Change Or Remove A Program, which opens Control Panel, Programs, Installed Programs; and Change A Setting, which opens Control Panel.
- **Control Panel**   Accesses Control Panel in Windows Explorer. As with any Control Panel view, you can list the Control Panel categories by clicking the arrow button to the right of the Control Panel link in the Address path. Click the category you want to access in the list.
- **Desktop**   Accesses the desktop in Windows Explorer. Based on your selection, the task-bar is updated to include additional tasks, such as: Open, which opens a selected item;

Share, which allows you to share the selected item; and Previous Versions, which allows you to access previous versions of files.

- **Network**   Accesses the base page for the computers and devices on your network. Network Center and Connect To A Network icons on the taskbar provide quick access to these features.

- **Public**   Access the base page for publicly shared files and folders. A Share Settings icon on the taskbar provides quick access to configure network file and printer sharing.

- **Recycle Bin**   Accesses the Recycle Bin in Windows Explorer. The Empty The Recycle Bin task on the taskbar allows you to permanently delete any items placed in the Recycle Bin. The Restore All Items task on the taskbar allows you to restore all of the deleted items placed in the Recycle Bin.

Working with the Windows Explorer Quick Search Box

Working with the Start menu Search box is discussed in Chapter 2, in the "Using the Search Box on the Start Menu" section. The Quick Search box in Windows Explorer works much like the Search box on the Start menu. However, there are some important differences.

With the Quick Search box, you must click in the Search box prior to typing your search text. Because of this, searches are performed using the following technique:

1. Click in the Search box, and then enter the search text.

2. To start the search, click the Search button (which is to the right of the Search box and depicts a magnifying glass) or press Enter.

   By default, Windows Explorer searches for the search text in the current folder location and in subfolders of the current location only. Windows Search Service matches the search text to words that appear in the title of any file or folder, the properties of any file or folder, and the contents of text-based documents.

Tip   Windows Search Service does not search the entire computer by default (unless of course you are searching from the Computer page). To search the entire computer or the Internet, click the arrow button to the right of the Search box, and then select Search The Computer or Search The Internet as appropriate.

From the experts
Control the search by using filters

Okay, so Windows Vista has this amazing search feature, but it's not working the way you expect it to–either the search is extremely slow or it just doesn't return the results you're look for–and you're wondering why. First of all, it's important to point out that Windows Search Service probably isn't to blame for the lack (or wealth) of results.

Windows Search Service indexes only the documents contained in the %SystemDrive%\Users folders, and it can be a very slow process to search nonindexed resources. You can index additional folders on a computer using the Indexing And Search Options utility in Control Panel.

Indexing frequently searched folders will speed up the search process, but it won't resolve the problem of Windows Search Service returning too much data. To get more meaningful results, you'll need to use filters. Filters can be added by clicking the arrow button to the right of the Search box and then selecting Advanced Filter Pane. With the Advanced Filter Pane displayed, you can easily filter results based on the kind of document you're looking for. By default, Windows Search Service searches all documents types. If you're searching for e-mails, documents, or pictures, you can narrow the search and the results by clicking the related Show Results For buttons. If you're looking for a different kind of file, click the More Kinds button to display other types of files for which you want to show results. For more information about fine-tuning searching and indexing, refer to the *Microsoft Windows Vista Administrator's Pocket Consultant* (Microsoft Press, 2006).

William Stanek
Author, MVP, and series editor for the Microsoft Press Administrator's Pocket Consultants

Working with the Windows Explorer View Panes, Views, and Organize Options

In Windows Vista, Windows Explorer no longer uses the Explorer bar. Instead, Windows Explorer uses view panes. View panes and the new Views and Organize options replace the classic menus that were previously available. Because of this, when you are working with folders and files, the taskbar displays View Panes, and Views and Organize buttons.

You configure and access View Panes using the Views and Organize buttons on the taskbar, shown in Figure 3-6. Depending on the location you are working with or the selected item, the taskbar might display additional tasks that you can perform, such as Open, Print, Share, or Previous Versions.

Figure 3-6   The taskbar in Windows Explorer

The view panes being used control Windows Explorer's layout. You can configure view panes using the options displayed when you click Organize and then click Layout. The following view panes are available:

■ **Navigation Pane**   Provides quick access to common locations and common types of files that you might be looking for. When selected, the Navigation Pane appears on the left in Windows Explorer.

■ **Preview Pane**   Provides an overview of the selected resource, such as the name, type of resource, size or number of items contained within, and last modification date. There are different previews for most base locations, including Current User, Computer, Network, and Recycle Bin. There are different previews for folders, virtual folders, and files. When selected, the Preview Pane appears at the bottom of Windows Explorer.

■ **Reading Pane**   Provides an easy way to determine the contents of a file or folder without having to open the file or folder. With files, the Reading Pane displays the contents of a selected image or document file (provided the image or document browser for that specific image or document is configured and available). You can use this feature to read text or document files without opening them. With folders, the Reading Pane displays an icon that represents the type of folder and the type of contents. You can use this feature to determine whether a folder contains music, documents files, pictures, or videos. When selected, the Reading Pane appears on the right in Windows Explorer.

■ **Search Pane**   Provides additional options for the Quick Search feature, allowing you to show results only for specific types of files and to select the start folder for a search.

> **Note**   Depending on the location you are working with, some view pane options might not be available. To add or remove a view pane, click the View Pane button, and then click the view pane that you want to add or remove.

The taskbar's Views button allows you to change the view of items in the folder. You can use Tiles view and Details view to get more information about items. Or use the Extra Large Icons, Large Icons, or Medium Icons views to display minimal information about items. The Organize button allows you to perform common tasks for arranging and editing the folder itself or selected items, such as Rename, Cut, Copy, Delete, and Select All.

Using Virtual Folders to Save Search Results

In addition to standard folders that can contain files and other folders, Windows Vista uses virtual folders. Virtual folders function like regular folders. Users dynamically define these virtual folders, which contain a list of files or folders that match specific search or filter criteria. For example, you can base the contents of a virtual folder on certain keywords, ratings, or document authors.

Using the Searches Folder

Within a user's profile folder is a folder named Searches (see Figure 3-7). Searches contains the default virtual folders available for the user and includes:

■ **Attachments**   A list of files originally received as attachments to e-mail messages.

■ **Favorite Music**   A list of recently played or frequently played music files.

- **Lasts 7 Days E-mail**   A list of e-mail messages received within the last 7 days.

- **Last 30 Days Documents**   A list of documents created or modified within the past 30 days.

- **Last 30 Days Pictures And Videos**   A list of pictures and videos created or modified within the past 30 days.

- **Shared By Me**   A list of files that you've shared on your computer.

- **Unread E-Mail**   A list of unread e-mail messages.

Figure 3-7   The Searches folder

Creating Virtual Folders

Virtual folders are stored as files with the .search file extension. For example, the Attachments virtual folder is actually a file named Attachments.search that contains the search details. If you find that you are frequently using the same search or filter criteria to find files and folders, you can create virtual folders to save your search results. To do this, perform a search using the search text and options and filters to get the set of results you want, and then save the search results as a virtual folder.

To save search results as a virtual folder, follow these steps:

1. Enter your search text in the Search box, setting any filters and options as necessary to get the desired results.

2. Right-click an open area in the main viewing area of Windows Explorer, and then select Save Search on the shortcut menu.

3. In the Save As dialog box, type a name for the search file. You must end the file name with the .search extension, such as 2006Reports.search.

Like the default virtual folders, virtual folders you create are stored by default in your Searches folder. You can find the files again later by accessing Searches and then accessing your virtual folder.

Managing File Properties and Metadata for Indexing and Searching

In Windows Vista, all files can have properties associated with them. The standard properties can be extended to include additional information referred to as *metadata*. Many types of document and picture files have metadata such as author, subject, categories, and keywords that can be used by Windows Search Service when indexing and searching files. The type of file determines the standard properties.

As with file contents, Windows Search Service indexes file properties to display search results of indexed folders faster. Because of this, you typically can search for any properties or metadata that you've added to a file.

Viewing and Configuring File Properties and Metadata

To view and configure a file's properties and metadata, follow these steps:

1. Right-click the file, and then select Properties.

2. In the Properties dialog box, click the Details tab, as shown in Figure 3-8.

Figure 3-8   The Properties dialog box

3. Click a property's entry to select it for editing, and then type the property value. Separate multiple values with a semicolon.

4. Click OK.

> **Note**   Most types of picture files have a Tags property. Windows Photo Gallery uses the Tags property to add keywords to pictures. When you tag a picture in Windows Photo Gallery, the keyword you specify is added as a tag.

Editing and Cleaning File Properties and Metadata

Although additional properties and metadata can be useful, there are times when you won't want this information to be saved with a file. For example, if you are publishing a file to a Web site or sending a file to someone as an attachment, you might not want this additional information to be associated with the file. Why? The additional information might be personal. It might also contain information about your organization that shouldn't be passed along to individuals outside the organization.

To clear out properties or metadata from a file, follow these steps:

1. Right-click the file, and then select Properties.

2. In the Properties dialog box, click the Details tab, as shown previously in Figure 3-8.

3. Click Remove Properties And Personal Information.

4. In the Remove Properties dialog box, select the individual properties to remove or select the Select All Properties check box.

5. Click OK.

> **Tip**   By default, Windows Explorer cleans properties from the original file you are working with. If you want to create a new copy of the file with the properties remove instead, select the Create A New Copy With The Properties Removed check box before clicking OK.

Chapter 4

Using Internet Explorer 7

Microsoft Internet Explorer 7 is included in Windows Vista and is available as a download to anyone using an earlier version of Microsoft Windows. This newest version of Internet Explorer reflects the input of the user community, many of whom have been asking for usability improvements for easier navigation and more continuity between windows. Internet Explorer 7 also promises to be the safest and most secure version of Internet Explorer produced so far. New safety and security features are provided as part of the Dynamic Security Protection package, which is designed to safeguard the integrity of the computer and any information you've entered into HTML forms on Web pages.

 Note This book was written using the Windows Vista Beta to provide early introduction to the operating system. More so than any other area of Windows Vista, the security features discussed in this book are subject to change. Some of the features might not be included in the final product, and some of the features might be changed substantially.

Introducing Internet Explorer 7

User experience was one of the key focuses in the redesign of Internet Explorer. New interface enhancements, such as tabs and integrated search, make Internet Explorer 7 much easier and much more intuitive to work with. However, these enhancements will take some getting used to, and the more pointers you have up front, the easier it'll be to work with Internet Explorer 7.

Getting Around in the Internet Explorer 7 Window

Internet Explorer 7 has many interface enhancements, as Figure 4-1 shows. These enhancements include:

■ The streamlined interface, which maximizes Web page display while reducing the toolbar size.

■ The use of tabs instead of separate windows, which handily organizes Internet Explorer windows and allows you to navigate between Web pages by clicking tabs.

■ The addition of a Web Search box as a standard feature on the toolbar.

Figure 4-1   The new interface in Internet Explorer 7

The enhancement that changes the way you use Internet Explorer is *tabbed browsing*. With tabbed browsing, you can view multiple Web pages in a single window. You switch from one Web page to another by clicking the tabs at the top of the browser frame. Internet Explorer still allows you to open new windows, but you typically don't need to do this.

When you want to access a new page and still have access to a current page, you display a new tab by pressing Ctrl+T or by clicking the New Tab button. The New Tab button is always displayed to the right of the last tab in the line of available tabs. Internet Explorer gives you several options for managing tabs. Whenever there are at least two tabs in use, Quick Tabs preview and Quick Tabs list buttons are added to the toolbar to the left of the tabs:

■ The Quick Tabs preview button depicts four open windows. Pressing Ctrl+Q or clicking this button displays a thumbnail preview of all tabbed pages in the current window. To access one of the tabbed pages, you simply click the page's thumbnail.

■ The Quick Tabs list button depicts a down arrow. When you click this button, Internet Explorer displays a list of open Web pages. To access one of these pages, you click its entry in the list.

Working with the Internet Explorer Toolbars

Tabbed browsing and Quick Tab options are just a few of the many ways Internet Explorer has changed. While these changes are fairly clear, some of the other changes are more subtle but just as powerful. By default, Internet Explorer 7 displays the following toolbars:

- Classic Menu bar
- Standard toolbar
- Address bar
- Status bar

The sections that follow discuss these toolbars and the related options.

Using the Classic Menu Bar and the Standard Toolbar: What's Changed

Figure 4-2 shows the Classic Menu bar and the standard toolbar. The Classic Menu bar is the menu bar used in previous versions of Internet Explorer. The standard toolbar is the main toolbar in Internet Explorer 7.

The standard toolbar is always displayed, unless you are using full-screen mode. On the far left of the standard toolbar, you'll find the Favorites Center button and the Add To Favorites button.

Figure 4-2   The Classic Menu and the standard toolbar in Internet Explorer 7

Favorites Center is a new feature that provides a single location to view and access the following:

- **Favorites**   Lists of your favorite pages for quick access.
- **Feeds**   Lists of Really Simple Syndication (RSS) feeds to which you've subscribed.
- **History**   Lists of pages you've accessed by date, site, most visited, or order visited.

RSS feed integration is a new feature in Internet Explorer 7. RSS feeds can contain news headlines, lists, and other information provided by businesses or individuals. Once you subscribe to an RSS feed, you can display it by:

1. Opening Internet Explorer.
2. Clicking the Favorites Center button.
3. Clicking the Feeds tab.
4. Selecting the feed you want to view.

> **Note**   You can also view RSS subscriptions by using the Feed Viewer gadget. See the "Working with Windows Gadgets" section in Chapter 3 for more information.

From the experts

RSS feeds made easy

RSS is a great way to keep up with the flood of news and opinion out there on almost any subject you're interested in. Until recently, I've been using a third-party RSS plug-in for Outlook, while many of my colleagues are using standalone third-party RSS news aggregators. But in Windows Vista with RSS functionality built right into Internet Explorer, I can subscribe to a feed simply by clicking the red RSS button that appears on most news media and tech Web sites (such as *http://technet.microsoft.com*) and then, as William has already explained, I can view my feeds in the Favorites Center anytime I want to read them. I'm definitely switching to Internet Explorer 7 on Vista as my news aggregator—once I finish "dogfooding" the beta versions!

Mitch Tulloch
Author and MVP–For more information, see http://www.mtit.com.

Other new features in Internet Explorer 7 have to do with home pages and printing. Internet Explorer 7 allows you to have more than one home page. The Home button on the right end of the standard toolbar allows you to access the default home page. The Home Options button (depicting a down arrow) to the right of the Home button allows you to:

- Display and select from a list of additional home pages that you've configured.

- Add, change, or remove home pages.

If you want to add the current page as a home page, click the Home Options button, and then select Change Home Page. In the Change Home Page dialog box, choose an appropriate option for configuring your home pages, and then click Yes.

The Print button on the right end of the standard toolbar allows you to print the current page. If you select the Print Options button to the right of the Print button and then select Print Preview, you can customize the print layout. The most important new option is the Change Print Size button, which lets you set the print size as a percentage of the actual page size. You can click the Change Print Size button and then select Shrink To Fit to ensure that a page prints properly.

Using the Classic Menu and the Standard Toolbar Menu Options

The Classic Menu features the Internet Explorer menus from earlier versions: File, Edit, View, Favorites, Tools, and Help. Once you get used to the new interface, however, you probably won't need the Classic Menu. By clicking Tools, Toolbars, Classic Menu, you can stop displaying the Classic Menu to further streamline the interface.

Instead of using the File menu to work with tabs, you can use the standard toolbar options. Clicking the New Tab button on the standard toolbar (or pressing Ctrl+T) creates tabs. If you right-click a tab, you can select Close to close the tab or select Close Other Tabs to close all tabs except for the currently selected one.

The Page menu on the standard toolbar combines many of the features of the Edit and View menus from the Classic Menu. One of the most useful new features is the Zoom option. Instead of simply increasing the font size of text, Zoom allows you to shrink or expand the entire page. You can shrink a page by selecting a Zoom size smaller than 100%. You can expand a page by selecting a Zoom size larger than 100%.

The Tools menu on the standard toolbar combines many of the features of the View and Tools menus from the Classic Menu. The options include:

- **Delete Browsing History**   Deletes all cached browsing information, including temporary files, page history, cookies, saved passwords, and Web form information. Thus, instead of having to access separate options to clear out this information, you can completely clear the cached browsing information with a single option.

- **Diagnose Connection Problems**   Helps you determine the possible cause of connection and access problems.

- **Full Screen**   Displays Internet Explorer in full-screen mode. You can toggle between full-screen mode and standard mode by pressing F11.

- **Internet Options**   Displays the Internet Options dialog box, which you can use to configure Internet Explorer.

- **Manage Add-Ons**   Displays a dialog box that depicts add-ons currently loaded in Internet Explorer. You can then enable, disable, or delete add-ons.

- **Phishing Filter**   Allows you to specify phishing filter options. Malicious Web sites use hidden forms and other phishing tactics to steal information you've previously entered into form fields. For more information, see the "Using the Internet Explorer Safety and Security Features" section later in this chapter.

- **Pop-Up Blocker**   Allows you to enable or disable pop-up blocking. You can also select Pop-Up Blocker Settings to configure pop-up blocking options.

- **Toolbars**   Allows you to configure which toolbars are displayed in the browser window.

- **Work Offline**   Sets Internet Explorer to work offline. When you are working offline, Internet Explorer attempts to retrieve pages you access from its offline browsing cache. If a page is available for offline browsing, Internet Explorer displays the page. Otherwise, Internet Explorer displays an error message.

Using the Address Bar: What's Changed

As shown in Figure 4-3, the Address bar in Internet Explorer 7 features Forward and Back buttons, an Address Path text box, a Path History button, Refresh and Stop buttons, and a Search box. To access a page from the currently selected tab, you can type an address in the Address Path field. At the far right side of the Address Path field is the Path History button, which depicts a down arrow. Clicking this button shows the paths from the history.

Figure 4-3   The Address bar in Internet Explorer 7

Internet Explorer 7 integrates a search feature directly into the browser window. To search the Web using the default search provider, click in the Search box, type your search text, and then press Enter or click the Search button. The Search Options button to the right of the Search button allows you to:

- Choose from the currently configured search providers.

- Find text on the current page rather than searching the Internet.

- Get a list of search providers from the Microsoft Web site, which can be configured.

- Change search default settings.

On most configurations of Internet Explorer 7, the default search provider is MSN Search.

Using the Status Bar: What's Changed

As in earlier versions, the status bar in Windows Vista displays browser status messages. The following new items have been added on the right end of the status bar:

- **A phishing status indicator**   Specifies the phishing status as it relates to the currently accessed site or page. On less well-known Web sites, the phishing filter status indicator displays a warning icon. Clicking this icon allows you to check the Web site, report the Web site, and configure phishing filter options. On trusted or well-known Web sites, such as MSN or Microsoft.com, the phishing filter status indicator is blank. That doesn't mean, however, that the phishing filter isn't active or available. If you click in the empty space to the immediate left of the Internet Security indicator, you can display all the standard phishing filter options.

- **An Internet Security indicator**   Specifies the current security zone and mode being used. There are separate security zones for Internet, Local Intranet, Trusted Sites, and Restricted Sites. When accessing sites in the Internet zone, Internet Explorer uses pro-tected mode by default. For more information, see the "Using the Internet Explorer Safety and Security Features" section later in this chapter.

- **A view magnifier**   Depicts the current Zoom setting. You can use Zoom settings to shrink or expand the textual and graphical contents of a Web page. Shrink the page by selecting a Zoom size smaller than 100%. Expand the page by selecting a Zoom size larger than 100%.

Using the Internet Explorer Safety and Security Features

The Dynamic Security Protection package in Internet Explorer 7 is a comprehensive suite of safety and security features designed to safeguard the integrity of the computer and your personal information. The components of Dynamic Security Protection can be organized into four key areas:

- Protected mode features
- Privacy reporting
- Phishing filters
- Parental controls

Protected mode features, privacy reporting, and phishing filters are discussed in the sections that follow. Parental controls are discussed in Chapter 9, "Protecting User Accounts and Using Parental Controls."

Understanding Internet Explorer Protected Mode

Unlike earlier versions of Internet Explorer, which have access to the operating system and running applications, Internet Explorer 7 operates in a protected mode, which isolates it from other applications in the operating system and prevents add-ons from writing content in any location beyond temporary Internet files folders without explicit user consent. Isolating Internet Explorer from other applications and restricting write locations prevents many types of malicious software from exploiting the computer. To further protect Windows Vista computers from malicious software, many other safeguards are in place, including:

- Add-on restrictions
- Domain and URL restrictions
- Security zone restrictions

Understanding the Internet Explorer Add-Ons Restrictions

By default, ActiveX controls that can run in Internet Explorer 7 are limited. Preinstalled ActiveX controls are disabled by default to prevent potentially vulnerable controls from being exposed to attack. Internet Explorer also has a special Add-Ons Disabled mode in which all browser extensions and add-ons are disabled (except for critical add-ons that are part of the browser core components). To start Internet Explorer in Add-Ons Disabled mode, click Start, point to All Programs, Accessories, System Tools, and click Internet Explorer (No Add-Ons), or right-click the Internet Explorer icon on the desktop and select Internet Explorer (No Add-Ons).

Internet Explorer 7 also makes its easier for you to manage installed add-ons by using the Manage Add-Ons dialog box, shown in Figure 4-4. These changes allow you to easily determine which add-ons have been downloaded and installed as well as which add-ons are currently loaded in Internet Explorer. Most downloaded add-ons can be easily disabled and deleted as well.

Figure 4-4   The Manage Add-Ons dialog box

To view and manage downloaded add-ons, follow these steps:

1. In Internet Explorer, click Tools, click Manage Add-Ons, and then select Enable Or Disable Add-Ons.

2. In the Show drop-down list, select Downloaded ActiveX Controls.

3. Click the downloaded add-on you want to work with.

4. To disable the add-on, click Disable. The add-on is then prevented from running in Internet Explorer.

5. To delete the downloaded add-on, click Delete ActiveX. The add-on is then permanently removed from Internet Explorer.

Understanding the Internet Explorer Domain and URL Restrictions

Internet Explorer 7 supports both standard English domain names and internationalized domain names. English domain names are domain names represented using the letters A–Z, the numerals 0–9 and the hyphen. Internationalized domain names are domain names represented using native language characters.

Because Internet Explorer supports internationalized domain names, Microsoft wanted to find a way to help ensure that international characters aren't used to make a site seem like something it isn't. This is where international domain name anti-spoofing comes into the picture. International domain name anti-spoofing is designed to protect you against sites that could otherwise appear as known, trustworthy sites. If you visit a site that uses characters that are visually similar to a known trusted site, Internet Explorer displays a warning notification.

Another protection added to Internet Explorer has to do with URL handling. Internet Explorer 7 features a redesigned URL handler, which protects the computer from possible URL parsing exploitations, such as URLs that attempt to run commands or URLs that perform suspect actions.

Understanding the Internet Explorer Security Zone Restrictions

As Figure 4-5 shows, security levels and zones are core parts of Internet Explorer's security features. You can display security options for Internet Explorer by clicking Tools, selecting Internet Options, and then clicking the Security tab in the Internet Options dialog box.

Figure 4-5   Configuring security levels and zone options in Internet Explorer

By default, Internet Explorer always runs in protected mode. You can enable or disable protected mode by selecting or clearing the Enable Protected Mode check box. The standard levels of security that you can use are:

- **High**   This level is appropriate for sites that might contain harmful content. Internet Explorer runs in its highest protected mode with maximum safeguards and in which less secure features are disabled.

- **Medium-high**   This level is appropriate for most sites. Internet Explorer prompts you prior to downloading potentially unsafe contents and disabling downloading of unsigned ActiveX controls.

> **Note**   Medium-high is a new security level in Internet Explorer 7, and it is also the default level for the Internet security zone.

- **Medium**   This level is appropriate only for trusted sites. In this mode, Internet Explorer prompts you prior to downloading potentially unsafe contents and disables downloading of unsigned ActiveX controls.

- **Medium-low**   This level is appropriate only for sites on your internal network. In this mode, Internet Explorer runs most types of content without prompting but does disable downloading of unsigned ActiveX controls.

- **Low**   This level is appropriate only for sites you absolutely trust, such as secure internal sites. In this mode, Internet Explorer uses minimal safeguards, and most content is downloaded and run without prompts.

To help you manage when the various security levels should be used, Internet Explorer defines four standard security zones:

- **Internet**   This zone is for Internet sites, except those listed in trusted and restricted zones. By default, the Internet zone uses medium-high security.

- **Local Intranet**   This zone is for all sites that are on your internal network (intranet). By default, the Local Intranet zone uses medium-low security.

- **Trusted Sites**   This zone is for all sites that you have specifically identified as trusted and requiring the lowest level of safeguarding against possible damage. By default, the Trusted Sites zone uses a custom security level that is close to medium security.

- **Restricted Sites**   This zone is for all sites that you have identified as restricted and requiring the highest level of safeguarding against possible damage. By default, the Restricted Sites zone uses high security.

You can change the default behavior by setting a new security level for a zone, if permitted. For example, you could increase security for the Internet zone by setting the security level to High. With any security levels except Restricted Sites, you can set a custom security level as well. With a custom security level, you configure individual security settings for content and downloads in any way desired.

From the experts
Navigating the security zones and levels changes

In addition to creating the new medium-high security level, Internet Explorer prevents you from using certain security levels in some security zones. When working with security zones and levels, you'll need to keep the following in mind:

- In the Internet security zone, only the high, medium-high, and medium security levels are available. However, you can set a custom security level that is less secure. If you select the Internet zone and click the Default Level button, the security level is set to Medium-High.

- In the Local Intranet security zone, any of the security levels can be used. If you select the Local Intranet zone and click the Default Level button, the security level is set to Medium-Low.

■ In earlier versions of Internet Explorer, trusted sites use a custom low security level. Now trusted sites use a custom medium security level by default. If you select the Trusted Sites zone and click the Default Level button, the security level is set to Medium.

■ In earlier versions of Internet Explorer, restricted sites use a custom high security level that you can reset to any other security level. Now restricted sites use a non-configurable high security level. However, you can set a custom security level that is less secure.

For the Internet and Restricted Sites zones, Internet Explorer displays a warning on the information bar specifying that your security settings put your computer at risk if you use a custom security level lower than the default security level. You can restore the default security level by right-clicking the information bar and then selecting Fix Settings For Me. When prompted, click Fix Settings to restore the defaults.

One of the best ways to manage Internet Explorer security is to use Group Policy. For more information about configuring security levels and using Group Policy with Internet Explorer, refer to the *Microsoft Windows Vista Administrator's Pocket Consultant* (Microsoft Press, 2006).

William Stanek
Author, MVP, and series editor for the Microsoft Press Administrator's Pocket Consultants

Managing Cookies and Privacy Reporting

Cookies are used to store information on your computer so that the information can be retrieved in other pages or in other browser sessions. Many Web sites use cookies to store information you've entered into online forms, such as an e-commerce site that remembers your name and e-mail address. Cookies might also be used to store your user name if you've logged on to a site, your site preferences, and other information about you. Internet Explorer privacy settings seek to ensure that the information tracked by cookies is used only by the appropriate parties.

In the Internet zone, privacy levels are used to restrict and block certain types of cookies. Internet Explorer distinguishes between the site you are browsing and other sites from which content might come. The Web site that you are currently visiting is considered a first party. Any other Web site from which content on a page might be displayed is considered a third party. For example, if you are browsing a page on *www.msn.com*, you might find that some of the content comes from stj.msn.com. In this instance, *www.msn.com* is a first party and *stj.msn.com* is a third party. By clicking Page and then clicking Web Page Privacy Policy, you can display a privacy report for the current page. As Figure 4-6 depicts, this report shows:

■ Whether cookies were restricted or blocked based on your privacy settings.

■ Which Web sites have content on the page.

- Whether a cookie for an individual site for accepted, restricted, or blocked.

Figure 4-6   A Web privacy report

When you are viewing the Web privacy report, you can click the Settings button to display the Internet Options dialog box with the Privacy tab selected. According to the privacy rules, cookies set by first-party sites are subject to different constraints than cookies set by third-party sites. By default, Internet Explorer uses a Medium privacy level, as shown in Figure 4-7. The Medium privacy level:

- Blocks third-party cookies that do not have a compact privacy policy.

- Blocks third-party cookies that save information that can be used to contact you without your explicit consent.

- Restricts first-party cookies that save information that can be used to contact you without your implicit consent.

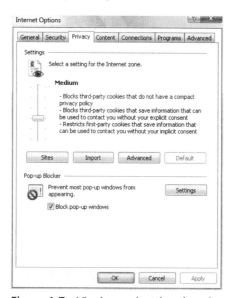

Figure 4-7   Viewing and setting the privacy level

In the Internet Options dialog box, you can configure other privacy levels using the options of the Privacy tab, including:

- **Block All Cookies** Blocks all cookies from all Web sites, and blocks reading of existing cookies by Web sites.

- **High** Blocks all cookies from Web sites that do not have a compact privacy policy, and blocks cookies that save information that can be used to contact you without your explicit consent.

- **Medium High** Blocks third-party cookies that do not have a compact privacy policy. Blocks third-party cookies that save information that can be used to contact you without your explicit consent. Blocks first-party cookies that save information that can be used to contact you without your implicit consent.

- **Medium** Blocks third-party cookies that do not have a compact privacy policy. Blocks third-party cookies that save information that can be used to contact you without your explicit consent. Restricts first-party cookies that save information that can be used to contact you without your implicit consent.

- **Low** Blocks third-party cookies that do not have a compact privacy policy. Restricts third-party cookies that save information that can be used to contact you without your implicit consent.

- **Accept All Cookies** Saves cookies from any Web site.

Protecting Your Computer from Phishing

Phishing is a technique whereby a site attempts to collect personal information about you without your knowledge or consent. Internet Explorer 7 has a phishing filter that proactively warns you against potential or known fraudulent sites and blocks the site if appropriate. You can manage this feature by clicking Tools, Phishing Filter.

> **Note** The phishing filter is always on by default. To turn off this feature, you can select Tools, Phishing Filter, Turn Off Automatic Website Checking. You can then manually check sites if desired by using the Check This Website option.

When you browse sites on the Internet, a warning icon is displayed on the status bar to help remind you when you aren't at a well-known site. The warning icon doesn't mean that the site has a known problem, rather it means that the site is probably a smaller and less widely known site. Most commercial sites, such as MSN.com and Microsoft.com, are considered well-known sites, and when you visit these sites in Internet Explorer, you won't see a warning icon.

Chapter 5
Collaborating, Connecting, and Sharing

Microsoft Windows Vista includes many features for collaborating, connecting, and sharing information. Windows Mail replaces Microsoft Outlook Express as the default program for e-mail. Windows Calendar is added to allow you to manage appointments and tasks using both personal and shared calendars. Windows Shared View is added to allow you to make virtual presentations over the network, share handouts, and collaborate with coworkers.

Note This book was written using the Windows Vista Beta to provide an early introduction to the operating system. More so than any other area of Windows Vista, the security features discussed in this book are subject to change. Some of the features might not be included in the final product, and some of the features might be changed substantially.

Messaging Essentials

Windows Mail is the new face of Outlook Express. While you will use Windows Mail primarily to send and receive e-mail messages, you can also use Windows Mail to browse and work with newsgroups. For managing personal and business contacts, Windows Vista provides a separate feature called Contacts.

Getting Started with Windows Mail

To start Windows Mail, click Start, point to All Programs, and then click Windows Mail. As Figure 5-1 shows, Windows Mail has an interface similar to earlier versions of Outlook Express. There are several important additions:

- **A Junk E-Mail folder**   Windows Mail uses Microsoft SmartScreen technology to help filter junk e-mail and keep it out of your Inbox. Windows enables junk e-mail filtering by default, and any suspected or actual junk e-mail messages are placed in the Junk E-Mail folder automatically.

■ **A Microsoft Help Groups folder**   Windows Mail is preconfigured for access to the msnews.microsoft.com newsgroups. These newsgroups allow you to ask questions about Microsoft products and to browse previous discussions of other users.

Figure 5-1   Using Windows Mail for e-mail and newsgroups

Before you can use Windows Mail for the first time, you'll need to configure your e-mail account. Once you configure Windows Mail, you can begin using its features to send and receive mail. You can also use Windows Mail to browse Microsoft Help newsgroups.

Configuring Windows Mail

When you first start using Windows Mail, the Internet Connection Wizard guides you through the process of configuring your e-mail account. As Figure 5-2 shows, you'll need to enter your display name and other essential information to configure your e-mail. To complete the configuration, you'll need to know:

■ Your e-mail address, such as *williamstanek@cpandl.com*

■ The incoming mail server name, such as *mail.cpandl.com*

■ The outgoing mail server name, such as *smtp.cpandl.com*

■ Your e-mail user name and password, given to you by your administrator or your Internet service provider (ISP).

Once you complete the configuration of your e-mail account, you'll be able to send and receive messages. You'll also be able to participate in the Microsoft Help newsgroups, as discussed in the next section.

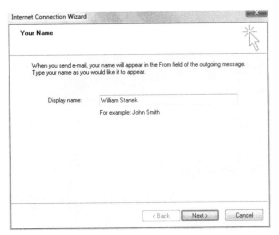

Figure 5-2 The Internet Connection Wizard

You can change your e-mail account information by following these steps:

1. In Windows Mail, click Tools, and then click Accounts.

2. Under the Mail heading, click your account, and then click Properties.

3. You can now change e-mail account settings such as user information, server information, and type of connection.

Accessing the Microsoft Help Newsgroups

Windows Mail not only allows you to manage your e-mail messages, but it also provides quick access to the Microsoft Help newsgroups through a Microsoft Help Groups node. The newsgroups are provided free of charge. If you are having trouble with your computer and Help And Support doesn't have the answers you are looking for, you might want to browse the Microsoft Help newsgroups to see if there is a discussion related to your issue. In many, but not all, cases, you'll find that someone had a similar problem and others have helped provide solutions or workarounds to the problem.

Access to the Microsoft Help newsgroups is not automatic, however. Before you can access the help newsgroups, you must select the ones you want to access and then subscribe to them by completing the following steps:

1. In Windows Mail, click the Microsoft Help Groups folder in the Folders view.

2. If you haven't subscribed to any newsgroups yet, you'll see a Windows Mail warning box stating this. Click Yes to see a list of available newsgroups.

3. Windows Mail will connect to the Internet to download a list of available newsgroups. The available newsgroups are then displayed in the Newsgroup Subscriptions dialog box, shown in Figure 5-3.

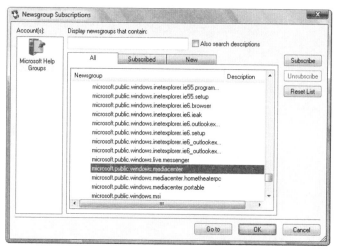

Figure 5-3   The Newsgroup Subscriptions dialog box

4. To subscribe to a newsgroup, click the newsgroup on the All tab, and then click the Subscribe button.

Newsgroups to which you've subscribed are then listed in the Folders view under the
Microsoft Help Groups folder, and you can access a newsgroup by double-clicking its entry.
You can also access newsgroups to which you've subscribed through the Subscribed tab in the
Newsgroup Subscriptions dialog box.

From the experts
Help is on the way

While the term "Microsoft Help Groups" is new with Vista, the underlying newsgroups
accessed by this feature aren't. The Microsoft public newsgroups have been around for
years, and sophisticated users who understood how to configure an NNTP newsreader
have been using them for years to get answers to their most difficult questions. Fortu-
nately, with Vista you don't even have to know what NNTP means (in case you're interested, it stands for Network News Transport Protocol) or which news server on the
Internet you need to connect to in order to access these groups (again if you're interested, the Microsoft public NNTP server is *news://msnews.microsoft.com*). Instead, you
only have to select the Microsoft Help Groups folder in Windows Mail and you immediately have access to this useful resource.

Which may bring a question to your mind: who answers all the questions posted to
these newsgroups? Usually MVPs, which stands for Most Valuable Professional. The
MVP program was developed by Microsoft to identify individuals who actively participate in online (and offline) communities to share their knowledge and expertise with
users of Microsoft products. MVPs are essentially volunteers who work a lot with
Microsoft products and enjoy helping others by answering their questions. Maybe

after you've worked with Vista for a while, you can begin answering questions in these newsgroups too, and if you do this, you may one day be recognized by Microsoft and awarded MVP status! For more information about the Microsoft MVP program, see *http://mvp.support.microsoft.com.*

Mitch Tulloch
Author and MVP–For more information, see http://www.mtit.com.

Searching Your Mail

Like the Start menu and Windows Explorer, Windows Mail also has a Search box. You can use the Search box to quickly search for messages containing the text you've entered. The Search feature matches complete or partial words in the message header and in the message text. This means that the complete text of your messages is searched, including but not limited to the From, To, Subject, Received, and Sent fields.

You can search your messages in the currently selected folder by completing the following steps:

1. Click in the Search box.

2. Type your search text.

Matches are returned as you type. If you want to search newsgroups, select the Newsgroups folder and then start your search.

 Tip   You can move the insertion point to the Search box by pressing Ctrl+E. You can clear the Search box by pressing Esc.

Working with Contacts

Although Windows Mail allows you to quickly send e-mail messages to contacts and to create contacts, contacts are managed separately through the Contacts window. The Contacts window allows you to create and manage both contacts and contact groups. A contact group is a collection of contacts and it allows you to send messages to all contacts that are part of the group using a single identifier. You can open the Contacts window, shown in Figure 5-4, by clicking Start, pointing to All Programs, and then clicking Contacts.

Windows Vista stores contacts and contact groups in the %UserProfile%\Contacts folder. Each contact is stored as a separate .contact file. Each contact group is stored as a separate .group file. Because contacts are stored separately from e-mail, they can more easily be used with other programs. As an example, both Windows Mail and Microsoft Outlook could make use of the files, and therefore both programs would have the same set of contacts.

Figure 5-4   The Contacts window

Once you've accessed Contacts, you can create a new contact or contact group by clicking New Contact or New Contact Group. To edit an existing contact or contact group, follow these steps:

1. Open the Contacts window.

2. Double-click the contact entry to display a Properties dialog box.

3. Make the necessary changes in the Properties dialog box.

4. Click OK.

Using Windows Calendar

Windows Calendar is a separate program for managing appointments and tasks. If you've worked previously with the calendar feature of Microsoft Outlook, you are probably familiar with how calendaring works. Windows Calendar offers similar features for tracking appointments and to-do tasks.

Getting Started with Windows Calendar

Most versions of Windows Vista include Windows Calendar. You can start Windows Calendar by clicking Start, pointing to All Programs, and then clicking Windows Calendar.

You can use Windows Calendar to manage appointments and tasks using both personal and shared calendars. While the ability to share calendars isn't new—the feature is included in Microsoft Outlook—what is new is the ability to easily create multiple calendars for different people or different purposes and then easily publish these calendars to share them with others.

Windows Calendar can be used at home and at work:

- At home, you can use Windows Calendar to help you keep track of appointments and tasks that you need to complete. You can create calendars for your spouse and children to help track their appointments and tasks as well.

- At work, you can use Windows Calendar to help you keep track of appointments and tasks for yourself and your entire team. You can create calendars for your team members and coworkers to help track their appointments and tasks.

Because calendars and their respective appointments and tasks are color-coded (see Figure 5-5), you can quickly and easily differentiate between one person's appointments and tasks and another's. Windows Calendar also makes it easy for you to access any available calendars and for you to allow others to access your calendars. If you want to access someone else's calendar, you can ask that person to publish the calendar so that you can subscribe to it. If you want others to be able to access your calendar, you can publish your calendar as a shared calendar.

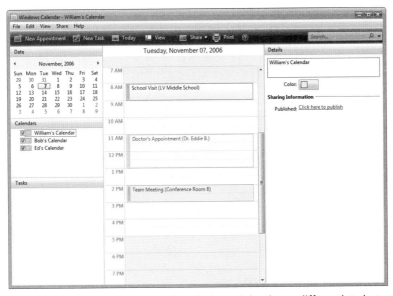

Figure 5-5 Using color-coding in Windows Calendar to differentiate between one person's appointments and tasks and another's

Searching for Appointments and Tasks

Like the Start menu and Windows Explorer, Windows Calendar also has a Search box. You can use the Search box to quickly search for appointments and tasks containing the text you've entered. The Search feature matches complete or partial words in the appointment and task details of all the calendars you've created as well as in all the calendars to which you've subscribed.

You can search calendars by completing the following steps:

1. Click in the Search box.

2. Type your search text.

   Matches are returned as you type.

Tip If you double-click an item in the search results, Windows Calendar displays the related calendar view and the item details. To clear the search results, click the Close button in the Search Results pane.

Performing Key Calendar Tasks

You can use the toolbar in the main Calendar window (see Figure 5-6) to navigate the calendar, change views, and perform essential tasks. From left to right, the buttons on the toolbar are:

- **New Appointment**   Creates a new (blank) appointment in the selected calendar.
- **New Task**   Creates a new (blank) task in the selected calendar.
- **New Calendar**   Creates a new (blank) calendar.
- **Today**   Shows the current date. Clicking this button accesses the current date in the calendar.
- **View**   Provides options that set the calendar to the Day, Work Week, Week, or Month view. Also has options for displaying or hiding the Navigation pane and the Details pane.
- **Share**   Allows you to manage the sharing options for a selected calendar.
- **Print**   Prints appoints on the selected calendar according to the options you select for print style and print range.

Figure 5-6   The Windows Calendar main toolbar

Creating and Using Appointments

Windows Calendar can help you track appointments for yourself and any calendars to which you've subscribed. All appointments can have a title and location associated with them. On the calendar, the title is shown first, followed by the location in parentheses (see Figure 5-7). When you create an appointment, you can specify start and end times or you can specify that an appointment runs all day. Windows Calendar also allows you to:

- Specify whether appointments repeat daily, weekly, monthly, or yearly.
- Add reminders to appointments so that you are notified a specified amount of time prior to an appointment.

- List and invite attendees based on your configured contacts and contact groups. Invitations are sent by e-mail to attendees.

- Add notes to an appointment in the form of a reference URL or text.

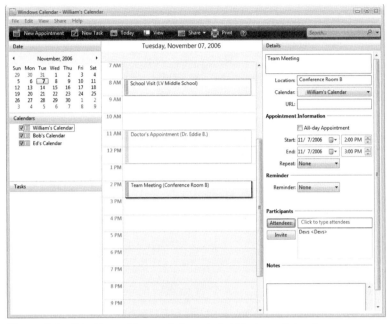

Figure 5-7   Working with appointments in Windows Calendar

You can create an appointment by following these steps:

1. Start Windows Calendar. Under the Calendars section, select the calendar you want to work with.

2. In the Day or Week view, right-click the date and time the appointment starts, and then select New Appointment.

3. If you prefer to work in the Month view, right-click the date on which the appointment occurs, and then select New Appointment.

4. Press Ctrl+D to view the appointment details, or click the Details button in the Day, Week, or Month view on the right.

5. In the text box provided at the top of the Details view, type a title for the appointment.

6. In the Location text box, type the location for the appointment.

7. Use the Appointment Information options to see the start and end times for the appointment. If the appointment should repeat, also set the repeat options.

8. If you want to be reminded prior to the appointment, use the Reminder list options to set the reminder.

9. If you want to specify participants, such as for a meeting, click the Attendees button. You can then select the contacts, contact groups, or both that should be listed as attendees.

10.   If you want to send invitations to attendees, click Invite. You will then be able to send an e-mail message to the attendees using your default e-mail program, such as Windows Mail.

11.   If you want to add notes to the appointment in the form of a reference URL or text, type this information in the boxes provided under the Notes heading.

Any appointments created on your personal calendar or on calendars to which you've subscribed are displayed in the Day, Week, and Month views. If the Details view is hidden, double-clicking an appointment displays the Details view for the appointment. If the Details view is open, clicking an appointment displays the Details view for the appointment.

> **Tip**   When you are working with multiple calendars, be sure to use color-coding to help you distinguish between calendars. If you click a calendar under the Calendars heading, you can specify the color to associate with the calendar.

Creating and Using Tasks

Windows Calendar can help you track the to-do tasks for yourself and any calendars to which you've subscribed. In Windows Calendar, tasks are listed under the Tasks heading, as shown in Figure 5-8. Tasks have two basic states:

■   **Open**   An open task is one that has not yet been completed.

■   **Completed**   A completed task is one that has been finished.

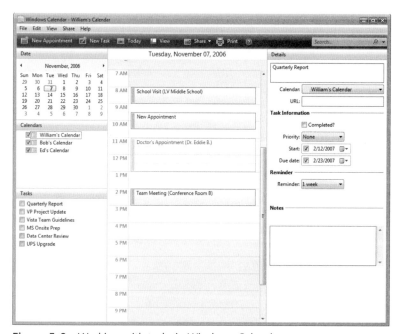

Figure 5-8   Working with tasks in Windows Calendar

When you create a task, you can specify a priority to indicate the task's relative importance. Windows Calendar also allows you to:

- Specify a date when you expect work on the task to start.

- Specify a due date for when the task must be completed.

- Add reminders so that you are notified a specified amount of time prior to a task's expected start date. The reminder will also notify you of when the task is due.

- Add notes to the task in the form of a reference URL or text.

You can create a task by following these steps:

1. Start Windows Calendar. Under the Calendars section, select the calendar you want to work with.

2. Click the New Task button on the toolbar.

3. Press Ctrl+D to view the task details, or click the Details button in the Day, Week, or Month view on the right.

4. If you want to add notes to the task in the form of a reference URL or text, type this information in the boxes provided under the Notes heading.

5. In the text box provided at the top of the Details view, type a title for the task.

6. If desired, use the Priority list to set the task's relative priority.

7. Use the Start options to set the task's expected start date.

8. Use the Due Date options to specify the date when the task must be completed.

9. If you want to be reminded prior to the task's expected start date, use the Reminder list options to set the reminder.

Any tasks created on your personal calendar or calendars to which you've subscribed are displayed under the Tasks heading. If the Details view is hidden, clicking a task and then pressing Ctrl+D displays the Details view for the task. If the Details view is open, clicking a task displays the Details view for the task.

You can mark a task as completed by using the check box provided under the Tasks heading. In the Details view, you can also mark a task completed by selecting the Completed check box under Task Information.

 Tip   Windows Calendar allows you to forward tasks via e-mail. To do this, right-click the task, and then select Forward.

Creating and Using Multiple Calendars

You might find that you need multiple calendars. For example, you might want one calendar for tracking office meetings and appointments, and another calendar for tracking personal meetings and your kids' appointments. Windows Calendar makes it easy to create and work with multiple calendars. If you want to create a new calendar, all you need to do is click File, New, Calendar or right-click an open area under the Calendars headings and select New, Calendar. A New Calendar entry is then added under the Calendars heading. The entry is selected and highlighted so that you can set the name of the new calendar by typing the calendar name and then pressing Enter.

When you are creating appointments and tasks in Windows Calendar, the calendar you've selected under the Calendars heading is the default. Tasks and appointments are created by default in the selected calendar. Calendars have two key properties that you can manage: a title and an associated color. You can edit calendar details by clicking a calendar under the Calendars heading and displaying the Details view. If the Details view is hidden, clicking a calendar and then pressing Ctrl+D displays the Details view for the calendar. If the Details view is open, clicking a calendar displays the Details view for the calendar.

Publishing and Subscribing to Calendars

Windows Calendar is designed to make sharing calendars easy. Any calendars you've created can be published to a folder on a Web server so that they can be accessed and subscribed to by other users. To share a calendar, follow these steps:

1. In Windows Calendar, click the calendar you want to work with under the Calendars heading.

2. If the Details view is hidden, press Ctrl+D to display it.

3. Under the Sharing Information heading, select Click Here To Publish.

4. Use the Publish Calendar dialog box to publish the calendar and associated information to a designated folder on a Web server, as shown in Figure 5-9.

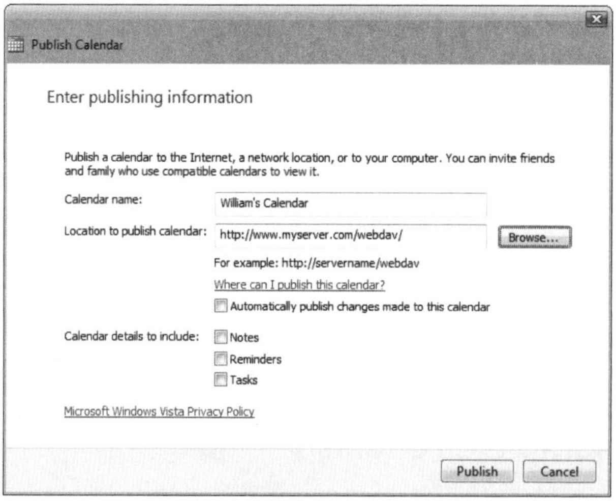

Figure 5-9   Entering the publishing information for the calendar

5.   Click Publish.

> **Note**   Windows Calendar uses Web Distributed Authoring and Versioning (WebDAV) to upload, download, view, and edit calendar data on the designated Web server. If you do not have adequate permissions to access the Web server and publish data via WebDAV, the publish operation will fail. Both Internet Information Services (IIS) 6 and IIS 7 support WebDAV. Be sure to obtain the appropriate URL from your network administrator before you attempt to publish your calendar.

To subscribe to a previously published calendar, follow these steps:

1.   In Windows Calendar, click the Share button on the toolbar and then click Subscribe. This displays the Subscribe To A Calendar dialog box, shown in Figure 5-10.

Figure 5-10   Subscribing to a published calendar

2.   In the Calendar To Subscribe To text box, type the URL path to the folder in which the calendar is published, such as **http://www.myserver.com/webdav/**.

3.   Click Next, and then follow the prompts.

> **Note**   WebDAV permissions determine whether you can subscribe to the calendar. If you do not have adequate permissions to access the Web server and subscribe to the calendar via WebDAV, the subscribe operation will fail.

Using Windows Shared View

Windows Shared View allows you to make virtual presentations over the network, share handouts, and collaborate with coworkers. When you work with Windows Shared View, you are able set up or join a Windows Shared View session. Because Windows Shared View establishes connections with other computers, you'll need to create exceptions on your computer's firewall and on any other firewalls between your computer and the computers participating in the Windows Shared View session.

Getting Started with Windows Shared View

Most versions of Windows Vista include Windows Shared View, which uses the People Near Me feature for sharing information. Windows Shared View also requires that you enable file synchronization and configure a Windows Firewall exception. The first time you run Windows Shared View, you are prompted to automatically configure these options.

You can start and configure Windows Shared View for first use by following these steps:

1. Click Start, point to All Programs, and then click Windows Shared View.

2. In the Windows Shared View Setup dialog box, click Enable File Synchronization And Windows Firewall Exception to continue to set up Windows Shared View.

3. In the Set Up People Near Me dialog box, type the display name you want to use, and then click OK. The default display name is your Windows logon display name.

4. The main Windows Shared View window appears in which you can start a new session, join a session near you, or open an invitation file.

Windows Shared View uses the concept of sessions to define the virtual space in which you make virtual presentations over the network, share handouts, and collaborate with coworkers. To control entry into a Windows Shared View session, each session has a session name and a session password. You must know the session name and the session password to join a session.

Starting a New Windows Shared View Session

You can start a new Windows Shared View session by completing these steps:

1. Start Windows Shared View.

2. Click Start A New Session in the main window.

3. In the Session Name text box, type a session name or accept the default value.

4. In the Password text box, enter a password for the session that is at least eight characters long. If you want to view the characters in the password, select the View Characters check box.

5. Click the Create A Session button. Windows Shared View then creates the session, and you can create presentations, share handouts, and more.

Note   The People Near Me concept is also used to control session visibility. Typically, users with computers on the same network are considered to be People Near Me and are listed in the People Near Me window. The default new session options allow People Near Me to see collaboration sessions. Users can then join a session if they know the session password. If you click the Options link when creating a new session, you can elect to hide the session from People Near Me, which would require a user to know both the session name and the session password to access the session.

Running a Windows Shared View Session

After Windows Shared View creates a session, you can use the options in the main window, shown in Figure 5-11, to invite people to the session, start a presentation, and share handouts. When you invite people to a collaboration session, you can choose people to invite from a list of those nearby by clicking the person's name in the Name list and then clicking Send Invitations. If you click the Invite Others option, you can invite people via e-mail or by creating an invitation file and saving it in a location others can access.

Figure 5-11   Using Windows Shared View

When you start a presentation, meeting participants will be able to view elements on your screen. If you want to limit the presentation to a specific application, you can choose a single running application to share for the presentation. For example, if you have a document open in Microsoft Office PowerPoint, you can select PowerPoint and then click Present to begin using PowerPoint to conduct your presentation. During the collaboration session, other users could take control of PowerPoint as well to add notes, share their slides, etc. Generally, only one person at a time can control the shared application. An additional option for presentations is to select Desktop as the program to share. If you select Desktop and then click Present, participants can see all running applications and items on your desktop.

When you share handouts, a selected file is copied to each participant's computer. One participant at a time can then make changes to the copy of the handout, and those changes will be made to all participants' handouts. The original file will not be changed, however.

Joining a Windows Shared View Session

You can join a Windows Shared View session by completing these steps:

1. Start Windows Shared View.
2. Click Join A Session Near Me in the main window.
3. Click the session to join.
4. In the Password field, enter a password for the session.
5. Click the Join A Session button.

Once you join a Windows Shared View session, you can begin participating. As with other participants, you can start a presentation, share a handout, and invite others to join the session. When you want to leave the session, click File and then select Leave Session.

Setting Your Participant Status

When you join a session, you are listed as one of the participants. If you need to work on something else or step away from your computer, you can change your participant status to let other participants know you are busy or away. To set a busy, away, or be right back status, click your name under the Participants heading, and then select the Busy, Be Right Back, or Away option. Your status is then updated in the Participants list.

When you are free or you return to your computer, you can change your status back to available. To do this, click your name under the Participants heading, and then select the Available option. Your name in the Participants list will then reflect a normal (available) status.

Sending Notes to Participants

From within Windows Shared View, you can easily send a note to a participant. To send a note to a participant, follow these steps:

1. Right-click the participant's name, and then select Send A Note.
2. In the Send A Note dialog box, type the text of the note.
3. Click Send.

The recipient sees the note in a You Received A Note dialog box. To reply to the note, the recipient can:

1. Click Reply.
2. In the Send A Note dialog box, type the text of the note.
3. Click Send.

Leaving a Session and Sharing Stored Files

Windows Shared View creates copies of shared files on each participant's computer. Any one participant can make changes to a shared copy of a file, and these changes are then made on all shared copies of the file on other participants' computers. The original file remains untouched in its original location.

When you leave a Windows Shared View session by clicking File and then selecting Leave Session, copies of shared files on your computer are not saved. If you want to save the copies of the shared files, you must do so before leaving the session. To save the copies of the shared files on your computer, follow these steps:

1. Click File, and then select Save Shared Files.

2. Use the Browse For Folder dialog box to select the save location.

3. Click OK.

The shared files are then saved to the designated location.

Chapter 6

Managing Programs and Multimedia

The available programs and the types of files those programs can work with are at the heart of everything you can do with a computer. If programs aren't installed and configured properly, you might have trouble working with various types of files and multimedia. You might find that the wrong programs are used to open files of particular types, that you waste time switching between programs, or that media files on removable media—such as audio, video, and pictures on CDs and DVDs—just aren't handled in the ways you need them to be handled. Indeed, in earlier versions of Microsoft Windows, it isn't always easy to manage installed programs, file associations, and AutoPlay options.

Windows Vista corrects many of these deficiencies by making it easier than ever before to manage programs, multimedia, and related settings. To do this, Windows Vista includes:

■ **Software Explorer** A component of Windows Defender, which lets you easily determine and manage startup programs, currently running programs, network-connected programs, and programs that use Winsock.

■ **Programs** A category in Control Panel that provides tasks for viewing installed programs, adding and removing programs, viewing installed updates, and more.

■ **Default Programs** A Control Panel page that lets you easily track and configure global default programs for the computer, personal default programs for yourself or another user, AutoPlay settings for multimedia, and file associations for programs. You can find Default Programs on the Programs page in Control Panel.

Most versions of Windows Vista also provide enhanced tools for managing your multimedia, including Windows Media Player for playing digital media such as music and videos; Windows Movie Maker for creating movies using pictures, videos, and music; and Windows Photo Gallery for viewing, editing, organizing, and sharing pictures and videos.

Note   This book was written using the Windows Vista Beta to provide an early introduction to the operating system. More so than any other area of Windows Vista, the security features discussed in this book are subject to change. Some of the features might not be included in the final product, and some of the features might be changed substantially.

Navigating Your Computer's Startup, Running, and Network-Connected Programs

Windows Vista includes Windows Defender for safeguarding your computer from spyware. To be able to do its job in tracking potentially malicious programs on your computer, Windows Defender must also track all the programs running on a computer and identify how those programs are being used. The component that handles these tasks is Software Explorer.

You access Software Explorer in Windows Defender. Click Start, point to All Programs, and click Windows Defender. Click Tools on the Windows Defender toolbar, and then click Software Explorer. Using the Software Explorer, you can quickly determine a computer's:

- Startup programs
- Currently running programs
- Network-connected programs

Exploring Your Startup Programs

Any programs configured to start automatically when you log on are considered to be *startup programs*. In Software Explorer, you select Startup Programs in the Category list to view currently configured startup programs.

Tip   In Windows Vista, you specify startup programs for all users by adding a program short-cut to the %SystemRoot%\ProgramData\Microsoft\Windows\Start Menu\Programs\Startup folder. You specify startup programs for yourself or another user by adding a program shortcut to the %UserProfile%\AppData\Roaming\Microsoft\Windows\Start Menu\Programs\Startup folder. Both folders are hidden and can be viewed only by changing the default Folder Options. Registry settings for the current user or local machine can also be used to configure startup programs.

As shown in Figure 6-1, startup programs are grouped by software publisher by default. You can group programs by startup type by right-clicking in the left pane and then selecting Startup Type on the shortcut menu.

Figure 6-1 Viewing startup programs in Software Explorer

To view details about a startup program's configuration, click the program in the left pane. The details listed for each startup program include:

- **File Name**   The executable file name.
- **Display Name**   The application name that Windows Vista uses.
- **Description**   A description of the program.
- **Publisher**   The company that published the software.
- **File Type**   The type of file listed in the File Name field, such as whether a file is an application file or an application extension file.
- **Startup Value**   The options or parameters passed to the program at startup.
- **Verified**   Specifies whether the file has been digitally verified as authentic.
- **File Path**   Shows the complete file path to the executable file.
- **File Size**   The size of the executable file in bytes.
- **File Version**   The version and revision number of the executable file.
- **Date Installed**   The date and time the file was installed.
- **Startup Type**   Specifies how you have configured the program to start automatically, such as whether the startup program is in the All Users Startup folder or in the user's personal Startup folder.
- **Location**   The folder path where the startup program shortcut was created or the Run registry key value was set.

- **Classification**   The classification of the executable file as either allowed or not allowed.

- **Ships With OS**   Specifies whether the executable file ships with the operating system.

When you select a startup program in the left pane, you can easily remove, enable, or disable a startup program:

- Click Remove to delete the shortcut or registry value that sets the program to start automatically.

- Click Disable to configure the program so that it doesn't start automatically, without removing the shortcut or registry value that sets the program to start automatically.

- Click Enable to allow a previously disabled startup program to run automatically at logon.

Determining Your Currently Running Programs

In earlier versions of Windows, Task Manager is the primary way to determine which programs and processes are running. In Windows Vista, you typically will use the Currently Running Programs view in Software Explorer to determine which programs are currently running. You can then access Task Manager from Software Explorer if you need to manage running programs or processes.

As shown in Figure 6-2, Software Explorer displays currently running programs when you select Currently Running Programs in the Category list. Software Explorer groups running programs by software publisher by default. To group programs by user, right-click in the left pane and then select User Name on the shortcut menu.

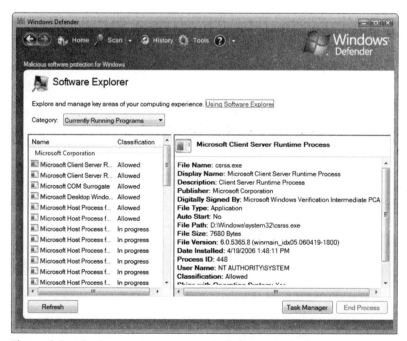

Figure 6-2   Viewing running programs in Software Explorer

You can view details about a running program's configuration by clicking the program in the left pane. The details listed for each running program are similar to those for startup programs. There are two important exceptions:

- Process ID lists the process ID number of the related process.
- User Name lists the user account under which the process is running.

The key tasks you can perform in the Currently Running Programs list are:

- **Terminate a process**   When you select a top-level process or an application's main process in the program list, you can end the process by clicking Terminate and then clicking Yes when prompted to confirm the action.

- **Run Task Manager**   When you click the Task Manager button, Windows Vista opens the Task Manager, and you can then manage processes as you would in earlier versions of Windows.

Examining Network-Connected Programs

In Software Explorer, you select Network Connected Programs in the Category list to view programs that are connected to the local area network (LAN), the Internet, or both. When you select a network-connected program, you can view the configuration details, as shown in Figure 6-3.

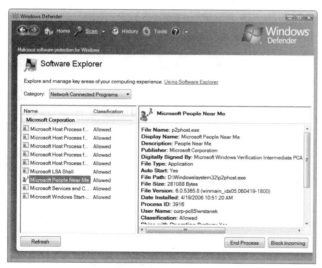

Figure 6-3   Viewing network-connected programs in Software Explorer

The details listed for each network-connected program include a list of active connections according to the following criteria:

- **Protocol**   The TCP/IP protocol being used.
- **Local Address**   The local IP address and port number being used.

- **Foreign Address**   The remote IP address and port number being used (if any).
- **State**   The state of the port being used, such as whether it is listening for incoming requests.

When you select a user-started program in the left pane, you can easily stop the program or block incoming connections to the program:

- Click Terminate to stop the program.
- Click Block Incoming to block incoming connections to the program.

Working with Your Computer's Programs

In earlier versions of Windows, you used the Add Or Remove Programs utility to add new programs, change or remove programs, add or remove Windows components, and set program access and defaults. In Windows Vista, these functions are provided by separate features that don't always work as they have in the past.

When you want to work with programs and updates, you'll use the Programs category in Control Panel, which provides tasks for:

- Viewing, adding, removing, and repairing installed programs.
- Viewing and checking for installed updates.
- Configuring Default Programs.
- Setting Advanced Options for Windows features.

To access the Programs category, click Start and then click Control Panel. In Control Panel, click the link for the Programs category heading.

Viewing, Adding, Removing, and Repairing Installed Programs

Windows Vista considers any program you've installed on a computer or made available for a network installation to be an installed program. The operating system provides separate features for viewing, adding, removing, and repairing installed programs.

You can view, add, remove, or repair installed programs by following these steps:

1. In Control Panel, click Programs.
2. Under Installed Programs, click View Installed Programs.

   The Installed Programs page is displayed (see Figure 6-4) with a list of programs you've installed.

3. In the Name list, right-click the program you want to work with, and then select Remove to uninstall the program, Change to modify the program, or Repair to repair the program.

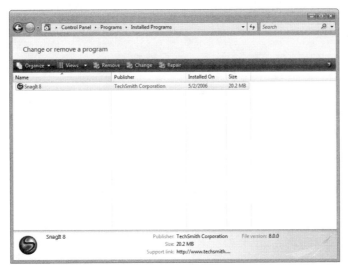

Figure 6-4   Working with installed programs

Viewing and Checking for Installed Updates

Windows Update allows a computer to connect automatically to the Microsoft Windows Update Web site or a designated update server to obtain any necessary operating system updates. This allows the computer to automatically download and install critical updates, security updates, update rollups, and service packs.

As in earlier versions of Windows, you must enable Windows Update for the feature to work. Once the feature is enabled, you can work with installed updates by using the options in the Programs category of Control Panel. To view, change, or remove installed updates, follow these steps:

1.   In Control Panel, click Programs.

2.   Under Installed Updates, click View Installed Updates.

     The Installed Updates page is displayed with a list of updates that have been installed.

3.   In the Name list, right-click the update you want to work with, and then select Remove to uninstall the update or Change to modify the update.

To check for updates by follow these steps:

1.   In Control Panel, click System And Maintenance.

2.   Under Windows Update, click Check For Updates.

Configuring Default Programs

Default programs and their related settings have important roles on your computer. They determine which programs are used with which types of files and how Windows handles files on CDs, DVDs, and portable devices. To configure default programs and settings, click

Programs in Control Panel, and then click Default Programs. You can then configure default programs and settings using the Default Programs page, shown in Figure 6-5.

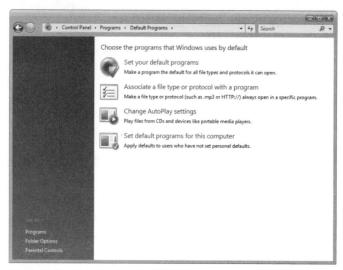

Figure 6-5   Configuring default programs and related settings

Program defaults allow you to specify which program should be used for certain activities, such as Web browsing or sending e-mail, and which programs are accessible from the Start menu, desktop, and other locations.

Note   Unlike earlier versions of Windows, Windows Vista makes it easy to set personal defaults as well as global defaults for programs, and those defaults apply not only to the specific file types the programs can use, such as .htm and .html files, but also to the specific protocols the programs can use, such as http:// and https://.

When working with personal and global default programs, keep the following in mind:

- Personal default programs apply to the currently logged on user and make a program the default for all file types and protocols it can open. To set personal defaults, click the Programs in Control Panel, click Default Programs, and then click Set Your Default Programs. Afterward, follow the prompts.

- Global default programs apply to all users who haven't set personal defaults and make a program the default for all file types and protocols it can open. To set global defaults, click Programs in Control Panel, click Default Programs, and then click Set Default Programs For This Computer. Afterward, follow the prompts.

In Windows Vista, AutoPlay options make it easy to specify how Windows handles files on CDs, DVDs, and portable devices. As Figure 6-6 shows, you can configure separate AutoPlay options for each type of CD, DVD, and media your computer can handle.

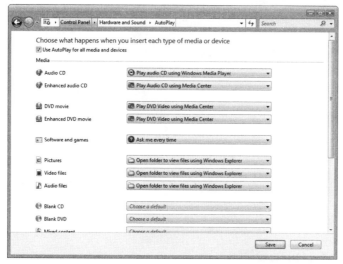

Figure 6-6   Configuring default programs and related settings

You can configure AutoPlay options by following these steps:

1.   Click Programs in Control Panel.

2.   Click Default Programs, and then click Change AutoPlay Settings.

3.   Use the Media selection list for the type of media for which you want to set the default AutoPlay option. Repeat as necessary.

4.   Click Save to save your settings.

Setting Advanced Options for Windows Features

In earlier versions of Windows, you used the Add/Remove Windows Components option of the Add Or Remove Programs utility to add or remove the Windows components a computer used. In Windows Vista, operating system components are considered Windows features that can be turned on or off rather than added or removed.

You can turn on or off Windows features by following these steps:

1.   Click Programs in Control Panel.

2.   Click Turn On Or Off Windows Features.

3.   Use the Windows Features dialog box, shown in Figure 6-7, to turn Windows features on or off.

4.   Click OK.

Figure 6-7   Turning Windows features on or off

Getting into Your Multimedia

Windows Vista has more features to support multimedia than any earlier version of Windows. Depending on which version of Windows Vista you are using, your computer might include Windows Media Player 11, Windows Movie Maker 6, Windows Photo Gallery, or any combination of these three programs.

Getting Started with Windows Media Player

Windows Media Player 11 plays digital media, including music and videos from files on your computer as well as CDs, DVDs, and other media you insert. It can also serve as an Internet radio player.

The first time you start Windows Media Player by clicking Programs, All Programs, Windows Media Player, you'll have to specify how Windows Media Player should be configured. As shown in Figure 6-8, you can either accept the default configuration or set a custom configuration. The default configuration works well in most instances.

As Figure 6-9 shows, the Windows Media Player main window has been streamlined considerably from earlier versions. Not only does this make working with Windows Media Player more intuitive, but you'll find that it is also much easier to organize your media. The key interface enhancements you should note are:

■ **Navigation toolbar**   The Navigation toolbar is the top toolbar. It provides browser-like Back and Forward buttons that let you navigate to pages you've viewed previously. It also has quick access buttons: Now Playing, Library, Rip, Burn, Sync, and Musicmatch.

■ **Address toolbar**   The Address toolbar allows you to navigate through the media available on your computer. It includes View Options and Layout Options buttons as well as a Quick Search box and a Show/Hide List Pane button.

■ **Controls toolbar**   The Controls toolbar is in the lower portion of the main window. It provides basic controls for playing music, videos, and pictures as well as going to previous or next items. The buttons are Turn Shuffle On/Off, Turn Repeat On/Off, Stop, Previous, Play, Next, Mute, Volume Control, View Full Screen, and Switch To Skin Mode.

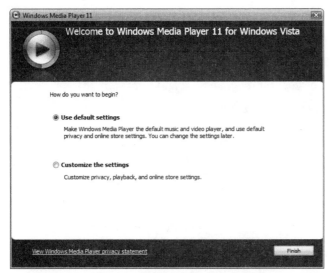

Figure 6-8   Configuring Windows Media Player for the first time

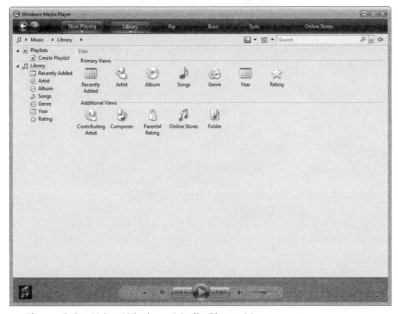

Figure 6-9   Using Windows Media Player 11

Navigating the Windows Media Player Quick Access Buttons

Figure 6-10 shows the Navigation toolbar in Windows Media Player 11. The Navigation toolbar's quick access buttons are used as follows:

- **Now Playing**   Allows you to watch what's currently playing.
- **Library**   Allows you to create play lists and manage content.
- **Rip**   Allows you to copy music from audio discs to your computer.
- **Burn**   Allows you to burn files to discs.
- **Sync**   Allows you to synchronize content to and from your portable devices.
- **Musicmatch**   Allows you to find online music sources.

Figure 6-10   The Navigation toolbar in Windows Media Player 11

If you click the lower portion of any quick access button, you'll see an options menu that provides additional related options. For example, the Rip options menu allows you to set the default format and bit rate for the music you are ripping. The default format is Windows Media Audio, and the default bit rate is 128 kilobits per second (Kbps).

> **Tip**   To get the best quality, you should set the bit rate to 192 Kbps. However, this increases the size of ripped files on your hard drive.

Searching and Browsing Media Categories in Windows Media Player 11

Figure 6-11 shows the Address toolbar in Windows Media Player 11. Like the Address toolbar in Windows Explorer, the Address toolbar in Windows Media Player displays your current location as a series of links separated by arrows. This allows you to see your current location in relation to the locations you've navigated.

Figure 6-11   The Address toolbar in Windows Media Player 11

On the far left of the Address path is the Select A Category icon. This icon depicts the type of media you are currently working with. You'll see different icons for each type of media you can work with, including:

- Music
- Pictures
- Video
- Recorded TV
- Other Media

You navigate each link in the Address path in several different ways:

- You can access a top-level page anywhere along the path that's displayed on the Address bar by clicking the link for that view page. For example, you could open the Music page by clicking the Music link.

- You can access a second-level page of any page displayed on the Address bar by clicking the arrow to the right of the page icon. This displays a list of the second-level pages for the currently selected page. To access one of these pages, you click the desired page in the list. For example, if you're working with music and click the My Library options button, you can view your music organized by Artist, Album, Songs, Genre, Parental Rating, Folder, and so on.

At the far right of the Address toolbar is the Show/Hide List Pane button. Click this button to display your current playlist, where you can drag items to the list to add them. Click this button again to close the current playlist view.

The Address toolbar also includes a Search box. You can use the Search box to quickly search for the media information associated with the currently selected type of media. The Search feature matches complete or partial words included in the media information.

You can search your media by completing the following steps:

1. Click in the Search box.

2. Type your search text.

    Windows Media Player returns matches as you type.

Click the Clear button to clear the search results.

Playing and Previewing Your Media

Figure 6-12 shows the Controls toolbar in Windows Media Player 11. The Controls toolbar is displayed in the lower portion of the main window. From left to right, the controls on the toolbar are:

- **Turn Shuffle On/Off**   Toggles the shuffle feature on or off.
- **Turn Repeat On/Off**   Toggles the repeat feature on or off.
- **Stop**   Stops playing or displaying the current file.
- **Previous**   Goes to the previous file. If you click and hold this button, you can rewind.
- **Play**   Plays the current file.
- **Next**   Goes to the next file. If you click and hold this button, you can fast forward.
- **Mute**   Mutes the sound.
- **Volume Control**   Adjusts the sound level.

- **View Full Screen**   Displays player in full screen mode, when allowed.
- **Switch To Skin Mode**   Displays mini-player with custom framing.

Figure 6-12   The Controls toolbar in Windows Media Player 11

Getting Started with Windows Movie Maker

Windows Movie Maker lets you create movies using pictures, videos, narration, and music. You start Windows Movie Maker by clicking Programs, All Programs, Windows Movie Maker. As Figure 6-13 shows, the main window has three areas:

- **Tasks pane**   Provides quick access to common tasks for importing, editing, and publishing movies.
- **Work area**   Provides the main work area, which you can divide into multiple view areas depending on the tasks you are performing.
- **Storyboard/timeline**   Allows you to organize the pictures, videos, narration, and music included in the movie according to a storyboard or timeline.

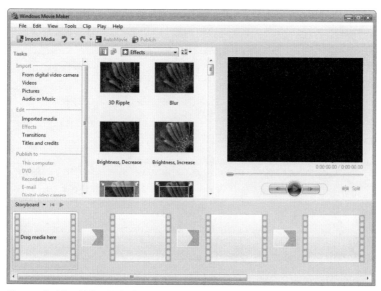

Figure 6-13   Using Windows Movie Maker

Movies are managed as projects. Once you open a project or create a new project, you can import pictures, videos, narration, and music for use in the project and then create your movie by putting these elements on the storyboard or project timeline in the order in which you want them to appear.

You can add titles and credits to a project as well. Titles can be inserted at the beginning of the project, before a selected clip, or as an overlay of a selected clip. Credits are added to the end of a project. When you have finished creating the movie, you can save it and then publish it so that other people can play your movie.

Getting Started with Windows Photo Gallery

Windows Photo Gallery allows you to view, edit, organize, and share pictures and videos. To start Windows Movie Make, click Programs, point to All Programs, and click Windows Photo Gallery. As Figure 6-14 shows, the main window has four key elements:

- **Navigation toolbar**   The Navigation toolbar is the top toolbar. It provides browser-like Back and Next buttons that let you navigate to pages you've viewed previously. It also has quick access buttons: File, Fix, Info, Print, Create, E-Mail, and Open.

- **Views pane**   Provides quick access for organizing and displaying pictures and videos by type, tags, date, ratings, and so on.

- **Preview/work area**   Displays thumbnail previews of pictures and videos when you select a particular category or type, and also provides the main work area for when you are performing tasks such as fixing a selected picture.

- **Controls toolbar**   The Controls toolbar is displayed in the lower portion of the main window. Basic controls are provided for manipulating a selected picture or video. You can change the default thumbnail size and the display size. You can also rotate pictures clockwise or counterclockwise.

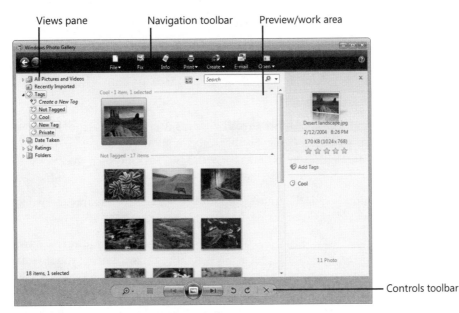

Figure 6-14   Using Windows Photo Gallery

Navigating the Windows Photo Gallery Quick Access Buttons

Figure 6-15 shows the Navigation toolbar in Windows Photo Gallery. The Navigation toolbar's quick access buttons are used as follows:

- **File**   Allows you to add files and folders and manipulate existing files.

- **Fix**   Allows you to edit a selected picture using auto adjust, adjust exposure, adjust color, crop picture, and fix red eye options.

- **Info**   Displays an Information pane for a selected picture or video that provides details about the related file. You can use the Information pane to add a star rating, to add tags as keywords, and to add captions to a selected picture or video.

- **Print**   Allows you to print a selected picture or video.

- **Create**   Allows you to create a DVD or movie using selected pictures and videos.

- **E-Mail**   Allows you to e-mail selected pictures and videos.

- **Open**   Allows you to open a selected picture or video in another program.

Figure 6-15   The Navigation toolbar in Windows Photo Gallery

Searching and Browsing Pictures and Videos in Windows Photo Gallery

The Views pane, shown as a separate panel on the left side of Windows Photo Gallery, and the Quick Search box, shown in the right corner of Windows Photo Gallery, provide quick access for organizing and displaying pictures and videos by type, tags, date, ratings, and so on.

The Views pane includes several top-level categories and subcategories. Selecting a category or subcategory displays related pictures, videos, or both. The categories are used as follows:

- **All Pictures And Videos**   Under the All Pictures And Videos category are Pictures and Videos subcategories. These subcategories allow you to return quickly a list of all videos or all pictures in folders that Windows Photo Gallery has been configured to use.

- **Recently Imported**   Select Recently Imported to see a list of pictures and videos recently imported from a digital camera or other media source.

- **Tags**   Under the Tags category, you'll find a list of all the tags you've used with pictures and videos. Tags are keywords that aid in searching and organizing your media. Clicking Create A New Tag allows you to create a new tag to be used as a keyword. Clicking Not Tagged displays all pictures and videos that you haven't tagged. You can drag a picture or video from the Not Tagged category to a named tag category to add the tag to that item.

- **Date Taken**   Use Date Taken to navigate through pictures and videos according to the year, month, and date they were created.

- **Ratings**   Use Ratings to navigate through pictures and videos according to the star rating you've assigned to them. Assign a low star rating to your least favorite pictures, and a high start rating to your favorite pictures.

- **Folders**   Use Folders to determine which folders are associated with Windows Photo Gallery and to navigate through pictures and videos using views of these folders.

From the experts
The curse of digital cameras

Digital cameras make it easy to take thousands of pictures. It gets hard when you want to find pictures, though, because they're probably named something like IMG_1322 or DSC3243.

Tags make it much easier to find your pictures. When you load your pictures from your camera, Windows Vista prompts you to assign a tag to that batch of pictures. So, pictures will have tags by default. You can also use Windows Photo Gallery to drag-and-drop thumbnails to assign tags to pictures. Your pictures still won't have useful names, but it won't matter because you can search for and group pictures according to their tags.

Tony Northrup
Author, MCSE, and MVP–For more information, see http://www.northrup.org.

 Tip   By default, only the %UserProfile%\Pictures folder and the Public Pictures folders are used by Windows Photo Gallery. To specify that additional folders should be used, right-click the Folders category in the Views pane, and then select Add Pictures And Videos To Gallery.

The work area of Windows Photo Gallery includes a Thumbnail Views button and a Quick Search box. You can use the Thumbnail Views button to display view and grouping options. You can use the Search box to quickly search for pictures and videos. The Search feature matches complete or partial words in the media information associated with pictures and videos. This allows you to search on file name, tags, and other information associated with pictures and videos.

You can search your media by completing the following steps:

1. Click in the Search box.

2. Type your search text.

   Windows Movie Maker returns matches as you type.

Click the Clear button to clear the search results.

Playing and Previewing Your Pictures and Videos

Figure 6-16 shows the Controls toolbar in Windows Photo Gallery. The Controls toolbar is displayed in the lower portion of the main window. From left to right, the controls on the toolbar are:

- **Magnify**   Used to magnify or shrink the thumbnail views of currently displayed items.
- **Set Default Thumbnail Size**   Restores the default thumbnail size.
- **Stop**   Stops playing or displaying the current file.
- **Previous**   Goes to the previous picture or video.
- **Play Slide Show**   Plays a slide show of the currently listed pictures or videos.
- **Next**   Goes to the next picture or video.
- **Rotate Counterclockwise**   Rotates the selected picture or video counterclockwise.
- **Rotate Clockwise**   Rotates the selected picture or video clockwise.
- **Delete**   Deletes the selected picture or video.

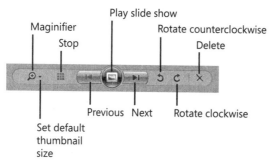

Figure 6-16   The Controls toolbar in Windows Photo Gallery

Chapter 7

Working with Laptops and Tablet PCs

Microsoft Windows Vista includes many enhancements for laptops and Tablet PCs. Because some of these enhancements have been discussed in earlier chapters, this chapter explores changes related to energy saving options, Tablet PC pens, and networked projectors. This chapter also describes Windows Mobility Center and how it can be used to quickly configure common mobile PC options.

Note This book was written using the Windows Vista Beta to provide an early introduction to the operating system. More so than any other area of Windows Vista, the security features discussed in this book are subject to change. Some of the features might not be included in the final product, and some of the features might be changed substantially.

Optimizing Performance and Saving Energy

Optimizing performance and saving energy is an issue with all computers, but especially with laptops and Tablet PCs, which run on battery power when they are disconnected from primary power. To help manage power consumption, Windows Vista uses *power plans*. Power plans are similar to the power schemes used in earlier versions of Microsoft Windows, but they are much easier to work with because the configuration interface has been streamlined and made more intuitive. Most power management settings are configured within a specified power plan. A few power options, however, are configured globally.

Note As you read through the sections that follow, keep in mind that mobile PCs have additional options for turning off and shutting down. You can turn off a mobile PC by using the sleep button or by closing the lid. You can shut down a mobile PC by pressing and holding its power button. The way these buttons are used can be configured, as you'll see.

Getting to Know the Windows Vista Power Plans

Windows XP includes six power schemes, which are used to automatically manage the monitor, hard disks, standby mode, and hibernation mode, and provides a number of other options to control power settings. Windows Vista simplifies power configuration by providing three preferred plans:

- **Balanced** The default (active) plan, which uses a balanced approach to managing power. This plan balances energy consumption and system performance. The processor speeds up when more resources are used and slows down when less are needed.

- **High Performance** A high-power usage plan that optimizes the computer for performance. This plan ensures that you always have enough power for using graphics-intensive programs or playing multimedia games.

- **Power Saver** A low-power usage plan designed to reduce power consumption. This plan slows down the processor to maximize the battery life.

Tip On laptops and Tablet PCs, the notification area of the taskbar includes a Power icon. Moving the mouse pointer over this icon shows the battery state and the power plan you are using. You can right-click the Power icon to display a shortcut menu with options for quickly accessing the Power Options utility and Windows Mobility Center.

The basic settings of power plans are used to control when a computer turns off its display and when it powers down. By default, both the Balanced plan and the Power Saver plan configure Windows Vista to turn off the display after 20 minutes of inactivity and to power down the computer after 1 hour of inactivity. The High Performance plan, on the other hand, configures Windows Vista to turn off the display after 20 minutes of inactivity but to never automatically power down. You can also create your own power plans.

Caution Standby and hibernation are not configurable as basic power options because Windows Vista handles power down and shutdown in different ways. As discussed in the "Turning Off and Shutting Down Computers Running Windows Vista" section in Chapter 1, Windows Vista enters a sleep state when you turn off the computer (in most instances), and it is only when you shut down that the power is turned off completely. If you want to configure Hibernation, you'll need to use the Power Options dialog box.

Note When running on battery, laptops and Tablet PCs continue to use battery power in the sleep state, but at a very low rate. If the battery runs low on power while the computer is in the sleep state, the current working environment of the laptop or Tablet PC is saved to the hard disk and then the computer is shut down completely. This is similar to the hibernate state used with Windows XP.

The advanced settings of the power plans are used to control every facet of power management, including both the basic settings and these additional settings:

- Requiring a password on wakeup
- Setting power saving mode for wireless adapters and PCI Express links
- Configuring sleep and hibernate options
- Defining power button and lid configuration
- Setting the permitted minimum and maximum processor state

The differences in the advanced settings are what really set the power plans apart from each other. For example, the High Performance plan allows the computer's processor to always run at 100 percent power consumption; the Balanced plan sets a minimum power consumption rate of 5 percent and a maximum rate of 100 percent; and the Power Save plan sets a minimum power consumption rate of 5 percent and a maximum rate of 50 percent.

From the experts
Want to save money?

Well-run businesses always try to keep an eye on the bottom line to save on unnecessary costs. Using power plans is one way to do this. A typical desktop PC including flat-screen monitor consumes around $100 to $150 (US) worth of electricity per year. If your company has hundreds of PCs, you might be able to save several thousand dollars per year simply by implementing appropriate power plans that turn off the display and put computers to sleep when they aren't being used.

In a business environment that has Active Directory deployed, power plans can easily be enforced on your desktop PCs using Group Policy. One thing to remember when you do this: the more aggressive (that is, more efficient in regard to energy savings) a power plan is, the greater its potential impact may be on performance for users. For example, a plan that puts computers to sleep after only ten minutes of inactivity may actually make users *less* productive if they need to keep waking their computers up to use them! The bottom line is that power plans aren't just for mobile computers like laptops—they're also great for saving energy costs in large desktop deployments.

Mitch Tulloch
Author and MVP—For more information, see http://www.mtit.com.

Selecting and Configuring a Power Plan

You can access and switch between power plans in Control Panel by following these steps:

1. Click Start, and then click Control Panel.
2. In Control Panel, click System And Maintenance, and then click Power Options.
3. As shown in Figure 7-1, you can specify the power plan to use by selecting it in the Preferred Plans list.

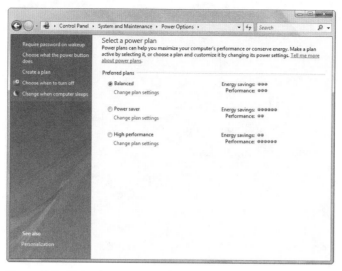

Figure 7-1   Selecting a power plan

You can change the options of a specific power plan by following these steps:

1. Access the Power Options utility in Control Panel.

2. Click Change Plan Settings for the plan you want to work with.

3. Use the Turn Off Display list to specify whether or when the computer's display automatically turns off (see Figure 7-2).

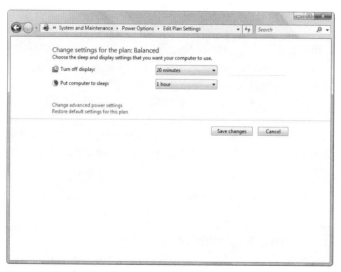

Figure 7-2   Configuring power plan options

4. Use the Put Computer To Sleep list to specify whether or when the computer automatically enters sleep mode.

5. If you want to configure advanced power options, click Change Advanced Power Settings.

Understanding Your Computer's Power Button and Password Protection On Wakeup Options

Windows Vista allows you to define global Power Button and Password Protection On Wakeup options that apply to all plans. When you work with these settings, keep the following in mind:

■ By default, pressing and holding a computer's power button shuts down the computer. Pressing a laptop or Tablet PC's sleep button or closing the lid turns off the computer and puts it in sleep mode. You can also configure a computer so that pressing the power button puts it in either sleep or hibernate mode. When a computer hibernates, the state of the computer is saved to the hard disk and then the computer is shut down completely.

■ By default, all power plans use Password Protection On Wakeup. This option ensures that when your computer wakes up from sleep mode, no one can access your computer without first entering a password to unlock the screen.

You can set the Power Button and Password Protection On Wakeup options by following these steps:

1. Click Start, and then click Control Panel.

2. In Control Panel, click System And Maintenance, and then click Power Options.

3. In the left pane, click Choose What The Power Button Does.

4. Use the When I Press The Power Button list to specify whether the computer should shut down, sleep, or hibernate when the power button is pressed (see Figure 7-3).

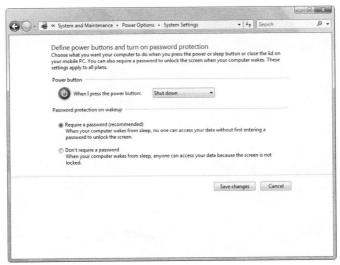

Figure 7-3   Setting Power Button and Password Protection On Wakeup options

5. Use the Password Protection On Wakeup options to specify whether the computer requires a password on wakeup.

Tapping and Flicking Your Tablet PC Pen

Tablet PCs use pens as input devices. Pens can be used to interact with items on the screen by tapping and flicking.

Tapping Your Pen

With pen taps, you can easily perform actions equivalent to using a mouse. Double-tapping the pen on the screen is equivalent to a double-click mouse action. Pressing and holding the pen to the screen is the equivalent to a right-click mouse action. You can also press the pen button to perform a right-click. On some tablet pens, you can grip the top of the pen to erase ink from the screen. By default, each tapping action of the pen is accompanied by some type of visual feedback.

You can set pen tap options by following these steps:

1. Click Start, and then click Control Panel.

2. In Control Panel, click Hardware And Sound, and then click Pen And Input Devices.

3. As shown in Figure 7-4, the Pen And Input Devices dialog box is displayed, with the Pen Options tab selected.

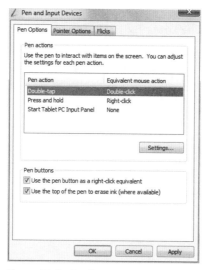

Figure 7-4   Setting pen tap options

4. To configure double-tapping, double-click Double-Tap in the Pen Action section. You can then adjust how quickly you can tap the screen and the distance the pointer can move between tapping.

5. Click OK.

6. To configure pressing and holding, double-click Press And Hold in the Pen Action section. You can then change the amount of time you must press and hold the pen to the

screen to perform the equivalent of a right-click and the amount of time to perform the right-click action.

7. Click OK to save the settings.

To view or change visual feedback options, follow these steps:

1. Click Start, and then click Control Panel.

2. In Control Panel, click Hardware And Sound, and then click Pen And Input Devices.

3. In the Pen And Input Devices dialog box, click the Pointer Options tab, as shown in Figure 7-5.

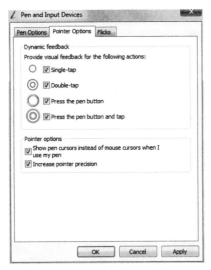

Figure 7-5 Setting visual feedback options

4. A different type of visual feedback is provided for each pen tap action. If you don't want to see visual feedback for a tap action, clear the related check box.

5. If you don't want pen cursors to be shown instead of mouse cursors when you use the pen, clear the Show Pen Cursors Instead Of Mouse Cursors When I Use My Pen check box.

6. Click OK to save the settings.

Flicking Your Pen

You can easily perform navigation and editing actions by flicking the pen in a specific direction. Navigational and editing flicks are configured separately. By default, only the following navigational flicks are enabled:

- Flick left to go back—equivalent to clicking the Back button in Windows Explorer.

- Flick right to go forward—equivalent to clicking the Forward button in Windows Explorer.

- Flick up to scroll up—equivalent to using a scroll bar to scroll up the page in an extended document.

- Flick down to scroll down—equivalent to using a scroll bar to scroll down the page in an extended document.

If you enable editing flicks, the default configuration is as follows:

- Flick up-left to copy.

- Flick up-right to paste.

- Flick down-left to undo.

- Flick down-right to delete.

You can set pen flick options by following these steps:

1. Click Start, and then click Control Panel.

2. In Control Panel, click Hardware And Sound, and then click Pen And Input Devices.

3. In the Pen And Input Devices dialog box, select the Flicks tab, as shown in Figure 7-6.

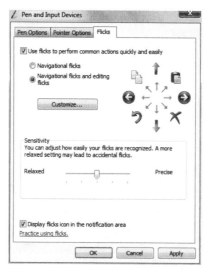

Figure 7-6 Setting pen flick options

4. Use the Active Flicks Set options to configure the types of flicks allowed. If you want both navigational and editing flicks, select the Navigational Flicks And Editing Flicks option.

5. Use the Sensitivity slider to adjust how easily pen flicks are recognized. In most cases, you'll want the sensitivity to be midway between relaxed and precise. However, if you are having issues with accidental flicks, you might want to use a more precise setting.

6. Click OK to save the settings.

Using Windows Mobility Center

Windows Mobility Center provides a single location for managing mobile PC settings. You can access Mobility Center only if you are working with a laptop or a Tablet PC.

Getting Started with Windows Mobility Center

As shown in Figure 7-7, Mobility Center includes a series of control tiles that provide quick access to the most commonly used mobile PC settings. On a laptop or Tablet PC, you can access Mobility Center by right-clicking the Power icon in the taskbar's notification area and then selecting Mobility Center.

Tip   If you've disabled the display of the Power icon, you won't be able to access it on the taskbar. Another way to access Mobility Center is to click Start and then click Control Panel. In Control Panel, click Mobile PC, and then click Mobility Center.

Figure 7-7   Using Windows Mobility Center

Each configurable setting is featured on a separate control tile. The exact set of control tiles available depends on the type of mobile PC (either a laptop or a Tablet PC) and the mobile PC manufacturer. Typically, laptops have seven standard control tiles and Tablet PCs have seven or eight standard control tiles.

Configuring Your Mobile PC by Using Mobility Center

Most control tiles allow you to make direct adjustments to your mobile PC settings by using available options such as sliders to adjust the brightness, a selection list to change the power plan, or a toggle button to turn on or off presentation settings. The most common control tiles are:

- **Brightness**   Shows the current brightness setting. If brightness is configurable on your computer, you can use the slider provided to adjust the brightness of the display.

- **Volume**   Shows the current volume setting. If volume is configurable on your computer, you can use the slider provided to adjust the volume.

- **Battery Status**   Shows the status of the computer's battery. You can use the selection list provided to quickly change from one power plan to another. If you've created custom power plans, these are available as well.

- **Wireless Network**   Shows the status or your wireless network connection. Click Turn Wireless On to enable your wireless connection for use.

- **External Display**   Provides options for connecting a secondary display to give a presentation. If a secondary display is available and you've connected the cables, you can click Connect Display to connect to the display.

- **Sync Center**   Shows the status of file syncing. Click Sync to start a new sync using Sync Center.

- **Presentation Settings**   Shows whether you are in presentation mode. In presentation mode, the mobile PC's display and hard disk do not go into sleep mode due to inactivity. Click Turn On to enter presentation mode.

- **Tablet Display**   Shows the current display orientation. Click Change Orientation to change from landscape to portrait display or vice versa.

If your mobile PC includes other control tiles, the PC manufacturer probably provides them. You can learn more about these control tiles from the documentation that came with the mobile PC or by visiting the manufacturer's Web site.

Connecting to Networked Projectors

Increasingly, meeting rooms and conference centers have networked projectors set up for use during presentations. Before you use this type of projector, you must connect your laptop or Tablet PC to the local area network (LAN). Often this is as simple as plugging in an Ethernet cable to your laptop or ensuring that you are using the correct wireless network connection.

Once you are connected to the network in the conference or meeting room you are using, you can connect to the networked project by using the Connect To A Network Project Wizard, which walks you through the steps of finding the projector on the network and establishing a connection. To start and use the Connect To A Network Project Wizard, follow these steps:

1. Click Start, point to All Programs, Accessories, and then click Connect To A Network Projector.

2. Next specify how you want to connect to the projector, as shown in Figure 7-8.

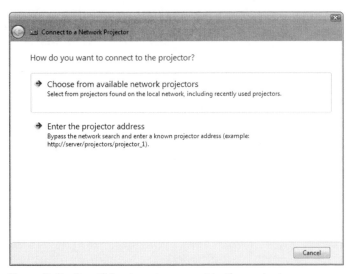

Figure 7-8   Specifying how to connect to the projector

3. If you want to select from projectors found on the local network, click Choose From Available Network Projectors. The wizard searches for projectors on the network and returns its results along with a list of any projectors you've used recently. Click the projector you want to use, provide the access password for the projector if necessary, and then click Next.

4. If you know the network address of the projector, click Enter The Projector Address. On the Enter The Network Address Of A Projector page, shown in Figure 7-9, type the network address of the project, such as **http://intranet.cpandl.local/projectors/projector18**. Enter any required access password, and then click Next.

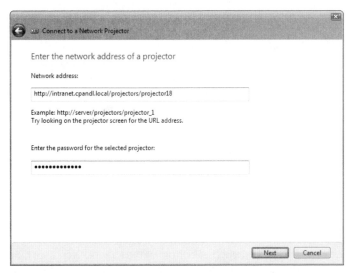

Figure 7-9   Specifying the project address and password

5. After you've established a connection to the projector, click Finish to exit the wizard and begin using the projector.

> **Tip**   Often the network address is written on the projector itself. The password might be controlled, however, so you'll need to know this beforehand.

Getting Acquainted with the Tablet PC Extras

When you are working with Tablet PCs, you'll find additional accessories on the computer. These accessories include:

- Input Panel
- Snipping Tool
- Sticky Notes
- Windows Journal

Entering Text Using the Tablet PC Pen

You use Input Panel to enter text using the Tablet PC pen instead of the computer keyboard. Input Panel converts any handwriting you enter using the pen to typed text. Input Panel supports several new features, including AutoComplete, Back-of-Pen erase, and additional scratch-out gestures.

Getting Started with the Tablet PC Input Panel

When you are working with a program that accepts handwriting input from a pen, such as Microsoft Office Word or Windows Mail, the Input Panel icon is displayed next to text entry areas when Input Panel is available, allowing you to display Input Panel by tapping the icon. You can then use the pen to write and insert the converted text by clicking the Insert button. In Input Panel, the Insert button is displayed below and to the right of your converted text.

If it is not already running, you can start Input Panel by clicking Start, pointing to All Programs, and then selecting Input Panel. Input Panel has changed in several ways since it was introduced with Microsoft Windows XP Tablet PC Edition. When you run Input Panel, it appears as a tab on the left side of the screen. To open Input Panel, move the mouse pointer over the tab and then click. Input Panel will then slide out from the edge of the screen. Clicking the Close button hides Input Panel.

> **Tip**   By default, Input Panel floats in the window. You can move Input Panel by dragging it to a desired position or docking it at the top or bottom of the screen. If you then hide Input Panel, it will reappear in the same location the next time you open it. The Input Panel tab remains available even if the program you are using is running in full-screen mode.

Input Panel provides three input modes:

- **Writing pad**   Provides a space for continuously writing with the pen as if you were writing on a lined sheet of paper. Each word you write is converted to text separately and displayed. If you click the word, you can correct letter case, change punctuation around the word, modify the letters, or delete letters.

- **Character pad**   Provides a space for entering single letters, digits, or symbols. Each character you write is converted to text separately. Clicking below a character displays an options menu with a list of related characters, such as those that are alternatives to the character you've entered or frequently confused with the character you've entered.

- **On-screen keyboard**   Provides an on-screen keyboard that allows you to use pen taps to select characters to use.

Figure 7-10 shows Input Panel in writing pad mode. The buttons on the right provide quick access to common functions. You can:

- Click Num to display the number pad, which contains the digits 0 through 9 and arithmetic symbols.

- Click Sym to display the symbols pad, which contains options for the most commonly used characters.

- Click Web to display the Web pad, which contains character shortcut options for entering URLs.

Figure 7-10   Using Input Panel in writing pad mode

Using AutoComplete, Back-Of-Pen Erase, and Scratch-Out Gestures

AutoComplete works much like AutoComplete in other Microsoft programs. As you enter text, AutoComplete lists possible matches based on items that you've entered before. If an item in the list matches the text that you want to enter, simply tap the suggestion to enter it in the text entry area.

> **Tip**   If you don't want to use AutoComplete, you can disable it in the Options dialog box. In Input Panel, click Tools, and then click Options. On the Settings tab, clear the Suggest Matches In Input Panel When Possible check box, and then click OK.

The Back-Of-Pen Erase feature allows Input Panel to support Tablet PC pens that have erasers. If the Tablet PC pen has an erase function, you can use it to delete entries from Input Panel.

Another way to delete entries is to use Scratch-Out Gestures. As in Windows XP, the Windows Vista Input Panel supports the Z-shaped scratch-out gesture. If you draw a Z over an entry or a series of entries, the entry or entries are deleted.

Windows Vista allows you to use several additional scratch-out gestures. These additional scratch-out gestures are:

- **Strikethrough scratch-out**   If you draw a horizontal line across an entry or a series of entries, the entry or entries are deleted. The horizontal line can be drawn right to left or left to right.

- **Angled scratch-out**   If you draw a line at an angle across an entry or a series of entries, the entry or entries are deleted. The line can be drawn at an angle from the upper right to the lower left or from the upper left to the lower right.

- **Vertical scratch-out**   If you draw an M or a W over an entry or a series of entries, the entry or entries are deleted. The M or W should be larger than the entries you are deleting.

- **Circular scratch-out**   If you draw a circle over an entry or a series of entries, the entry or entries are deleted. The circle can be drawn around or within the entries.

> **Tip**   If you'd rather use only the Z-shaped scratch out, you can disable the other types of scratch-out gestures by using the Options dialog box. In Input Panel, click Tools, and then click Options. On the Gestures tab, select the Only The Z-Shaped Scratch-Out Gesture option, and then click OK.

Capturing Screen Snips

You use Snipping Tool to capture and mark up snippets of documents. Snipping Tool is designed to work with the Table PC pen and includes pen selection, highlighter, and eraser features. Snipping Tool captures any screen elements that you select, including text and images. A captured element is referred to as a *snip*.

You can open Snipping Tool by clicking Start, pointing to All Programs, and then selecting Snipping Tool. Snipping Tool has two modes:

- New Snip mode for capturing snips
- Edit mode for working with snips

Using the Snipping Tool New Snip Mode

Snipping Tool starts in New Snip mode, which is the mode for capturing a snip. In the main snipping window, you can start a capture by clicking the New Snip button on the toolbar. In New Snip mode, the snipping window is displayed in the foreground, and the rest of the screen is brightened automatically to make it easier to distinguish the Snipping Tool interface elements from the background elements you are capturing.

Figure 7-11 shows Snipping Tool in New Snip mode. From left to right, the buttons on the toolbar are used as follows:

- **New** starts a new capture using the current capture mode.
- **Capture mode** (the options button to the right of the New button) sets the capture mode.
- **Stop** cancels the current capture.
- **Options** sets capture options.

Figure 7-11   Using Snipping Tool in New Snip mode

Snipping Tool has four capture modes:

- **Free Form Snip**   With freeform snip mode, you outline the area that you want to snip by drawing freehand around it. To capture a snip in this mode, click and then drag to outline the area you want to capture.
- **Rectangular Snip**   With rectangular snip mode, you outline the area that you want to snip by drawing a rectangle around it. To capture a snip in this mode, click and then drag around the area that you want to capture.
- **Window Snip**   With window snip mode, you capture an entire window as a snip. To capture a snip in this mode, move the mouse pointer over the window that you want to capture, and then click.
- **Full-Screen Snip**   With full-screen snip mode, you capture the full screen as a snip. The full screen is captured automatically after you select this mode.

The default capture mode is rectangular. To change the capture mode, click the Capture Mode button, and then select a new capture mode. You then click the New button to start the capture.

From the experts
Using Snipping Tool for screen captures

Snipping Tool is a great general-purpose screen capture utility. By default, snips are captured using a single-file Hypertext Markup Language (HTML) format that can recognize separate text and image components. You can also capture snips as JPEG, PNG, or GIF image files so that the entire snip is handled as a single picture. To change the capture mode, click Tools, click Options, and then use the Capture Snip As list to select the desired capture type. Regardless of the capture type, you can save the snip in HTML format or as a JPEG, PNG, or GIF image file.

By default, any snips you capture have a thick red selection line around them. This is meant to help you easily distinguish snips from other content if you later add the snips to other documents. Using Snipping Tool options, you can change the color of the line or clear the option altogether so that a selection line is not displayed around snips. To clear the selection line, click Tools, click Options, and then clear the Show Selection Line After Capturing Snips check box.

William Stanek
Author, MVP, and series editor for the Microsoft Press Administrator's Pocket Consultants

Using the Snipping Tool Edit Mode

After you've captured a snip, the Snipping Tool window changes to Edit mode. In this mode, you can mark up a snip by using the pen and also add highlights by using the highlighter. Figure 7-12 shows Snipping Tool in Edit mode. From left to right, the buttons on the toolbar are used as follows:

- **New Snip** switches to New Snip mode (and discards the current snip).

> **Caution**   If you click New Snip before saving a snip, the current snip is lost.

- **Save As** allows you to save the current snip as a single-file HTML document or as a JPEG, PNG, or GIF image.
- **Copy** copies the snip to the Windows Clipboard.
- **Send Snip** allows you to send the snip to someone in an e-mail message. Click the Options button to see additional send options, such as Send To E-Mail Recipient (As Attachment).
- **Pen** allows you to select the pen color. The default pen color is blue. To change the ink thickness, change the pen tip type, or select a custom color, click the Customize option.
- **Highlighter** allows you to highlight areas of the snippet.
- **Eraser** allows you to erase pen ink and highlights.

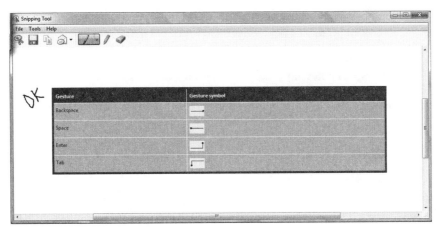

Figure 7-12   Using Snipping Tool in Edit mode

Creating Sticky Notes

The Sticky Notes accessory gives you a virtual scratch pad. You can use Sticky Notes to record both written and voice memos. Any sticky notes you create remain in the stack of sticky notes until you delete them.

To open Sticky Notes, click Start, point to All Programs, and then select Sticky Notes. As shown in Figure 7-13, Sticky Notes gives you a virtual work pad on which you can write notes using the pen. To add to the current work pad, simply use the pen to write the text of the note or click the Record button to record a voice note.

Figure 7-13   Using Sticky Notes

You can create a new note by clicking the New Note button. As you add notes, your stack of sticky notes grows. You can navigate the stack by using the Previous Note and Next Note buttons on the toolbar. The X/Y value on the toolbar shows you which note you are currently viewing and the total number of notes in the stack. In Figure 7-13, note 2 of 3 is displayed. If you no longer want a sticky note, click the Delete This Note button (the red X) on the toolbar, and then confirm the action by clicking Yes.

You can erase notes by moving the pen from side to side several times over the entries that you want to erase without lifting the pen. When you lift the pen, the entries are removed.

> **Tip**   If you use sticky notes regularly, you might want the Sticky Notes accessory to run automatically each time you start Windows Vista and log on. To configure Sticky Notes for automatic startup, click Tools, click Options, and then select Open At Startup.

Using Windows Journal

While Sticky Notes is useful for creating short notes or memos, you'll want to use Windows Journal for longer writing samples, such as reports, agendas, or meeting notes. Windows Journal gives you a virtual journal that you can use with the Tablet PC pen in much the same way you would use a stationery pad and an ink pen.

Getting Started with Windows Journal

You can open Windows Journal by clicking Start, pointing to All Programs, and then selecting Windows Journal. As shown in Figure 7-14, the Windows Journal main window looks like a notepad with lined paper, and you can use the Tablet PC pen to write your notes directly on the paper.

Figure 7-14   Using Windows Journal

Using Windows Journal is similar to using Sticky Notes. Your virtual journal can have a stack of pages just like a real journal. When a journal has multiple pages, you can navigate pages by clicking and dragging the scroll bar. Beneath the scroll bar are several buttons:

- **Previous**   Goes to the previous page. You can display the previous page by clicking the Previous button or by pressing Page Up on the keyboard. If you're on the first page of the journal, this button is dimmed.

- **Next**   Goes to the next page. You can display the next page by clicking the Next button or by pressing Page Down on the keyboard. If you're on the last page of the journal, this button is replaced by the New Page button.

- **New Page**   Creates a new page. You can add a new page to the end of the journal by clicking the New Page button. This button is available only if you're on the last page of the journal and you've written on the page.

When working with Windows Journal, you might also want to insert a page before the current page. You can insert a page by clicking New Page on the Insert menu.

Setting the Stationery Style

Windows Journal uses a college-ruled notepad as the default stationery style. You can easily change to narrow-ruled, wide-ruled, standard-ruled, or other stationery as well. To do this, follow these steps:

1. In Windows Journal, click Options on the Tools menu.

2. On the Stationery panel, make sure that the Stationery option is selected, and then click Default Page Setup.

3. In the Default Page Setup dialog box, click the Style tab.

4. Use the Line Style list to choose the style to use. Options include Standard Ruled, Narrow Ruled, Wide Ruled, Large Grid, Small Grid, and Blank.

5. Click OK twice.

Copying Handwriting and Replacing Text

With a few simple taps of the pen, you can convert handwriting to text, edit converted text, and copy converted text to the Clipboard. This allows you to use handwriting entered into Windows Journal as text in other programs.

To copy handwriting as text and edit it, follow these steps:

1. Press and hold the pen to the screen.

2. Drag the pen around the handwriting you want to select.

3. When you release the pen, a shortcut menu is displayed. Select Copy As Text to display the Copy As Text dialog box, as shown in Figure 7-15. Windows Journal converts the handwriting to text automatically.

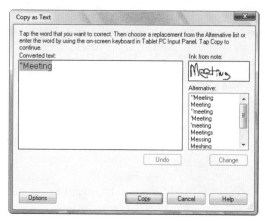

Figure 7-15   Copying handwriting as text

4.   Tap a word or character that you want to correct.

5.   Choose a replacement from the Alternative list.

6.   Click Copy to copy the text to the Clipboard.

Chapter 8

Improving Accessibility

As you saw in Chapter 7, Microsoft Windows Vista provides several accessories for Tablet PCs, including Input Panel, Snipping Tool, Sticky Notes, and Windows Journal. All of these accessories use Tablet PC pens, which improve accessibility by making it easier to work with computers. Additionally, people who might not be able to use a computer keyboard and mouse might be able to use a Tablet PC pen as an alternative input device.

As in earlier versions of Microsoft Windows, Windows Vista includes many other features that improve accessibility, including the Filter Keys, Sticky Keys, and High Contrast functions and the Narrator, Magnifier, and On-Screen Keyboard utilities. In Windows Vista, these features have all been enhanced, and most have completely redesigned interfaces. Windows Vista also includes speech recognition software. Using speech recognition, you can dictate documents and e-mail messages, and you can use your voice to control programs and browse the Web.

Note This book was written using the Windows Vista Beta to provide an early introduction to the operating system. More so than any other area of Windows Vista, the security features discussed in this book are subject to change. Some of the features might not be included in the final product, and some of the features might be changed substantially.

Accessing the Ease of Access Features in Control Panel

In Windows XP, you must go to three different places to manage accessibility settings. Some of the controls are located in the Accessibility Wizard, some in the Accessibility Utility Manager, and still others in the Accessibility Options utility in Control Panel. Windows Vista streamlines this myriad of programs and options. Instead of three separate programs, you can find all of the accessibility settings in one place, in the Ease Of Access Center.

To access the Ease Of Access Center, click Start and then click Control Panel. In Control Panel, click the link for the Ease Of Access category heading and then click Ease Of Access Center. As Figure 8-1 shows, the Ease Of Access Center has three main headings:

- **Quick Access**   You use the Quick Access options to turn common accessibility features on or off. These features include the Filter Keys, Sticky Keys, and High Contrast functions and the Narrator, Magnifier, and On-Screen Keyboard utilities. By default, Windows Vista uses the Narrator feature to read these options aloud and automatically highlights each option in turn. When an option is highlighted, you can press the Spacebar to select it.

- **Not Sure Where To Start?**   When you click Answer Questions That Windows Can Use To Recommend Settings, Windows Vista starts a recommendation wizard similar to, but more intuitive than, the Accessibility Wizard in Windows XP. The five questions in this recommendation wizard are designed to help Windows Vista determine and suggest the best accessibility options for you to use.

- **Explore All Available Settings**   You can use the additional options provided to quickly find related settings that might improve accessibility.

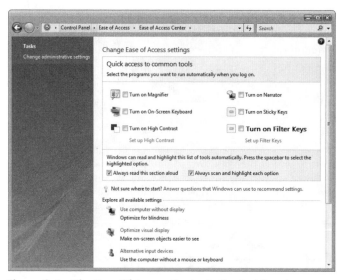

Figure 8-1   The Ease Of Access Center in Control Panel

Using Magnifier

Magnifier is a utility that enlarges part of the screen in a separate window to make it easier for those with limited vision to work with a computer. By default, the Magnifier window is docked at the top of the screen and displays the area around the cursor, the text you are editing, or the focus of the keyboard. You can resize the Magnifier window by moving the mouse pointer over the edge of the window and then dragging the window border. If you move the mouse pointer over the Magnifier window, you can click and drag the window to make it float.

The configuration options for Magnifier have changed considerably in Windows Vista. You can now specify whether the Magnifier window should float or be docked, and you can specify the docked position. To turn on and configure Magnifier, follow these steps:

1. Click Start, and then click Control Panel.

2. In Control Panel, click the Ease Of Access category link, and then select the Ease Of Access Center link.

3. Select the Turn On Magnifier check box. The Microsoft Screen Magnify dialog box is displayed, as shown in Figure 8-2.

Figure 8-2   Configuring Magnifier

4. Once you enable Magnifier, the program is started each time you log on. If you want the Magnifier window to be minimized at startup, select Minimize On Startup.

5. Use the Scale Factor list to set the magnification level of the Magnifier window. The default scale is 2x, or twice normal, and you can select a value as high as 16x.

6. If you want the Magnifier window to float rather than be docked, clear the Docked check box. You can also set the dock position as Top, Bottom, Left, or Right.

7. When you have finished configuring your settings, click Exit.

From the experts
More than accessible

While the accessibility tools are mainly designed to help users who have some form of visual or motor impairment, users without such impairments can sometimes benefit from using them as well. One notable example of this is the Magnifier. The intended use for this tool is enabling visually-impaired users to zoom in on any screen area where the mouse pointer is hovering. All the Magnifier does in this case, however, is increase the size of pixels on your desktop, so the result can look blocky and a bit blurry to the ordinary eye.

However, if you have XAML graphic files created by Windows Presentation Foundation (WPF) applications, you can use the Magnifier to actually zoom in on the graphic and see details in the Magnifier that aren't visible on your desktop because they're too small to be displayed. An architect or engineer might find the Magnifier useful like this to inspect details in a large graphic that must be scaled down to make fit the desktop. This kind of magnification effect is possible because the Vista desktop works differently than the desktop in previous versions of Windows. Specifically, instead of having applications render to the screen, the new Vista Desktop Window Manager (DWM) lets applications render directly to in-memory buffers. That means applications can render more detail than can actually be displayed on the screen and, for supported applications, the Magnifier can be used to make this extra detail visible. Note that you require full Aero support to make this work, so hardware that doesn't support the Aero experience can't use the Magnifier in this way. For more information about Windows Presentation Foundation and XAML, see *http://msdn.microsoft.com/windowsvista/about/*.

Mitch Tulloch
Author and MVP–For more information, see http://www.mtit.com.

Using the On-Screen Keyboard

The On-Screen Keyboard utility is designed to assist mobility-impaired users, allowing them to use a mouse or an alternative input device for typing. Similar to Input Panel, characters typed on the On-Screen Keyboard are inserted into the current application.

By default, the keyboard is configured to type characters when you click the keys. You can also configure the keyboard to use hovering to select characters or to accept input from a joystick. With hovering, you move the pointer over a character for a specified period of time, such as 1 second, to select that character. With a joystick, you move the joystick and then click the joystick button when over a character to select that character. As Figure 8-3 shows, the On-Screen Keyboard utility in Windows Vista has a slightly different look from Windows XP, but the functionality is the same.

Figure 8-3 The On-Screen Keyboard

To turn on the On-Screen Keyboard, click Start, and then click Control Panel. In Control Panel, click the Ease Of Access category link, select the Ease Of Access Center link, and then select the Turn On On-Screen Keyboard check box. Once you enable the On-Screen Keyboard, the program is started each time you log on and is displayed on top of all other windows by default.

Using Narrator

Narrator is a text-to-speech program that reads aloud what is displayed on the screen as you navigate the keyboard. You can use the program to read aloud menu commands, dialog box options, and characters typed.

To turn on Narrator, click Start, and then click Control Panel. In Control Panel, click the Ease Of Access category link, select the Ease Of Access Center link, and then select the Turn On Narrator check box. Once you enable Narrator, the program is started each time you log on.

As Figure 8-4 shows, the Microsoft Narrator dialog box options have changed considerably in Windows Vista:

- The default voice is Microsoft Anna, which is a more natural sounding voice than the voice of Microsoft Sam. By clicking the Voice Settings button, you can modify the voice options.

- By default, Narrator echoes user keystrokes, announces both system messages and scroll notifications, and automatically monitors screen elements. You can use the Preferences menu options to toggle these options on or off.

- By selecting Preferences and then clicking Background Message Settings, you can configure whether and when background messages are discarded if they have not been presented to the user.

Figure 8-4   Using Microsoft Narrator

Using Sticky Keys, Filter Keys, and High Contrast

For those who have difficulty pressing keys on keyboards or reading on-screen text, Windows Vista includes several other useful accessibility features. These features include:

- **Sticky Keys**   The Sticky Keys feature lets you press key combinations, such as Ctrl+Alt+Delete, one key at a time. The default settings for Sticky Keys are the same as in earlier versions of Windows. You can turn on Sticky Keys by selecting Turn On Sticky Keys in the Ease Of Access Center in Control Panel or by pressing the Shift key five times. Modifier keys are locked and selected automatically if you press them twice in a row. You can turn off Sticky Keys by pressing two keys at once.

- **Filter Keys**   The Filter Keys feature lets you automatically filter unintentional keystrokes. When this feature is enabled, you must press and hold a key for a specific length of time before it is accepted or repeated. You can turn on Filter Keys by selecting Turn On Filter Keys in the Ease Of Access Center in Control Panel or by pressing and holding the Shift key for 8 seconds.

- **High Contrast**   The High Contrast feature configures the appearance of the user interface to use high contrast between the colors for text and interface elements. You can turn on High Contrast by selecting Turn On High Contrast in the Ease Of Access Center in Control Panel. To configure the color scheme used, click the Setup High Contrast link in the Ease of Access Center.

Talking to Your Computer and Getting It to Listen by Using Speech Recognition

With the speech recognition software included in Windows Vista, you can dictate documents and e-mail messages and use your voice to control programs and browse the Web. Not only does this allow you to create documents quickly and perform common tasks, it can also reduce the risk of repetitive stress injuries.

Getting Started with Speech Recognition

Speech recognition allows you to control your computer by speaking. When you talk, the software uses context-sensitive controls to determine whether to convert your voice to text or whether you have given a control command. Text is entered into the document you are working with. Control commands are used to activate menus and to select options.

> **Tip**   Speech recognition works best when you use a high-quality microphone, such as a universal serial bus (USB) headset microphone or an array microphone. Although many high-quality microphones include noise cancellation technology, the environment in which you use the microphone should be relatively quiet, meaning that you probably wouldn't want to use speech recognition in a noisy call center.

Before you can use speech recognition, you must ensure that your computer has a sound card and that the sound card is properly configured. You must then connect a microphone to the sound card's microphone jack. Speaking into the microphone is what triggers the software.

Speech recognition software is easy to use and reliable. The software is designed to provide the best possible accuracy and the most complete end-to-end speech recognition solution available. The software accomplishes this by:

- Improving the user interfaces to provide a simple yet more efficient way to dictate text, make changes, and correct mistakes.

- Including an interactive tutorial that teaches you about the software while you are training the computer to understand your voice.

■ Improving accuracy by having the software learn as you use it and by prompting for clarification when you give a command that can be interpreted in multiple ways.

Primarily, speech recognition is intended for people who frequently use word processing applications, e-mail applications, and Web browsers. By using speech recognition with these programs, you can use spoken words to enter text and perform commands, thereby significantly reducing the use of the keyboard and mouse.

Speech recognition dictation works only in applications that support the Text Services Framework. Applications that support this framework include:

■ Microsoft Office Word

■ Microsoft Office Outlook

■ Microsoft Internet Explorer

■ Nearly all applications included with Windows Vista

Dictation won't work in applications that don't support the Text Services Framework, such as Microsoft Office PowerPoint, Microsoft Office Excel, WordPerfect, or Eudora.

Configuring Speech Recognition for First Use

Before you can use speech recognition for dictation and handling commands, you must configure the software for first use. To do this, follow these steps:

1. Click Start, point to All Programs, and then click Accessories.

2. Click Ease Of Access, and then click Speech Recognition. This starts the Set Up Speech Recognition Wizard (see Figure 8-5).

Figure 8-5   The Welcome To Speech Recognition page

3. On the Welcome To Speech Recognition page, shown in Figure 8-5, read the introductory text, and then click Next.

4. On the Select Microphone page, shown in Figure 8-6, select the type of microphone you are using.

Figure 8-6   The Select Microphone page

5. On the Set Up Your Microphone page, follow the instructions for setting up and positioning your microphone. The directions differ, depending on the type of microphone you are using. Click Next to continue.

6. On the Adjust The Microphone Volume page, shown in Figure 8-7, follow the instructions and read the sample text aloud. You won't be able to proceed until you've adjusted the microphone volume to the proper level while reading the sample text. Click Next to continue.

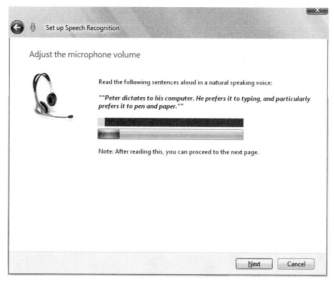

Figure 8-7   The Adjust The Microphone Volume page

7. The next page confirms that your microphone is now set up for use. Click Next.

8. On the Improve Speech Recognition Accuracy page, shown in Figure 8-8, specify whether the speech recognition software should scan your documents and e-mail messages to learn the words and phrases you use, and then click Next.

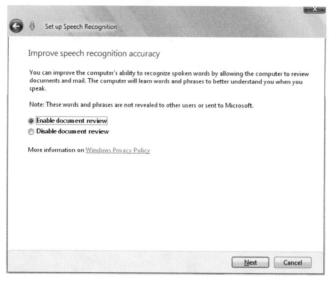

Figure 8-8 The Improve Speech Recognition Accuracy page

9. The next page is used to print a reference sheet with a list of speech commands. You can view the reference sheet by clicking the View Reference Sheet button. Click Next to continue.

10. The Run Speech Recognition At Startup check box is automatically selected on the Run Speech Recognition Every Time I Start Computer page. Clear this check box if desired. Click Next to continue.

11. Click Start Tutorial to take the speech tutorials and practice using the most common commands. The tutorial also trains the computer to recognize your voice.

Using Speech Recognition for Dictation

The most common way you'll use speech recognition is for dictating a document. This process involves:

1. Starting your word processing application.

2. Opening an existing document or creating a new document.

3. Dictating the body of the document.

4. Saving the document and exiting your word processing application.

You can use speech recognition to perform these tasks in Microsoft Office Word or WordPad by following these steps:

1. If speech recognition is not running, start it. Click Start, point to All Programs, and then click Accessories. Click Ease Of Access, and then click Speech Recognition.

2. Say "Start Listening."

3. Say "Open Word" or "Open WordPad" as appropriate.

4. Start dictating. Use the spoken-word commands for punctuation marks and special characters as necessary. For example, to insert a comma, you say "comma." To end a sentence with a period, you say "period."

5. To correct mistakes, say "correct" and the word that the computer typed by mistake. Select the correct word from the list offered, or say the correct word again. For example, if the computer misrecognized *rode* as *strode*, say "correct rode," and then select the right word from the list or say the word "strode" again.

6. To save the document, say "File," say "Save As," and then say the name of the document, such as "Quarterly Report." Complete the operation by saying "Save."

Part III
Securing Windows Vista

In this part of the book, you'll learn about the security features of Microsoft Windows Vista. Chapter 9, "Protecting User Accounts and Using Parental Controls," discusses new features for protecting user accounts, including User Account Control and parental controls. Chapter 10, "Protecting Your Computer," discusses the dramatic changes in the Windows Vista architecture that are designed to provide multiple layers of protection for your computer. The chapter introduces the new boot environment and new security features, such as Windows Service Hardening and Network Access Protection. The chapter also discusses computer security improvements that harden the operating system against attack. Chapter 11, "Protecting Your Data," introduces data protection and file encryption. A key focus of Chapter 11 is BitLocker Drive Encryption, which adds machine-level data protection to help protect data from being compromised on a lost or stolen computer. Chapter 12, "Networking Your Computer," examines enhancements for networking and restricting access to Windows Vista systems. Chapter 13, "Securing Your Network Connection," discusses security tools, including Windows Firewall and Windows Defender.

Chapter 9

Protecting User Accounts and Using Parental Controls

Microsoft Windows Vista includes many features to help you maintain control over your computer in response to constantly evolving security threats. Traditionally, security threats have been combated with software tools and operating system components, such as firewall and spyware software, and for this reason, Windows Vista includes Windows Firewall, Windows Defender, and many other security features. Beyond the traditional, Windows Vista also provides a fundamental change in the way security is implemented and managed in the form of User Account Control (UAC) and parental controls.

User Account Control dramatically changes the way user accounts are configured and used and also changes the way applications and system components make use of system-level privileges. Parental controls provide features to help keep your family safe on the Internet. These same features can be extended to organizations with youth volunteers and to organizations that provides services for youths.

Note This book was written using the Windows Vista Beta to provide an early introduction to the operating system. More so than any other area of Windows Vista, the security features discussed in this book are subject to change. Some of the features might not be included in the final product, and some of the features might be changed substantially.

Introducing User Account Control

User Account Control (UAC) is designed to address the need for a solution that is resilient to attack from an ever-growing array of malicious software (also called malware) programs. For those who have installed and used an earlier version of Microsoft Windows, UAC represents a significant change in the way user accounts are used and configured. It does this by reducing the need for administrator privileges and by carefully defining the standard user and administrator user modes.

Reducing the Need for Administrator Privileges

In earlier versions of Windows, most user accounts are configured as members of the local administrator's group to ensure that users can install, update, and run software applications without conflicts and to perform common system-level tasks. In Windows XP and earlier versions of Windows, some of the most basic tasks, such as clicking the taskbar clock to view a calendar, require administrator privileges, and this is why many user accounts are configured as local administrators. Unfortunately, configuring user accounts as local administrators makes individual computers and networks vulnerable to malicious software and also makes maintaining computers more difficult, as users might be able to make unapproved system changes.

Note   Malicious software programs exploit the system-level privileges provided to the local administrator. Not only does this allow malicious software to install itself, it also allows malicious software to damage files, change the system configuration, and steal your confidential data. Some organizations try to combat malicious software by locking down computers and requiring users to operate in standard user mode. While this can solve some problems with malicious software, it can also seriously affect productivity, as many applications designed for Windows XP will not function properly without local administrative rights. Why? Typically, Windows XP applications use local administrative rights to write to system locations during normal operations.

Through User Account Control, Windows Vista provides the architecture for running user accounts with standard user privileges while eliminating the need for using administrator privileges to perform common tasks. This fundamental shift in computing serves to better protect computers against malicious software while ensuring that users can perform their day-to-day tasks.

User Account Control is an architecture that includes a set of infrastructure technologies. These technologies require all users to run applications and tasks with a standard user account, limiting administrator-level access to authorized processes. Because of UAC, computers can be locked down to prevent unauthorized applications from installing and to stop standard users from making inadvertent changes to system settings.

Defining the Standard User and Administrator User Modes

In Windows Vista, there are two levels of users:

- **Administrator users**   Administrator users run applications with an administrator account and are members of the local Administrators group. When an administrator user starts an application, her access token and its associated administrator privileges are applied to the application at run time. This means that an application started by a member of the local Administrators group runs with all the rights and privileges of a local administrator.

- **Standard users** Standard users run applications with a user account and are members of the Users group. When a user starts an application, her access token and its associated privileges are applied to the application at run time. This means that an application started by a member of the Users group runs with the rights and privileges of a standard user.

In Windows Vista, many common tasks can be performed with a standard user account, and users should log on using accounts with standard user privileges. Whenever a user attempts to perform a task that requires administrator permissions, the user sees a Windows Security dialog box containing a warning prompt. The way the prompt works depends on whether the user is logged on with an administrator account or a standard user account:

- Users with administrator permissions are asked for confirmation.

- Users with standard accounts are asked to provide a password for an administrator account.

Administrator users run as standard users until an application or system component that requires administrative credentials requests permission to run. Windows Vista determines whether a user needs elevated permissions to run a program by supplying most applications and processes with a security token. Windows Vista uses the token as follows:

- If an application or process has an "administrator" token, elevated privileges are required to run the application or process, and Windows Vista will prompt the user for permission confirmation prior to running the application.

- If an application or process has a "standard" token or an application cannot be identified as an administrator application, elevated privileges are not required to run the application or process, and Windows Vista will start it as a standard application by default.

By requiring that all users run in standard user mode and by limiting administrator-level access to authorized processes, UAC reduces the exposure and attack surface of the operating system. The process of getting an administrator or standard user's approval prior to running an application in administrator mode and prior to performing actions that change system-wide settings is known as *elevation*, and this feature is known as Admin Approval Mode. Elevation enhances security and reduces the impact of malicious software by:

- Ensuring that users are notified when they are about to perform an action that could impact system settings, such as installing an application.

- Eliminating the ability for malicious software to invoke administrator privileges without a user's knowledge.

- Preventing users, and the applications they are running, from making unauthorized or accidental system-wide changes to operating system settings.

- Protecting administrator applications from attacks by standard applications and processes.

Elevation is a new feature and a permanent change to the Windows operating system.

> **Tip**   Elevation affects not only users and administrators, but developers as well. Developers must design their programs so that everyday users can complete basic tasks without requiring administrator privileges. A key part of this is determining which of the two levels of privilege their applications need to complete specific procedures. If an application doesn't need administrator privileges for a task, it should be written to require only standard user privileges. As an example, a standard user–compliant application should write data files only to a nonsystem location, such as the user profile folder.

Navigating the User Account Changes

User Account Control is designed to make it easier to protect computers while ensuring that users can perform the tasks they need to perform. As part of the restructuring for UAC, many changes have been made to user accounts and privileges. These changes are designed to ensure that there is true separation of user and administrator tasks, and that any tasks that have minimal system impact and potential for risk can be performed using standard user accounts. Administrators also have the ability to restrict privileges if they prefer.

Understanding Standard User Privileges

In Windows Vista, standard user accounts can be used to perform some tasks that previously required administrator privileges. New permissions for standard user accounts in Windows Vista include:

- Viewing the system clock and calendar and changing the time zone.
- Changing the display settings and installing fonts.
- Changing power management settings.
- Adding printers and other devices (where the required drivers are installed on the computer or are provided by an IT administrator).
- Downloading and installing updates using User Account Control–compatible installers.
- Creating and configuring virtual private network (VPN) connections. A VPN connection helps you establish a secure connection to a private network over the public Internet.
- Installing Wired Equivalent Privacy (WEP) to connect to secure wireless networks. WEP is a security protocol that provides a wireless network with the same level of security as a wired local area network (LAN).

Additionally, some maintenance tasks are now automatically scheduled processes, so users will not have to initiate these processes manually. Processes that are scheduled to run automatically include:

- **CareTaker**   Performs automated maintenance of the computer.

- **Consolidator** Performs automated consolidation of the computer's event logs.

- **AutomaticDefrag** Performs automatic defragmentation of the computer's hard disks.

- **AutomaticBackup** Performs automatic backup of the computer (once configured).

In earlier versions of Windows, nonadministrators couldn't easily tell whether they were allowed to perform an action. To make it easier for users to determine whether they can perform a task, Windows Vista uses a shield icon to identify tasks that require administrator privileges.

In Figure 9-1, two tasks are preceded by a shield icon: Change Settings and Change Product Key. These tasks require administrator privileges.

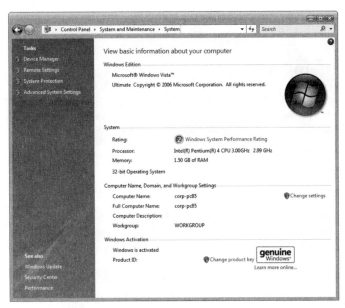

Figure 9-1   The shield icon indicates tasks that require administrator privileges

---

From the experts
Only legacy applications need the Power Users group

The terms *legacy application* and *legacy operating systems* take on new meanings with the introduction of Windows Vista. In Windows Vista, legacy application refers to an application developed for Windows XP or an earlier version of Windows, and legacy operating system refers to an operating system using Windows XP or an earlier version of Windows.

In earlier versions of Windows, the Power Users group was designed to give users specific administrator privileges to perform basic system tasks while running applications. As standard user accounts can now perform most common configuration tasks, Windows Vista does not require the use of the Power Users group.

Further, while Windows Vista maintains the Power Users group for legacy application compatibility, applications written for Windows Vista do not require the use of the Power User mode. Legacy applications that require administrative privileges use file and registry virtualization; compliant applications use standard user mode and adminis trator mode, as discussed previously. For more information about legacy application compatibility, refer to the *Microsoft Windows Vista Administrator's Pocket Consultant* (Microsoft Press, 2006).

William Stanek
Author, MVP, and series editor for the Microsoft Press Administrator's Pocket Consultants

Understanding File System and Registry Virtualization

Windows Vista uses application security tokens to determine whether elevated privileges are required to run applications or processes. With applications written for Vista, applications either have an "administrator" token or a "standard" token. If an application has an "administrator" token, it requires elevated privileges. If an application has a "standard" token, it doesn't require elevated privileges.

The token is a reflection of the required level of privileges. A standard user mode–compliant application should write data files only to nonsystem locations. If the application requires administrator privileges to perform a specific task, the application should request elevated privileges to perform that task. For all other tasks, the application should not run using elevated privileges.

Applications not written for the Windows Vista new user account architecture are considered legacy applications. Windows Vista starts these applications as standard user applications by default and uses file and registry virtualization to give legacy applications their own "virtualized" views of resources they are attempting to change. When a legacy application attempts to write a system location, Windows Vista gives the application its own private copy of the file or registry value so that the application will function properly. All attempts to write to protected areas are logged by default as well.

 Note   Virtualization is not meant to be a long-term solution. As applications are revised to support Windows Vista's new user account architecture, the revised versions should be deployed to ensure compliance with User Account Control and to safeguard the security of the computer.

Handling User Account Control

Applications written for Windows Vista use User Account Control to reduce the attack surface of the operating system. They do this by reducing the basic privileges granted to applications and by helping to prevent unauthorized applications from running without the user's consent. User Account Control makes it harder for malicious software to take over a computer by ensuring that existing security measures are not unintentionally disabled by standard users running in administrator mode. By helping to ensure that users do not accidentally change settings, User Account Control reduces the cost of managing computers and provides a more consistent environment that should also make troubleshooting easier. User Account Control also helps to control access to sensitive files and data by securing the Documents folder so that other users cannot change, read, or delete files created by other users of the same computer.

Applications that have been certified as compliant with the new Windows Vista architecture will have the Windows Vista–Compliant logo. Although the logo indicates that the program has been written to take advantage of User Account Control, it doesn't mean that the program will run only in standard user mode. Compliant applications run in the mode appropriate for the functions that they perform and elevate privileges to perform tasks as necessary. Administrators can modify the way User Account Control works as required.

Understanding and Setting Run Levels

In Windows Vista, an application can indicate the specific permission level it needs to function so that it will perform only authorized functions, making the code less vulnerable to exploits by malicious users or malicious software. A new feature in Windows Vista, called Windows Vista Trust Manager, can use this information prior to installing an application to determine whether to allow the application to be installed. If the application's required permissions are determined to pose no risk, the application can be installed without generating security alerts. However, if the application's installer writes to sensitive areas or performs tasks that could potentially harm the computer, Windows Vista displays security alerts describing the potential dangers of installing the application and asking for confirmation before proceeding.

Application Manifests and Run Levels are used to help track required privileges. Application Manifests allow administrators to define the application's desired security credentials and to specify when to prompt users for administrator authorization to elevate privileges. If privileges other than those for standard users are required, the manifest should contain runLevel designations. These runLevel designations identify the specific tasks that the application needs to elevate with an "administrator" token.

With User Account Control and Admin Approval Mode, you are prompted for consent prior to performing any task that requires elevated permission, and the Windows Security dialog box allows you to run the application on a one-time basis using elevated credentials. In the Windows Security dialog box, click Allow to start the application using an administrator account, or click an account, type the account's password, and then click Submit to start the application using a standard account.

Another way to use elevation is to mark an application or process to always run using elevated credentials without prompting the user for consent. To do this, follow these steps:

1. Log on to the computer as a member of the local Administrators group.

2. By using the Start menu, locate the program that you want to run always using elevated credentials.

3. Right-click the application's shortcut icon, and then click Properties.

4. In the Properties dialog box, select the Compatibility tab, as shown in Figure 9-2.

Figure 9-2   Marking an application to always run elevated

5. Under Privilege Level, select the Run This Program As An Administrator check box.

6. Click OK.

Note   If the Run This Program As An Administrator option is unavailable, it means that the application is blocked from always running elevated, the application does not require administrative credentials to run, or you are not logged on as an administrator.

Modifying User Account Control and Admin Approval Mode

Administrators can change the way User Account Control and Admin Approval Mode work in several different ways. They can:

- Disable running all users as standard users.
- Disable prompting for credentials to install applications.
- Change the elevation prompt behavior.

Each of these tasks is configured through Group Policy and can be configured on a per-computer basis through Local Group Policy or on a per-domain, per-site, or per-organizational-unit basis through Active Directory Group Policy. The sections that follow focus on configuring the related settings by using Local Group Policy.

Disabling Admin Approval Mode

By default, Windows Vista uses Admin Approval Mode to run programs for all users, including administrators, as standard users. This approach serves to better safeguard the computer from malicious software by ensuring that any time programs need administrator privileges, they must prompt the user for approval. To bypass the safety and security settings, you can modify this behavior so that administrators run programs as administrators and standard users run programs as standard users.

You can use the following procedure to disable Admin Approval Mode:

1. Log on to the computer as a member of the local Administrators group.
2. Click Start, point to All Programs, Accessories, and then click Run.
3. Type **secpol.msc** in the Open text box, and then click OK.
4. In the console tree, under Security Settings, expand Local Policies, and then select Security Options.
5. Double-click User Account Control: Run All Administrators In Admin Approval Mode.
6. Click Disabled, as shown in Figure 9-3, and then click OK.

Figure 9-3   Disabling Admin Approval Mode

Disabling Credential Prompting for Application Installation

By default, Windows Vista prompts users for consent or credentials prior to installing applications using elevated permissions. If you don't want users to have access to this prompt, you can disable User Account Control: Detect Application Installations And Prompt For Elevation under Security Options, and in this way block users from using this feature to install applications as administrators. This doesn't, however, block users from using other techniques to install applications as administrators.

You can use the following procedure to disable the User Account Control: Detect Application Installations And Prompt For Elevation feature:

1. Log on to the computer as a member of the local Administrators group.

2. Click Start, point to All Programs, Accessories, and then click Run.

3. Type **secpol.msc** in the Open text box, and then click OK.

4. In the console tree, under Security Settings, expand Local Policies, and then select Security Options.

5. Double-click User Account Control: Detect Application Installations And Prompt For Elevation.

6. Click Disabled, and then click OK.

Changing the Elevation Prompt Behavior

By default, Windows Vista handles security prompts for standard users and administrator users in different ways. Standard users are prompted for credentials. Administrators are prompted for consent. Using Group Policy, you can change this behavior in several ways:

- If you don't want standard users to have access to this prompt, you can specify that users shouldn't see the elevation prompt, and in this way block users from using this feature to run applications with elevated privileges. However, this doesn't block users from using other techniques to run applications as administrators.

- If you want to require administrators to enter credentials, you can specify that administrators should be prompted for credentials rather than consent.

- If you don't want administrators to have access to this prompt, you can specify that administrators shouldn't see the elevation prompt, and in this way block administrators from using this feature to run applications with elevated privileges. This doesn't, however, block administrators from using other techniques to run applications with elevated permissions.

You can use the following procedure to configure the elevation prompt for standard users:

1. Log on to the computer as a member of the local Administrators group.

2. Click Start, point to All Programs, Accessories, and then click Run.

3. Type **secpol.msc** in the Open text box, and then click OK.

4. In the console tree, under Security Settings, expand Local Policies, and then select Security Options.

5. Double-click User Account Control: Behavior Of The Elevation Prompt For Standard Users.

6. You can now:

   ❑ Block the elevation prompt by selecting No Prompt in the drop-down list.

   ❑ Enable the elevation prompt by selecting Prompt For Credentials in the drop-down list. (The default setting is Prompt For Credentials.)

7. Click OK.

You can use the following procedure to configure the elevation prompt for administrators:

1. Log on to the computer as a member of the local Administrators group.

2. Click Start, point to All Programs, Accessories, and then click Run.

3. Type **secpol.msc** in the Open text box, and then click OK.

4. In the console tree, under Security Settings, expand Local Policies, and then select Security Options.

5. Double-click User Account Control: Behavior Of The Elevation Prompt For Administrators In Admin Approval Mode.

6. You can now:

   ❑ Block the elevation prompt by selecting No Prompt in the drop-down list.

   ❑ Enable the elevation prompt to use consent by selecting Prompt For Consent in the drop-down list. (The default setting is Prompt For Consent.)

   ❑ Require the elevation prompt to obtain credentials by selecting Prompt For Credentials in the drop-down list.

7. Click OK.

Introducing Parental Controls

Computer and Internet safety are major concerns. Many parents don't want their children to play certain types of games or access certain types of materials on the Internet. To help with this issue, Windows Vista includes parental controls. Parental controls help keep your family safe whether they are using the computer to play games or browsing the Web.

Getting Started with Parental Controls

The term *parental controls* is somewhat of a misnomer. Children and young adults use computers at home, in school, at the library, and elsewhere, and keeping them safe in all of these environments is what parental controls are all about. If you don't want children and young adults to play certain types of games or access certain types of materials on the Internet, you can use parental controls to help control their access to the computer and to mature content.

You can set parental controls for standard user accounts on the local computer only. You cannot set parental controls for administrators, and you cannot set parental controls for domain user accounts. Any user designated as an administrator on the local computer can configure parental controls and view activity reports for users subject to parental controls.

You can access parental controls by completing the following steps:

1. Click Start, and then click Control Panel.

2. In a workgroup setting, click Set Up Parental Controls under the User Accounts And Family Safety heading. In a domain setting, click Set Up Parental Controls under the User Accounts heading.

3. On the main Parental Controls page, shown in Figure 9-4, you can now set up parental controls.

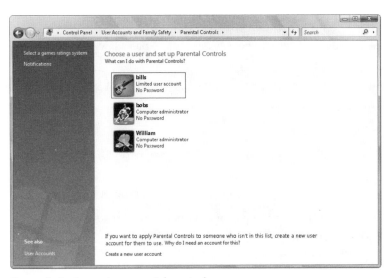

Figure 9-4 Accessing parental controls

Parental controls are configured using general settings for the computer as a whole as well as specific settings for individual users. General computer settings:

■ Control whether activity reports are active for specific users and how often you are reminded to read activity reports.

■ Determine whether an icon is displayed in the system tray when parental controls are running.

■ Determine the games rating system to use on the computer.

Individual user settings:

- Control allowed Web sites and allowed types of content.
- Set time limits for when the computer can be used.
- Determine the types of games that can be played according to rating, content, or title.
- Block specific programs by name.

Selecting a Games Rating System

Games rating systems, such as those used by the Entertainment Software Ratings Board (ESRB), are meant to help protect children and young adults from specific types of mature content in computer games and on the Internet. You can learn more about the available rating systems and configure a default rating system to use by following these steps:

1. Click Start, and then click Control Panel.

2. In Control Panel, click Set Up Parental Controls under the User Accounts And Family Safety category heading.

3. In the left panel of the main Parental Controls page, click Select A Games Rating System.

4. As Figure 9-5 shows, you can now review the games rating systems available. The default rating system used might depend on the country or region settings for the computer.

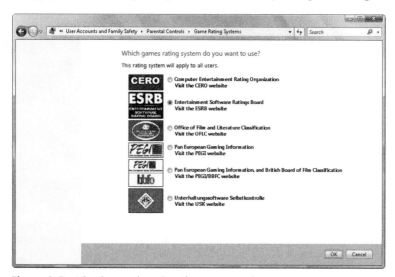

Figure 9-5   Viewing and setting the games rating system to use

Tip   When you click one of the links provided, the home page for the designated organization appears in Microsoft Internet Explorer. If you have questions about a rating system, the organization's Web site can answer them.

5. If you want to change the default rating system, click the rating system you want to use, and then click OK. Otherwise, click the Back button to go back to the Parental Controls page in Control Panel.

Configuring Notifications for Parental Controls

By default, when you configure parental controls, you are reminded weekly to read activity reports, and users subject to parental controls see an icon in the system tray when parental controls are running. If you want to change the way notification is handled, follow these steps:

1. Click Start, and then click Control Panel.

2. In Control Panel, click Set Up Parental Controls under the User Accounts And Family Safety category heading.

3. In the left panel of the main Parental Controls page, click Notifications.

4. As Figure 9-6 shows, you can now specify how often you would like to be reminded to read activity reports. You can specify that you want to be notified weekly, every two weeks, monthly, or never.

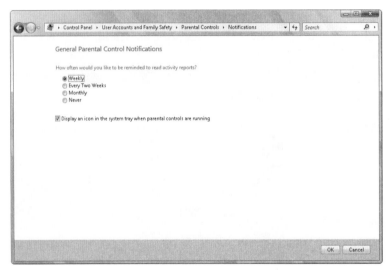

Figure 9-6   Setting general notifications

5. If you want to hide the parental controls icon rather than display it in the system tray, clear the Display An Icon In The System Tray When Parental Controls Are Running check box.

6. Click OK.

Configuring Parental Controls for User Accounts

Any standard user account can be configured to use parental controls. Parental controls can be used to control allowed Web sites and allowed types of content, set time limits for when the computer can be used, determine the types of games that can be played, and block specific programs by name. Parental controls can also be used to collect information about computer usage.

You can enable and configure parental controls by following these steps:

1. Click Start, and then click Control Panel.

2. In Control Panel, click Set Up Parental Controls under the User Accounts And Family Safety category heading.

3. On the Parental Controls page, click the user account for which you are configuring parental controls.

> **Note**   Only local administrators can set and manage parental controls. You cannot configure parental controls for local administrators.

4. To turn on parental controls and enforce settings, select On, Enforce Current Settings, as shown in Figure 9-7.

Figure 9-7   Enabling and configuring parental controls

5. To turn on activity reporting, select On, Collect Information About Computer Usage.

6. Web Restrictions determine allowed Web sites and allowed types of content. If you want to enforce Web Restrictions, click Web Restrictions. On the Web Restrictions page, shown in Figure 9-8, you can specify which parts of the Internet the user can access:

   ❑ Enable blocking by setting Do You Want To Block Some Web Content to Yes.

   ❑ Under Filter Web Content, choose a Web restriction level, and then select the content that you want to block.

❑ Click OK when you have finished.

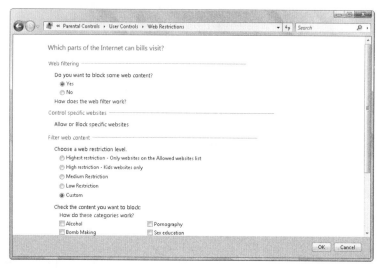

Figure 9-8   Setting Web restrictions

7. Time Limits specify the times when the computer can be used. If you want to enforce Time Limits, click Time Limits on the User Controls page. On the Time Limits page, shown in Figure 9-9, you can specify what times you allow and what times you block:

❑ Click and drag over allowed hours to change them to blocked hours.

❑ Click and drag over blocked hours to change them to allowed hours.

❑ Click OK when you have finished.

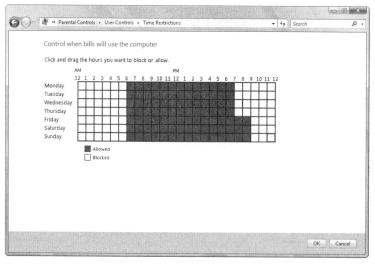

Figure 9-9   Setting time limits

8. Game Controls determine the types of games that can be played. If you want to control the types of games that can be played, click Games on the User Controls page. On the Game Controls page, shown in Figure 9-10, you can specify which types of games the user can play:

   ❑ Block all game play by setting Can <...> Play Games? to No.

   ❑ Block or allow games by rating and content types by clicking Set Game Ratings, choosing which game ratings are okay for the user to play, and then clicking OK.

   ❑ Block or allow specific games by clicking Block Or Allow Specific Games, choosing allowed or blocked games, and then clicking OK.

   ❑ Click OK when you have finished.

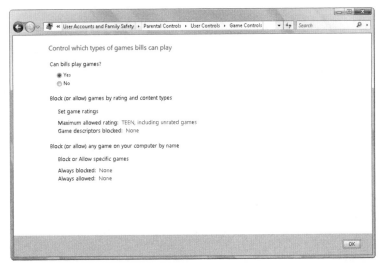

Figure 9-10   Setting game controls

9. Application Restrictions determine which programs can be run by the user. If you want to control application usage, click Block Specific Programs on the User Controls page. On the Application Restrictions page, shown in Figure 9-11, you can specify which types of applications can be run:

   ❑ Allow all programs to be run by selecting <...> Can Use All Programs.

   ❑ Restrict all programs except those specifically allowed by selecting <...> Can Only Use The Programs I Allow In This List.

   ❑ Set allowed programs using the options provided. If a program you want to allow isn't listed, click Browse, and then use the Open dialog box to select that program for use.

   ❑ Click OK when you have finished.

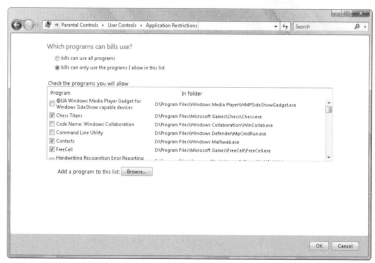

Figure 9-11 Setting application restrictions

10. On the User Controls page, click OK to save the settings.

Viewing and Using Activity Reports

An activity report for a user's account provides complete details about the user's computer and instant messaging usage and also provides details about general system modifications related to the account. Computer usage details include the following:

- The top 10 Web sites visited in the reporting period
- The most recent 10 Web sites blocked
- File downloads
- Logon times
- Applications run and games played
- E-mail messages sent and received
- Media played in media players
- Instant messaging

Instant messaging details include:

- Conversation initiation
- Link exchanges
- Webcam usage

- Audio usage
- Game play
- File exchanges
- SMS messages
- Contact list changes

General system details specify:

- Whether anyone made changes to parental controls for the account and, if so, who made those changes, how many changes he made, and when those changes were made.
- Whether general changes were made to the account and, if so, what changes were made.
- Whether system clock changes were made, such as in an attempt to circumvent time controls.
- Whether, for whom, and how many failed logon attempts were recorded in the security event logs.

You can turn on activity reports for a standard user by following these steps:

1. Click Start, and then click Control Panel.
2. In Control Panel, click Set Up Parental Controls under the User Accounts And Family Safety category heading.
3. On the Parental Controls page, click the user account for which you are configuring activity reports.
4. Turn on activity reporting by selecting On, Collect Information About Computer Usage.
5. Click OK to save the settings.

To view activity reports for a user, follow these steps:

1. Click Start, and then click Control Panel.
2. In Control Panel, click Set Up Parental Controls under the User Accounts And Family Safety category heading.
3. On the Parental Controls page, click the user account you want to work with.
4. Select Activity Reports to access the Activity Viewer page, shown in Figure 9-12.

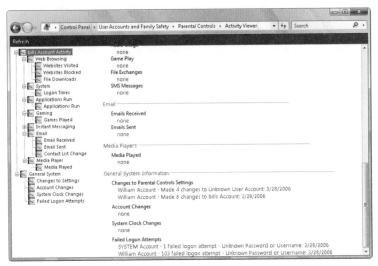

Figure 9-12   Viewing activity reports

By default, Activity Viewer provides summary details for all categories of information tracked. Using the options provided in the left pane, you can access detailed information for each category, which typically includes the date and time of the activity as well as other important details. For example, if you want to see a detailed list of Web sites visited, you can expand Account Activity, expand Web Browsing, and then select Websites Visited.

Chapter 10

Protecting Your Computer

Microsoft Windows Vista represents a fundamental shift in operating system architecture, so much so in fact that earlier versions of the Microsoft Windows operating system are considered legacy operating systems. The dramatic changes in the Windows Vista architecture are designed to provide multiple layers of protection for your computer and your data. These protections begin with a change in the way Windows Vista starts, and they extend through just about every facet of the operating system—from the way services run, to the way authentication is performed, to the way your computer uses encryption.

In this chapter, you'll learn about the most important architecture changes and how they create layers of protection for your computer. The changes that we'll look at include the new boot environment, which safeguards and enhances computer startup, and new security features as well as enhancements to existing security features.

Note This book was written using the Windows Vista Beta to provide an early introduction to the operating system. More so than any other area of Windows Vista, the security features discussed in this book are subject to change. Some of the features might not be included in the final product, and some of the features might be changed substantially.

Safeguarding and Enhancing Computer Startup

By using a pre-operating system boot environment, Windows Vista radically changes the way computers start up. Not only does this change serve to better protect the computer at startup, it also enhances the boot environment by making it extensible—and an extensible boot environment can be customized to the needs of various firmware interfaces.

Getting Started with the Windows Vista Boot Environment

Earlier versions of the Windows operating system use two files, named Ntldr and Boot.ini, to boot into the operating system. Ntldr handles the task of loading the operating system. In Boot.ini, you enter boot loader and operating system options that specify boot partitions according to hard disk controller, SCSI bus adapter, physical disk, and physical partition that should be used. You can add options that control the way the operating system starts, the way computer components are used, and the way operating system features are used.

To better control operating system startup and enhance pre-execution security, Windows Vista defines a pre-operating system boot environment and starts the operating system from within this environment. The boot environment has two key components: Windows Boot Manager and various boot applications that run in the boot environment. You can think of Windows Boot Manager as a mini-operating system that controls your startup experience and enables you to choose which boot application to run. Boot applications are used to load a specific operating system or operating system version. For example, a Windows Boot Loader application loads Windows Vista.

Windows Boot Loader is designed to work with the Boot Configuration Data (BCD) store. Entries in the BCD store contain boot configuration parameters and control how the operating system is started. BCD provides an extensible and interoperable interface for describing boot configuration data. BCD abstracts the underlying firmware, making it easier for Windows Vista to work with new firmware models, such as the Extensible Firmware Interface (EFI). BCD also provides the foundation for a variety of new features in Windows Vista, including the Startup Repair tool and Multi-User Install shortcuts.

The BCD store is contained in a file called the BCD registry file. On BIOS-based operating systems, the BCD registry file is located in the \Boot\Bcd directory of the active partition. On EFI-based operating systems, the BCD registry file is located on the EFI system partition.

On most computers, the BCD store contains multiple entries. If you examine the BCD store on a BIOS-based computer, the entries you see will include:

- A single Windows Boot Manager entry. There is only one boot manager, so there is only one boot manager entry.

- A Windows Boot Loader application entry for each Windows Vista operating system installed on the computer. For example, if you have installed two different versions of Windows Vista on different partitions, you will see two Windows Boot Loader entries.

- A single legacy operating system entry. This entry is not for a boot application. Instead, this entry uses Ntldr and Boot.ini to start up an earlier Windows operating system than Windows Vista. You will use this entry to start up Microsoft Windows Server 2003, Windows XP, and earlier operating systems if they are installed on a computer.

Modifying the Boot Environment

You must have administrative credentials to modify the BCD. Depending on what you want to change, you can use either of the following tools to modify BCD entries:

- **Startup And Recovery**   The Startup And Recovery dialog box, shown in Figure 10-1, enables you to select the default operating system to start if you have multiple operating systems installed on your computer. You can also specify time-out values for operating system selection lists and recovery options. To access these settings, click Start, and then click Control Panel. In Control Panel, click the System And Maintenance category heading link, and then click System. In the System utility, click Advanced System Settings in the left pane, and then on the Advanced tab of the System Properties dialog box, click Settings under Startup And Recovery.

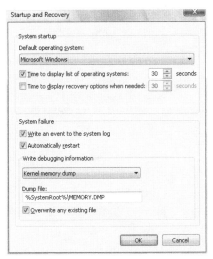

Figure 10-1   Using the Startup And Recovery dialog box to configure basic startup options

■ **System Configuration utility**   The System Configuration utility (Msconfig.exe), shown in Figure 10-2, allows you to control boot options. You can use the boot options to configure the computer to set the default operating system, to start the operating system in safe mode, to boot to the Windows prompt without loading the graphical components of the operating system, to force the computer to use standard VGA display settings, and more. To open the System Configuration utility, click Start, type **msconfig.exe** in the Search box, and then press Enter.

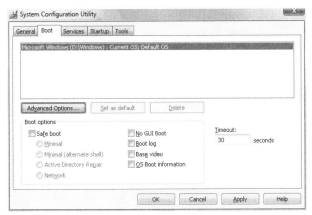

Figure 10-2   Using the System Configuration utility to configure advanced startup options

Developers and administrators have several other options for working with BCD entries. You can use the BCD Windows Management Instrumentation (WMI) provider to create scripts that modify the BCD store. Or you can use the BCDEdit command-line utility to view and manage the BCD store.

You can use BCDEdit to list the contents of the BCD store by following these steps:

1. Click Start, point to All Programs, and then click Accessories.

2. Right-click Command Prompt, and then select Run As Administrator.

> **Tip** You must run the command prompt with administrator credentials to perform administrative tasks at the command line. If you don't start the command prompt as an administrator, you will be denied permission to perform tasks that require administrator credentials.

3. Type **bcdedit** at the command prompt.

Listing 10-1 shows an example of the output from BCDEdit. As mentioned previously, this example output includes three entries: one for Windows Boot Manager, one for the Windows legacy operating system loader, and one for Windows Boot Loader. You can enter **bcdedit /?** at a command prompt to display options for this program.

Listing 10-1 Entries in the BCD store displayed using BCDEdit

```
Windows Boot Manager
--------------------
Identifier:             {bootmgr}
Type:                   10100002
Device:                 partition=C:
Description:            Windows Boot Manager
Locale:                 en-US
Inherit options:        {globalsettings}
Boot debugger:          No
Default:                {current}
Resume application:     {23432149-a32e-132a-ba28-ed8322b34395}
Display order:          {ntldr}
                        {current}
Timeout:                30

Windows Legacy OS Loader
------------------------
Identifier:             {ntldr}
Type:                   10300006
Device:                 partition=C:
Path:                   \ntldr
Description:            Legacy (pre-Longhorn) Microsoft Windows Operating System
Boot debugger:          No
```

```
Windows Boot Loader
-------------------
Identifier:             {current}
Type:                   10200003
Device:                 partition=D:
Path:                   \Windows\system32\winload.exe
Description:            Microsoft Windows
Locale:                 en-US
Inherit options:        {bootloadersettings}
Boot debugger:          No
Windows device:         partition=D:
Windows root:           \Windows
Resume application:     {23432149-a32e-132a-ba28-ed8322b34395}
No Execute policy:      OptIn
No integrity checks:    Yes
Kernel debugger:        No
EMS enabled in OS:      No
```

Safeguarding Your Computer

To keep pace with constantly evolving security threats, the Windows operating system must also evolve and provide new ways of protecting your computer. Windows Vista meets this challenge by expanding the security offerings of Windows XP in a variety of ways and by providing entirely new security features, such as Windows Service Hardening and Network Access Protection. Together these features offer additional layers of protection for your computer.

Getting to Know the Windows Vista Expanded Security Features

Windows Vista expands the security features offered in earlier versions of Windows in several ways. To ensure that organizations have a wide variety of authentication mechanisms to choose from, Windows Vista includes a new authentication architecture that is both extensible and customizable. Because the new architecture makes it easier for third-party developers to extend and customize the Windows Vista authentication mechanisms, this should lead to more choices for smart cards, biometrics, and other forms of strong authentication.

Windows Vista provides enhancements to the Kerberos authentication protocol and smart card logons. Deployment and management tools, such as self-service personal identification number (PIN) reset tools, make smart cards easier to manage. Windows Vista also has improved support for data protection at the document, file, folder, and machine level.

With integrated rights management, you can enforce policies regarding document access and usage. The Encrypting File System (EFS), which provides user-based file and folder encryption, has been enhanced to allow storage of encryption keys on smart cards, providing better protection of encryption keys. To extend the level of data encryption protection beyond files and folders, Windows Vista includes support for Trusted Platform Modules and BitLocker Drive Encryption. On a computer with appropriate enabling hardware, these features validate boot integrity and provide full disk encryption, which helps protect data from being compromised on a lost or stolen machine.

Getting Started with Network Access Protection

Business versions of Windows Vista include Network Access Protection (NAP) to prevent a Windows Vista–based client from connecting to your private network if the client lacks current security updates and virus signatures or otherwise fails to meet your computer health requirements. NAP is designed to protect client computers as well as your network from vulnerabilities that could otherwise be exploited if NAP wasn't used and enforced.

From the experts

NAP: Finally wired networks can be as secure as wireless networks

When remote access connections and wireless networks were new, they were popular targets for people who wanted to break into those networks. So, members of the security community put their heads together and developed some near-bullet-proof techniques for keeping the bad guys out—even if the "bad guy" was just a computer that hadn't been patched.

Many of us forgot our Ethernet networks, and did not provide the same security protections. Somehow, we felt safe inside our offices because wired networks are more difficult for an attacker to connect to. However, mobile users can still connect to a wired network and spread worms and viruses. Finally, with NAP, we have a good way to help protect wired, wireless, and remote access connections from traditional hackers as well as malicious software.

Tony Northrup
Author, MCSE, and MVP–For more information, see http://www.northrup.org.

Understanding Network Access Protection

Network Access Protection can be used to protect your network from local clients as well as remote access clients. At the heart of this feature are three components:

- **Network Access Protection Agent**   A software component that allows a client running Windows to participate in Network Access Protection. This agent runs as a service on computers running Windows Vista.

- **NAP Client Configuration**   A configuration tool that is used to define and enforce NAP requirements on clients. This tool is also used to specify health registration settings and designate trusted servers.

- **NAP Server Configuration**   A configuration tool that is used to manage NAP and define NAP policy.

The Network Access Protection Agent reports the health status of a client computer to a server called a Health Registration Authority. The report includes details about the client's overall security health, such as whether the client has current security updates and up-to-date virus signatures installed. The security mechanism by which a client computer communicates with a Health Registration Authority is configured through a designated Request Policy.

Request Policies can be configured to use:

- Any of a variety of private key algorithms, including asymmetric key algorithms based on Rivest-Shamir-Adleman (RSA), Digital Signal Algorithm (DSA), and other security specifications.

- Any of a variety of signed and unsigned hash algorithms, including RSA MD5 hashing and DSA SHA1 hashing.

- Any of a variety of Cryptographic Service Providers, including the Microsoft Enhanced Cryptographic Provider version 1.0, the Microsoft Enhanced RSA and AES Cryptographic Provider, and the Microsoft Enhanced DSS and Diffie-Hellman Cryptographic Provider.

You can access the NAP Client Configuration tool, shown in Figure 10-3, by following these steps:

1. Click Start, and then click Control Panel.

2. In Control Panel, click the System And Maintenance category heading link, and then click Administrative Tools.

3. Double-click NAP Client Configuration.

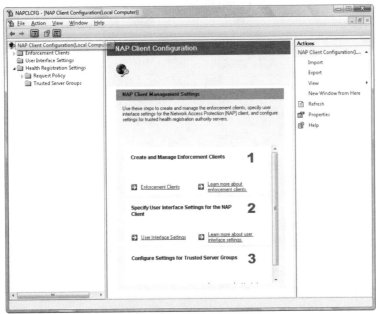

Figure 10-3   Using the NAP Client Configuration console to manage NAP

Using Network Access Protection

Using the NAP Client Configuration tool, administrators can configure separate enforcement policies for Dynamic Host Configuration Protocol (DHCP) clients, remote access clients, and terminal services clients. Enforcement policy can also be configured for virtual private network (VPN) clients that use Extensible Authentication Protocol (EAP).

Administrators can use NAP to enforce health requirements for all computers that are connected to an organization's private network, regardless of how those computers are connected to the network. You can use NAP to improve the security of your private network by ensuring that the latest updates are installed before users connect to your private network. If a client computer does not meet the health requirements, you can:

- Prevent the computer from connecting to your private network.
- Provide instructions to users on how to update their computers. (In some cases, you can update their computers automatically.)
- Limit access to your network so that users with out-of-date computer security can access only designated servers on your network.

To allow NAP to be enforced when a computer is acting as a DHCP client, follow these steps:

1. Start the NAP Client Configuration tool.

2. In the left panel, select Enforcement Clients.

3. Double-click DHCP Quarantine Enforcement Client.

4. In the DHCP Quarantine Enforcement Client Properties dialog box, select the Enable This Enforcement Client check box, as shown in Figure 10-4.

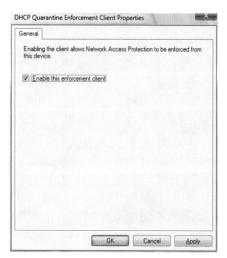

Figure 10-4   Enforcing NAP when DHCP is used

You can enable enforcement for other types of connections using a similar procedure:

- To enforce remote access NAP, open NAP Client Configuration tool, double-click Remote Access Quarantine Enforcement Client, and then select the Enable This Enforcement Client check box.

- To enforce terminal services NAP, open NAP Client Configuration tool, double-click TS Gateway Quarantine Enforcement Client, and then select the Enable This Enforcement Client check box.

- To enforce VPN protection, NAP Client Configuration tool, double-click EAP Quarantine Enforcement Client, and then select the Enable This Enforcement Client check box.

You configure the actual NAP policies that apply to clients by using the NAP Server Configuration tool.

Understanding Windows Service Hardening

Earlier versions of Windows grant wide access to the system-level services running on the computer. Many of these services run under the LocalSystem account, where any breach could:

- Grant wide access to the data on the computer.

- Allow malicious programs to modify the system configuration.

- Open the computer to other types of attacks.

Windows Vista uses Windows Service Hardening to provide an additional layer of protection so that services cannot be compromised. Following the security principle of defense-in-depth, Windows Service Hardening:

- Restricts critical Windows services from performing abnormal activities that affect the file system, registry, network, or other resources that could be used to allow malicious software to install itself or attack other computers. Services can be restricted from replacing system files or modifying the registry. Unnecessary Windows privileges, such as the ability to perform debugging, have also been removed on a per-service basis.

- Limits the number of services that are running and operational by default to reduce the overall attack surface in Windows. Some services are now configured to start manually as needed rather than automatically when the operating system starts.

- Limits the privilege level of servers by limiting the number of services that run in the LocalSystem account. Some services that previously ran in the LocalSystem account now run in a less privileged account, such as the Local Service or Network Service account. This reduces the overall privilege level of the service, which is similar to the benefits derived from User Account Control (UAC). (UAC is discussed in Chapter 9.)

Windows Service Hardening introduces entirely new features, which are used by Windows services as well. Like user accounts, each service has a security identifier that is used to manage the security permissions granted to the service. Per-service security identifiers (SIDs) enable per-service identity. Per-service identity, in turn, enables access control partitioning through the existing Windows access control model, covering all objects and resource managers that use access control lists (ACLs). Services can now apply explicit ACLs to resources that are private to the service, and this prevents other services as well as the user from accessing those resources.

All services now have write-restricted access tokens. A write-restricted access token can be used in cases where the set of objects written to by the service is bounded and can be configured. Write attempts to resources to which the service was not granted explicit access fail. Further, services are assigned a network firewall policy to prevent network access outside the normal bounds of the service program. The firewall policy is linked directly to the per-service SID.

While Windows Service Hardening cannot prevent a vulnerable service from being compromised, it does go a long way toward limiting how much damage an attacker can do in the unlikely event the attacker is able to identify and exploit a vulnerable service. When combined with other Windows Vista components and other defense-in-depth strategies, such as Windows Firewall and Windows Defender, computers running Windows Vista have much more protection than computers running earlier versions of Windows.

Improving Computer Security

To improve computer security and harden the operating system against attack, Windows Vista modifies many areas of the local computer security configuration. Some of the most far reaching changes have to do with security settings for local policies, which can be managed through Active Directory Group Policy or through Local Group Policy. To manage Active Directory Group Policy, you can use the Group Policy Object Editor or the Group Policy Management Console. To manage Local Group Policy on a local computer, you can access security settings by using the Security Configuration Management console. The sections that follow discuss changes to Audit Policy, User Rights Assignment, and Security Options.

Navigating Audit Policy Changes

Audit Policy is used to collect information regarding resource and privilege use. By enabling auditing policies, you can configure security logging to track important security events, such as when a user logs on to the computer or when a user changes account settings.

You can follow these steps to access Audit Policy in the Local Security Settings console:

1. Click Start, point to All Programs, Accessories, and then click Run.
2. Type **secpol.msc** in the Open text box, and then click OK.

3. Expand the Local Polices node in the left pane, and then click the Audit Policy node, as shown in Figure 10-5.

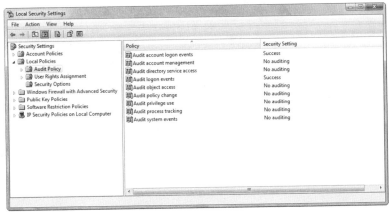

Figure 10-5   Using the Local Security Settings console to manage Audit Policy

Table 10-1 provides an overview of the default Audit Policy configuration used in Windows XP and Windows Vista. As the table shows, in Windows XP, auditing is not enabled by default. In Windows Vista, however, successful logons are tracked for all types of accounts.

Table 10-1   Comparing Audit Policy in Windows XP and Windows Vista

Policy	Default Security Setting in Windows XP	Default Security Setting in Windows Vista
Audit Account Logon Events	No auditing	Success
Audit Account Management	No auditing	No auditing
Audit Directory Service Access	No auditing	No auditing
Audit Logon Events	No auditing	Success
Audit Object Access	No auditing	No auditing
Audit Policy Change	No auditing	No auditing
Audit Privilege Use	No auditing	No auditing
Audit Process Tracking	No auditing	No auditing
Audit System Events	No auditing	No auditing

Navigating User Rights Assignment Changes

User Rights Assignment policies determine what a user or group can do on a computer. Follow these steps to access User Rights Assignment policies in the Local Security Settings console:

1. Click Start, point to All Programs, Accessories, and then click Run.

2. Type **secpol.msc** in the Open text box, and then click OK.

3. Expand the Local Polices node in the left pane, and then click the User Rights Assignment node, as shown in Figure 10-6.

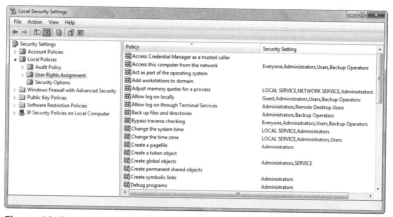

Figure 10-6 Using the Local Security Settings console to manage User Rights Assignment policies

As Table 10-2 shows, the default user rights have changed substantially between Windows XP and Windows Vista. A key reason for these changes has to do with User Account Control. User Account Control provides a new layer of protection for computers by ensuring that there is true separation of user and administrator accounts. Because of User Account Control, there are many changes to user rights assignment in Windows Vista.

Table 10-2 Comparing User Rights Assignment in Windows XP and Windows Vista

Policy	Default Security Setting in Windows XP	Security Setting in Windows Vista
Access Credential Manager As A Trusted Caller	Not Applicable	No default setting
Access This Computer From The Network	Everyone, Administrators, Users, Power Users, Backup Operators	Everyone, Administrators, Users, Backup Operators
Act As Part Of The Operating System	No default setting	No default setting
Add Workstations To Domain	No default setting	No default setting
Adjust Memory Quotas For A Process	LOCAL SERVICE, NETWORK SERVICE, Administrators	LOCAL SERVICE, NETWORK SERVICE, Administrators
Allow Log On Locally	Not Applicable	Guest, Administrators, Users, Backup Operators
Allow Logon Through Terminal Services	Administrators, Remote Desktop Users	Administrators, Remote Desktop Users
Back Up Files And Directories	Administrators, Backup Operators	Administrators, Backup Operators
Bypass Traverse Checking	Everyone, Administrators, Users, Power Users, Backup Operators	Everyone, Administrators, Users, Backup Operators
Change The System Time	Administrators, Power Users	LOCAL SERVICE, Administrators
Change The Time Zone	Not Applicable	LOCAL SERVICE, Administrators, Users

Table 10-2   Comparing User Rights Assignment in Windows XP and Windows Vista

Policy	Default Security Setting in Windows XP	Security Setting in Windows Vista
Create A Pagefile	Administrators	Administrators
Create A Token Object	No default setting	No default setting
Create Global Objects	Administrators, INTERACTIVE, SERVICE	Administrators, SERVICE
Create Permanent Shared Objects	No default setting	No default setting
Create Symbolic Links	No default setting	Administrators
Debug Programs	Administrators	Administrators
Deny Access To This Computer From The Network	SUPPORT, Guest	Guest
Deny Logon As A Batch Job	No default setting	No default setting
Deny Logon As A Service	No default setting	No default setting
Deny Logon Locally	SUPPORT, Guest	Guest
Deny Logon Through Terminal Services	No default setting	No default setting
Enable Computer And User Accounts To Be Trusted For Delegation	No default setting	No default setting
Force Shutdown From A Remote System	Administrators	Administrators
Generate Security Audits	LOCAL SERVICE, NETWORK SERVICE	LOCAL SERVICE, NETWORK SERVICE
Impersonate A Client After Authentication	Administrators, SERVICE	Administrators, SERVICE
Increase A Process Working Set	No default setting	Users
Increase Scheduling Priority	Administrators	Administrators
Load And Unload Device Drivers	Administrators	Administrators
Lock Pages In Memory	No default setting	No default setting
Log On As A Batch Job	SUPPORT, Administrator	Administrators, Backup Operators
Log On As A Service	NETWORK SERVICE	
Log On Locally	Guest, Administrators, Users, Power Users, Backup Operators	Not applicable
Manage Auditing And Security Log	Administrators	Administrators
Modify An Object Label	Not Applicable	No default setting
Modify Firmware Environment Values	Administrators	Administrators

Table 10-2   Comparing User Rights Assignment in Windows XP and Windows Vista

Policy	Default Security Setting in Windows XP	Security Setting in Windows Vista
Perform Volume Maintenance Tasks	Administrators	Administrators
Profile Single Process	Administrators, Power Users	Administrators
Profile System Performance	Administrators	Administrators
Remove Computer From Docking Station	Administrators, Users, Power Users	Administrators, Users
Replace A Process Level Token	LOCAL SERVICE, NETWORK SERVICE	LOCAL SERVICE, NETWORK SERVICE
Restore Files And Directories	Administrators, Backup Operators	Administrators, Backup Operators
Shut Down The System	Administrators, Users, Power Users, Backup Operators	Administrators, Users, Backup Operators
Synchronize Directory Service Data	No default setting	No default setting
Take Ownership Of Files Or Other Objects	Administrators	Administrators

When you compare the user rights assigned in Windows Vista to those assigned in Windows XP, you'll see many changes. Windows Vista phased out the Power Users group and now maintains this group only for backward compatibility with legacy applications. As a result, the Power Users group is not granted user rights in Windows Vista.

Windows Vista includes several new user rights, including:

- **Access Credential Manager As A Trusted Caller**   Allows a user or group to establish a trusted connection to Credential Manager. In Windows Vista, Credential Manager is used to manage a user's credentials. A *credential* is an association of all the information needed for logging on and being authenticated on a particular server or at a particular site, such as a user name and password or certificate. Credentials provide identification and proof of identification. Examples of credentials are user names and passwords, smart cards, and certificates.

- **Allow Log On Locally**   Allows a user or group to log on at the keyboard. This user right was originally named Log On Locally and has been renamed in Windows Vista so that there are now both Allow Log On Locally and Deny Log On Locally user rights.

- **Change The Time Zone**   Allows a user or group to change the time zone. As users have this right by default, users are able to change the computer's time zone without using administrator privileges.

In Windows Vista, users—or more specifically, processes started by users—can now increase the working set for a process. This change is important for applications that run using standard user credentials. Why? The working set of a process is the amount of physical memory assigned to that process by the operating system. Windows Vista restricts the tasks that applications can perform and the system areas to which they can write. If user privileges could not be used to increase the working set of a process, an application running in standard user mode could run out of memory.

Navigating Security Options Changes

Security Options enable or disable security settings for a computer. Follow these steps to access Security Options in the Local Security Settings console:

1. Click Start, point to All Programs, Accessories, and then click Run.

2. Type **secpol.msc** in the Open text box, and then click OK.

3. Expand the Local Polices node in the left pane, and then click the Security Options node, as shown in Figure 10-7.

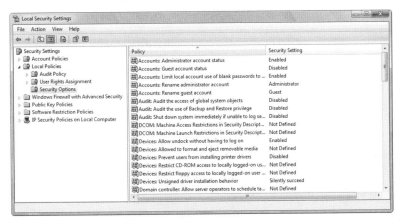

Figure 10-7   Using the Local Security Settings console to manage Security Options

As Table 10-3 shows, the default security options have changed substantially between Windows XP and Windows Vista. As with User Rights Assignment, many of the changes are because of User Account Control.

Table 10-3   Comparing Security Options in Windows XP and Windows Vista

Policy	Default Security Setting in Windows XP	Security Setting in Windows Vista
Accounts: Administrator Account Status	Not Applicable	Enabled
Accounts: Guest Account Status	Not Applicable	Disabled
Accounts: Limit Local Account Use Of Blank Passwords To Console Logon Only	Enabled	Enabled
Accounts: Rename Administrator Account	Administrator	Administrator
Accounts: Rename Guest Account	Guest	Guest

Table 10-3   Comparing Security Options in Windows XP and Windows Vista

Policy	Default Security Setting in Windows XP	Security Setting in Windows Vista
Audit: Audit The Access Of Global System Objects	Disabled	Disabled
Audit: Audit The Use Of Backup And Restore Privilege	Disabled	Disabled
Audit: Shut Down System Immediately If Unable To Log Security Audits	Disabled	Disabled
DCOM: Machine Access Restrictions In Security Descriptor Definition Language (SDDL) Syntax	Not Defined	Not Defined
DCOM: Machine Launch Restrictions In Security Descriptor Definition Language (SDDL) Syntax	Not Defined	Not Defined
Devices: Allow Undock Without Having To Log On	Enabled	Enabled
Devices: Allowed To Format And Eject Removable Media	Administrators	Not Defined
Devices: Prevent Users From Installing Printer Drivers	Disabled	Disabled
Devices: Restrict CD-ROM Access To Locally Logged-On User Only	Disabled	Not Defined
Devices: Restrict Floppy Access To Locally Logged-On User Only	Disabled	Not Defined
Devices: Unsigned Driver Installation Behavior	Warn But Allow Installation	Silently Succeed
Domain Controller: Allow Server Operators To Schedule Tasks	Not Defined	Not Defined
Domain Controller: LDAP Server Signing Requirements	Not Defined	Not Defined
Domain Controller: Refuse Machine Account Password Changes	Not Defined	Not Defined
Domain Member: Digitally Encrypt Or Sign Secure Channel Data (Always)	Enabled	Enabled
Domain Member: Digitally Encrypt Secure Channel Data (When Possible)	Enabled	Enabled
Domain Member: Digitally Sign Secure Channel Data (When Possible)	Enabled	Enabled
Domain Member: Disable Machine Account Password Changes	Disabled	Disabled
Domain Member: Maximum Machine Account Password Age	30 Days	30 Days
Domain Member: Require Strong (Windows 2000 Or Later) Session Key	Disabled	Disabled
Interactive Logon: Do Not Display Last User Name	Disabled	Disabled

Table 10-3   **Comparing Security Options in Windows XP and Windows Vista**

Policy	Default Security Setting in Windows XP	Security Setting in Windows Vista
Interactive Logon: Do Not Require Ctrl+Alt+Del	Not Defined	Not Defined
Interactive Logon: Message Text For Users Attempting To Log On		
Interactive Logon: Message Title For Users Attempting To Log On	Not Defined	Not Defined
Interactive Logon: Number Of Previous Logons To Cache (In Case Domain Controller Is Not Available)	10 Logons	10 Logons
Interactive Logon: Prompt User To Change Password Before Expiration	14 Days	14 Days
Interactive Logon: Require Domain Controller Authentication To Unlock Workstation	Disabled	Disabled
Interactive Logon: Require Smart Card	Not Defined	Disabled
Interactive Logon: Smart Card Removal Behavior	No Action	No Action
Microsoft Network Client: Digitally Sign Communications (Always)	Disabled	Disabled
Microsoft Network Client: Digitally Sign Communications (If Server Agrees)	Enabled	Enabled
Microsoft Network Client: Send Unencrypted Password To Third-Party SMB Servers	Disabled	Disabled
Microsoft Network Server: Amount Of Idle Time Required Before Suspending Session	15 Minutes	15 Minutes
Microsoft Network Server: Digitally Sign Communications (Always)	Disabled	Disabled
Microsoft Network Server: Digitally Sign Communications (If Client Agrees)	Disabled	Disabled
Microsoft Network Server: Disconnect Clients When Logon Hours Expire	Enabled	Enabled
Network Access: Allow Anonymous SID/Name Translation	Not Applicable	Disabled
Network Access: Do Not Allow Anonymous Enumeration Of SAM Accounts	Enabled	Enabled
Network Access: Do Not Allow Anonymous Enumeration Of SAM Accounts And Shares	Disabled	Disabled
Network Access: Do Not Allow Storage Of Credentials Or .NET Passports For Network Authentication	Disabled	Disabled
Network Access: Let Everyone Permissions Apply To Anonymous Users	Disabled	Disabled

Table 10-3   **Comparing Security Options in Windows XP and Windows Vista**

Policy	Default Security Setting in Windows XP	Security Setting in Windows Vista
Network Access: Named Pipes That Can Be Accessed Anonymously	COMNAP, COMNODE, SQL\QUERY, SPOOLSS, LLSRPC, Browser	SQL\QUERY, SPOOLSS, Netlogon, Lsarpc, Samr, Browser
Network Access: Remotely Accessible Registry Paths	(Multiple paths defined as accessible)	Not Defined
Network Access: Remotely Accessible Registry Paths And Sub-Paths	Not Applicable	Not Defined
Network Access: Restrict Anonymous Access To Named Pipes And Shares	Not Applicable	Enabled
Network Access: Shares That Can Be Accessed Anonymously	COMCFG, DFS$	
Network Access: Sharing And Security Model For Local Accounts	Guest Only – Local Users Authenticate As Guest	Classic – Local Users Authenticate As Themselves
Network Security: Do Not Store LAN Manager Hash Value On Next Password Change	Disabled	Enabled
Network Security: Force Logoff When Logon Hours Expire	Disabled	Disabled
Network Security: LAN Manager Authentication Level	Send LM & NTLM Responses	Send NTLMv2 Response Only
Network Security: LDAP Client Signing Requirements	Negotiate Signing	Negotiate Signing
Network Security: Minimum Session Security For NTLM SSP Based (Including Secure RPC) Clients	No Minimum	No Minimum
Network Security: Minimum Session Security For NTLM SSP Based (Including Secure RPC) Servers	No Minimum	No Minimum
Recovery Console: Allow Automatic Administrative Logon	Disabled	Disabled
Recovery Console: Allow Floppy Copy And Access To All Drives And All Folders	Disabled	Disabled
Shutdown: Allow System To Be Shut Down Without Having To Log On	Enabled	Enabled
Shutdown: Clear Virtual Memory Pagefile	Disabled	Disabled
System Cryptography: Force Strong Key Protection For User Keys Stored On The Computer	Not Applicable	Not Defined
System Cryptography: Use FIPS Compliant Algorithms For Encryption, Hashing, And Signing	Disabled	Disabled

Table 10-3   Comparing Security Options in Windows XP and Windows Vista

Policy	Default Security Setting in Windows XP	Security Setting in Windows Vista
System Objects: Default Owner For Objects Created By Members Of The Administrators Group	Object Creator	Object Creator
System Objects: Require Case Insensitivity For Non-Windows Subsystems	Enabled	Enabled
System Objects: Strengthen Default Permissions Of Internal System Objects (for example, Symbolic Links)	Enabled	Enabled
System Settings: Optional Subsystems	Not Applicable	Posix
System Settings: Use Certificate Rules On Windows Executables For Software Restriction Policies	Not Applicable	Disabled
User Account Control: Behavior Of The Elevation Prompt For Administrators In Admin Approval Mode	Not Applicable	Prompt For Consent
User Account Control: Behavior Of The Elevation Prompt For Standard Users	Not Applicable	Prompt For Credentials
User Account Control: Detect Application Installations And Prompt For Elevation	Not Applicable	Enabled
User Account Control: Only Elevate Executables That Are Signed And Validated	Not Applicable	Disabled
User Account Control: Run All Administrators In Admin Approval Mode	Not Applicable	Enabled
User Account Control: Switch To The Secure Desktop When Prompting For Elevation	Not Applicable	Enabled
User Account Control: Virtualize File And Registry Write Failures To Per-User Locations	Not Applicable	Enabled

Some of the most significant security changes in Windows Vista have to do with the following default settings for network access and network security:

■ **Remote registry access**   In Windows XP, multiple registry paths are remotely accessible by default. In Windows Vista, no areas of the registry are remotely accessible by default. This change improves registry security. Additionally, Windows Vista includes a new security option to manage access to registry subpaths.

■ **Anonymous access to named pipes and shares**   Windows Vista adds a security option to restrict anonymous access to named pipes and shares. This change blocks anonymous access to named pipes and shares.

■ **Sharing and security model for local accounts**   In Windows XP, the default sharing and security model for local accounts is to authenticate local users as guests. In Windows

Vista, local users are authenticated as themselves. This change enhances security by ensuring that users must have appropriate permissions to access all areas of the file system.

■ **Storing LAN Manager hash values**   In Windows XP, when a user changes a password, the LAN Manager hash value used to help in subsequent authentication can be stored on the computer. Windows Vista ensures that these hash values are not stored on the computer. This improves security by requiring a user to obtain a new hash value anytime a password is changed.

■ **LAN Manager authentication**   In Windows XP, client computers use LM and NTLM authentication and never use NTLM version 2 session security. In Windows Vista, client computers use NTLM version 2 authentication only and can also use NTLM version 2 session security if the server supports it. Because NTLM version 2 is more secure than LM and NTLM, the authentication process is more secure.

Chapter 11
Protecting Your Data

Many of the security features in Microsoft Windows Vista are designed to protect your computer from attack by individuals accessing the computer over the network or from the Internet. When the attacker is in your home or office, however, most of these remote access security features fall short in protecting your data. If someone can boot your computer to another operating system, that person could change your computer's configuration or make other unapproved modifications. He or she could also gain access to your most sensitive data. To protect your data from individuals who have direct access to your computer, Windows Vista includes Trusted Platform Module Services architecture and BitLocker Drive Encryption. Together these features ensure that your computer is protected from many types of attacks by individuals who have direct access to your computer.

Note This book was written using the Windows Vista Beta to provide an early introduction to the operating system. More so than any other area of Windows Vista, the security features discussed in this book are subject to change. Some of these features might not be included in the final product, and some of the features might be changed substantially.

Introducing Trusted Platforms

Both Microsoft Windows XP and Windows Vista include the Encrypting File System (EFS) for encrypting files and folders. Using EFS, you can protect your sensitive data so that it can be accessed only by using your public key infrastructure (PKI) certificate. Encryption certificates are stored as part of the data in your user profile. As long as you have access to your profile and the encryption key it contains, you can access your files.

While EFS offers excellent protection for you data, it doesn't safeguard the computer from attack by someone who has access to the console. In a situation where you've lost your computer, your computer has been stolen, or an attacker is logging on to your computer, EFS might not protect you, because the unauthorized user might be able to gain access to the computer before it starts up. He could then access the computer from another operating system and change your computer's configuration. He might then be able to hack into your account so that he can log on as you or configure the computer so that he can log on as a local administrator. Either way, the unauthorized user could eventually gain full access to your computer and your data.

To seal a computer from physical attack and wrap it in an additional layer of protection, Windows Vista includes the Trusted Platform Module Services architecture. Using Trusted Platform Module Services architecture, you can create a trusted platform with enhanced security and within which your computer's data is protected even when the operating system is offline. How the Trusted Platform Module Services architecture does this and how you can use Trusted Platform Module Services architecture is what this section is all about.

In Windows Vista, Trusted Platform Module Services provide the infrastructure necessary to take advantage of Trusted Platform Module (TPM) Security Hardware. Trusted Platform Module Services protect a computer by using a dedicated hardware component called a TPM. A *TPM* is a microchip that is usually installed on the motherboard of a computer, where it communicates with the rest of the system by using a hardware bus. Computers running Windows Vista can use a TPM to provide enhanced protection for data, to ensure early validation of the boot file's integrity, and to guarantee that a disk has not been tampered with while the operating system was offline.

A TPM has the ability to create cryptographic keys and encrypt them so that they can be decrypted only by the TPM. This process, which is referred to as *wrapping* or *binding*, protects the key from disclosure. A TPM has a master wrapping key called the Storage Root Key (SRK), which is stored within the TPM itself to ensure that the private portion of the key is secure.

Increasingly, new business computers have TPMs installed. Computers that have a TPM can create a key that has not only been wrapped but also *sealed*. The process of sealing the key ensures that the key is tied to specific platform measurements and can be unwrapped only when those platform measurements have the same values that they had when the key was created, and this is what gives TPM-equipped computers increased resistance to attack.

> **Note**   Because a TPM stores private portions of key pairs separately from memory controlled by the operating system, keys can be sealed to the TPM to provide absolute assurances about the state of a system and its trustworthiness. TPM keys are *unsealed* (or decrypted) only when the integrity of the system is intact. Further, because the TPM uses its own internal firmware and logical circuits for processing instructions, it does not rely on the operating system and is not subject to external software vulnerabilities.

The TPM can also be used to seal and unseal data that is generated outside of the TPM, and this is where the true power of the TPM lies. In Windows Vista, the feature that accesses the TPM and uses it to seal your computer is called BitLocker Drive Encryption.

When you use BitLocker Drive Encryption and a TPM to seal the boot manager and boot files of a computer, the boot manager and boot files can be unsealed only if they are unchanged since they were last sealed. This means that you can use the TPM to validate a computer's boot files in the pre-operating system environment. When you seal a hard disk by using the TPM, the hard disk can be unsealed only if the data on the disk is unchanged since it was last sealed. This guarantees that a disk has not been tampered with while the operating system was offline.

From the experts
Should you use BitLocker?

BitLocker makes your data more secure in the event an attacker is able to bypass operating system security and directly access your data. In other words, BitLocker can safeguard your computer if an attacker has physical access to your computer. That's very important to business travelers because confidential data can be leaked when someone loses a laptop.

However, BitLocker is not without its drawbacks. First, you need a way to manage the encryption key because, if you lose the key, you can't start your computer or access your files. While enterprises that use domains can centrally manage BitLocker keys using Active Directory, no similar solution is available for using BitLocker in workgroup environments. Second, recovering a computer is more difficult when BitLocker is enabled. Normally, if a hard disk is starting to fail or you've removed a hard disk from a computer, you can connect the hard disk to a different computer to copy and recover the data. With BitLocker, you can't do this easily, and you must first unlock the drive. Because of this, regular backups are a must (which can be a challenge for traveling users). Finally, BitLocker only protects your computer when it is off. That means BitLocker won't protect your computer from malicious software or attackers on the Internet.

With those factors in mind, you *should* use BitLocker in enterprise environments where the risk of data theft is greater than the cost of managing the encryption keys.

Tony Northrup
Author, MCSE, and MVP–For more information, see http://www.northrup.org.

Getting Started with TPM Management

To take advantage of the Trusted Platform Module Services architecture, a computer running Windows Vista must be equipped with a compatible TPM and compatible BIOS. Windows Vista supports TPM version 1.2 and requires Trusted Computing Group (TCG)–compliant BIOS. BIOS that is TCG-compliant is BIOS that supports the Static Root of Trust Measurement specification as defined by the Trusted Computing Group. You can learn more about this specification at *http://www.trustedcomputinggroup.org*.

> **Note**   The TPM Services architecture in Windows Vista provides the basic features required to configure and deploy TPM-equipped computers. This architecture can be extended by using BitLocker Drive Encryption, which is discussed in detail in the "Using BitLocker Drive Encryption" section later in this chapter.

You manage the TPM by using the Trusted Platform Module Management console, shown in Figure 11-1. To start this console, follow these steps:

1. Click Start, point to All Programs, Accessories, and then click Run.

2. Type **tpm.msc** in the Open text box, and then click Enter.

3. Manage the computer's TPM configuration by using the commands listed under Actions.

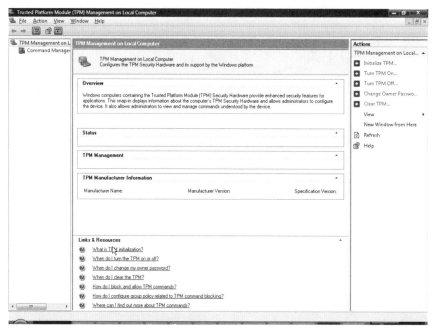

Figure 11-1   Managing the TPM by using the Trusted Platform Module Management console

Managing the TPM

Before you can use the TPM, you must initialize the TPM for first use and turn on the TPM. Once the TPM is enabled, you can manage the TPM configuration. The sections that follow discuss:

- Initializing the TPM for first use.
- Turning off and clearing the TPM.
- Changing the TPM owner password.

> **Caution**   While understanding how TPMs are managed is important for getting a complete understanding of using the Trusted Platform Module Services architecture, managing TPMs isn't something inexperienced users or administrators should attempt. Only experienced administrators should attempt to manage TPMs, and even then, only as necessary.

Initializing a TPM for First Use

Initializing a TPM configures it for use on a computer. The initialization process involves turning on the TPM and then setting ownership of the TPM. Although Windows Vista supports remote initialization of a TPM, you must have local access to the computer to turn on the TPM. On some new computers, the TPM is turned on by default. If this is the case with the computer you are working with, you can complete the initialization of the TPM remotely.

To initialize the TPM on your computer for first use, complete the following steps:

1.   Log on locally to the computer with local administrator credentials.

2.   Start the Trusted Platform Module Management console.

3.   Under Actions, click Initialize TPM to start the TPM Initialization Wizard. On the Welcome page, click Next.

4.   The next step depends on the state of the TPM:

      ❑   If the TPM Initialization Wizard detects a BIOS that does not meet Windows Vista requirements, you will not be able to continue with the wizard. Instead, you will be alerted to consult the computer manufacturer's documentation for instructions on turning on the TPM.

      ❑   If the TPM is turned off, the TPM Initialization Wizard displays the Turn On The TPM Security Hardware page. Follow the instructions for turning on the TPM. Click Shutdown (or Restart), and then follow the BIOS screen prompts. After the computer restarts, confirm that you want to turn on the TPM when prompted.

      ❑   If the TPM is already turned on, the first page you see is the Create The TPM Owner Password page. For details about setting the owner password, see the next procedure.

The second part of initializing the TPM for first use is setting ownership. By setting ownership of the TPM, you are assigning a password that helps ensure that only the authorized TPM owner can access and manage the TPM. The TPM password is required to turn off the TPM if you no longer want to use it and to clear the TPM if the computer is to be recycled.

To set the ownership of the TPM on your computer, complete the following steps:

1.   Log on locally to the computer with local administrator credentials.

2.   Start the Trusted Platform Module Management console.

3. Under Actions, click Initialize TPM to start the TPM Initialization Wizard. On the Welcome page, click Next.

4. On the Create The TPM Owner Password page, select Automatically Create The Password (Recommended), and then click Next.

5. On the Save Your TPM Owner Password page, click Save, and then select a location to save the password. Ideally, you'll save the TPM ownership password to removable media, such as a universal serial bus (USB) flash drive.

6. Click Save again. The password file is saved as *computer_name*.tpm.

7. Click Print if you want to print a hard copy of your password. Be sure to save the printout containing the password in a secure location.

8. Click Initialize. The initialization process might take several minutes to complete.

9. When initialization is complete, click Close. The status of the TPM is displayed under Status in the TPM Management console.

Turning Off and Clearing the TPM

New computers that have a TPM might arrive with the TPM turned on by default. If you decide not to use the TPM, you should turn off and clear the TPM. If you want to reconfigure or recycle a computer, you should also turn off and clear the TPM. Windows Vista supports remotely turning off and clearing a TPM as well as using scripts to turn off and clear a TPM.

To turn off the TPM, complete the following steps:

1. Log on locally to the computer with local administrator credentials.

2. Start the Trusted Platform Module Management console.

3. Under Actions, click Turn TPM Off.

4. In the Turn Off The TPM Security Hardware dialog box, select one of the following methods for entering your password and turning off the TPM:

   ❑ If you have the removable media on which you saved your TPM owner password, insert it, and then click I Have A Backup File With The TPM Owner Password. In the Select Backup File With The TPM Owner Password dialog box, click Browse, and then use the Open dialog box to locate the .tpm file saved on your removable media. Click Open, and then click Turn TPM Off.

   ❑ If you do not have the removable media on which you saved your password, click I Want To Type The TPM Owner Password. In the Type Your TPM Owner Password dialog box, type your password (including dashes), and then click Turn TPM Off.

   ❑ If you do not know your TPM owner password, click I Don't Have The TPM Owner Password, and then follow the instructions provided to turn off the TPM without entering the password. Because you are logged on locally to the computer, you will be able to turn off the TPM.

Clearing the TPM cancels the TPM ownership and finalizes the shutdown of the TPM. You should clear the TPM only when a TPM-equipped client computer is to be recycled or when the TPM owner has lost the TPM owner password and recovery information was not backed up.

To clear the TPM, complete the following steps:

1. Log on locally to the computer with local administrator credentials.

2. Start the Trusted Platform Module Management console.

3. Under Actions, click Clear TPM.

> **Caution**   Clearing the TPM resets it to factory defaults and finalizes its shutdown. As a result, you will lose all created keys and data protected by those keys.

4. In the Clear The TPM Security Hardware dialog box, select a method for entering your password and clearing the TPM:

   ❑ If you have the removable media on which you saved your TPM owner password, insert it, and then click I Have A Backup File With The TPM Owner Password. In the Select Backup File With The TPM Owner Password dialog box, click Browse, and then use the Open dialog box to locate the .tpm file saved on your removable media. Click Open, and then click Clear TPM.

   ❑ If you do not have the removable media on which you saved your password, click I Want To Type The TPM Owner Password. In the Type Your TPM Owner Password dialog box, enter your password (including dashes) and then click Clear TPM.

   ❑ If you do not know your TPM owner password, click I Don't Have The TPM Owner Password, and then follow the instructions provided to clear the TPM without entering the password. Because you are logged on locally to the computer, you will be able to clear the TPM.

5. The status of the TPM is displayed under Status in the TPM Management console.

Changing the TPM Owner Password

If you suspect that the TPM owner password has been compromised, you can change the password by using the Trusted Platform Module Management console. To change the TPM owner password, complete the following steps:

1. Log on locally to the computer with local administrator credentials.

2. Start the Trusted Platform Module Management console.

3. Under Actions, click Change Owner Password.

4. Follow the prompts to provide the current password and change the password.

Using BitLocker Drive Encryption

BitLocker Drive Encryption is designed to protect computers from attackers who have physical access to a computer. Without BitLocker Drive Encryption, an attacker could start the computer with a boot disk and then reset the administrator password to gain full control of the computer. Or the attacker could access the computer's hard disk directly by using a different operating system to bypass file permissions. BitLocker Drive Encryption prevents this by entering recovery mode at startup if there are any offline changes to boot files, operating system files, or encrypted volumes. In this way, BitLocker Drive Encryption dramatically reduces the risk of an attacker gaining access to confidential data by using offline attacks.

Introducing BitLocker Drive Encryption

BitLocker Drive Encryption is the feature in Windows Vista that makes use of a computer's TPM. BitLocker Drive Encryption can use a TPM to validate the integrity of a computer's boot manager and boot files at startup, and to guarantee that a computer's hard disk has not been tampered with while the operating system was offline. BitLocker Drive Encryption also stores measurements of core operating system files in the TPM.

Every time the computer is started, Windows Vista validates the boot files, the operating system files, and any encrypted volumes to ensure they have not been modified while the computer was offline. If the files have been modified, Windows Vista alerts the user and refuses to release the key required to access Windows. The computer then goes into a recovery mode, prompting the user to provide a recovery key before allowing access to the boot volume. Recovery mode is also used if a disk drive is transferred to another system.

BitLocker Drive Encryption can be used in both TPM and non-TPM computers:

- If a computer has a TPM, BitLocker Drive Encryption uses the TPM to provide enhanced protection for your data and to assure early boot file integrity. This helps protect the data on your computer from unauthorized viewing by encrypting the entire Windows volume and by safeguarding the boot files from tampering.

- If a computer doesn't have a TPM or its TPM isn't compatible with Windows Vista, BitLocker Drive Encryption can be used to encrypt entire volumes and in this way protect the volumes from tampering. This configuration, however, doesn't allow the added security of early boot file integrity validation.

On computers with a compatible TPM, BitLocker Drive Encryption can use one of two TPM modes:

- **TPM-only**   In this mode, only the TPM is used for validation. When the computer starts up, the TPM is used to validate the boot files, the operating system files, and any encrypted volumes. Because the user doesn't need to provide an additional startup key, this mode is transparent to the user and the user logon experience is unchanged. However, if the TPM is missing or the integrity of files or volumes has changed, BitLocker will enter recovery mode and require a recovery key or password to regain access to the boot volume.

■ **Startup key**   In this mode, both the TPM and a startup key are used for validation. When the computer starts up, the TPM is used to validate the boot files, the operating system files, and any encrypted volumes. The user must have a startup key to log on to the computer. A startup key can be either physical, such as a USB flash drive with a machine-readable key written to it, or personal, such as a personal identification number (PIN) set by the user. If the user doesn't have the startup key or is unable to provide the correct startup key, BitLocker will enter recovery mode. As before, BitLocker will also enter recovery mode if the TPM is missing or the integrity of boot files or encrypted volumes has changed.

On computers without a TPM or on computers that have incompatible TPMs, BitLocker Drive Encryption uses USB Flash Drive Key mode. As the name implies, this mode requires a USB flash drive containing a startup key. The user inserts a USB flash drive in the computer before turning it on. The key stored on the flash drive unlocks the computer. If the user doesn't have the startup key or is unable to provide the correct startup key, BitLocker will enter recovery mode. BitLocker will also enter recovery mode if the integrity of encrypted volumes has changed.

Preparing a Computer for BitLocker Drive Encryption

Before you can use BitLocker Drive Encryption, you must prepare the computer. On a computer with a compatible TPM, you must create a BitLocker Drive Encryption partition on your hard drive and then initialize the TPM as discussed in the "Initializing a TPM for First Use" section earlier in this chapter. On a computer without a compatible TPM, you need only to create a BitLocker Drive Encryption partition on your hard drive.

The way you create the BitLocker Drive Encryption partition depends on whether the computer has an operating system installed. If the computer doesn't have an operating system installed, follow the procedure discussed "Creating the BitLocker Drive Encryption Partition on a Computer with No Operating System." If the computer has an operating system installed, follow the procedure discussed in the "Creating the BitLocker Drive Encryption Partition on a Computer with an Operating System" section later in this chapter.

> **Note**   Enterprise computers shipped with Windows Vista installed might already have a BitLocker Drive Encryption partition. These computers might also have the TPM turned on. Check with the computer manufacturer.

Creating the BitLocker Drive Encryption Partition on a Computer with No Operating System

BitLocker Drive Encryption requires a separate partition on the computer's hard disk that must be at least 450 megabytes (MB) and set as the active partition. This section describes how to create the BitLocker Drive Encryption partition on a computer with no operating system and a single hard drive.

> **Note**   Due to changes in the operating system, some of the steps in this procedure might change. Do not attempt this procedure without first performing it on a test computer.
>
> In this procedure, you will start the computer from the installation media and then create two partitions on the computer. The first partition is the primary partition for the operating system and your data. The second partition is a smaller partition for BitLocker Drive Encryption.

> **Caution**   Do not perform this procedure on a computer with an operating system. Performing this procedure will erase all data on your hard disk. You must back up any data before beginning this procedure. If you have a drive that already has the operating system installed on a single partition, don't perform this procedure. Instead, you will need to repartition the drive as discussed in the next section, "Creating the BitLocker Drive Encryption Partition on a Computer with an Operating System."

You can partition a drive with no operating system for BitLocker Drive Encryption by following these steps:

1. Start the computer with the installation media in the computer's CD-ROM or DVD-ROM drive.

2. When prompted, press any key to boot from the installation media.

3. When Windows has finished loading the Setup environment, you'll see the Installation Windows dialog box. In the Installation Windows dialog box, select System Recovery Options.

4. Clear any operating systems listed in the System Recovery Options, and then click Next.

5. Click Command Line Window.

6. In the command-line window, type **diskpart**.

7. Select the hard disk for use by typing **select disk 0**.

8. Erase the existing partition table by typing **clean**.

9. Create a primary partition by typing **create partition primary**.

10. Designate the partition as drive C by typing **assign letter=c**.

11. Format the partition by typing **format**.

12. Shrink the partition by 450 MB at the end by typing **shrink minimum=450**.

13. Create a primary partition in the space remaining after the Shrink command by typing **create partition primary**.

14. Set the new partition as active by typing **active**.

15. Designate the partition as drive D by typing **assign letter=d**. If drive D is already in use, you might need to use a different drive letter.

16. Format the partition by typing **format**.

17. Quit the DiskPart application by typing **exit**.

18. Close the Command Prompt window by typing **exit**.

19. If possible, return to the main installation screen by clicking Close. Restart the computer and then press any key to boot from the installation media when prompted.

20. Click Install Now, and proceed with the installation process. Install Windows Vista on drive C.

21. If the computer has a TPM, you will need to initialize it as described in the "Initializing a TPM for First Use" section earlier in this chapter.

Creating the BitLocker Drive Encryption Partition on a Computer with an Operating System

BitLocker Drive Encryption requires a separate partition on the computer's hard disk that must be at least 450 MB and set as the active partition. This section describes how to create the BitLocker Drive Encryption partition on a computer with an operating system and a single hard drive.

> **Caution**   Due to changes in the operating system, some of the steps in this procedure might change. Do not attempt this procedure without first performing it on a test computer. After testing and before performing this procedure, back up your computer and all data.
>
> In this procedure, you will start the computer from the installation media. You will then shrink the current partition to create a partition for BitLocker Drive Encryption. Afterward, you will copy key boot files from the encrypted C partition to the active D partition.

You can create an additional partition on a drive with an operating system by following these steps:

1. Start the computer with the installation media in the computer's CD-ROM or DVD-ROM drive.

2. When prompted, press any key to boot from the installation media.

3. When Windows has finished loading the Setup environment, you'll see the Installation dialog box. In the Installation Windows dialog box, select System Recovery Options.

4. Clear any operating system in the System Recovery Options and click Next.

5. Click Command Line Window.

6.   In the command line window, type **diskpart**.

7.   Select the hard disk for use by typing **select disk 0**.

8.   Select the current partition by typing **select partition 1**.

9.   Shrink the current partition by 450 MB at the end by typing **shrink minimum=450**.

10. Create a primary partition in the space remaining after the Shrink command by typing **create partition primary**.

11. Set the new partition as active by typing **active**.

12. Designate the partition as drive D by typing **assign letter=d**.

> **Note**   If drive D is already in use, you might need to use a different drive letter. Throughout the rest of this procedure, you'll then need to provide this drive letter whenever drive d is referenced.

13. Format the partition by typing **format**.

14. Quit the DiskPart application by typing **exit**.

15. Make new boot sectors at the beginning of the new partition. If you have the Bootsect tool, type **x:\boot\bootsect /nt60 ALL**. If you have the Fixntfs tool, type **x:\boot\ fixntfs −LH −ALL**.

16. Remove the read-only, system, and hidden attributes from the boot manager files by typing **attrib −r −s −h c:\bootmgr**.

17. Copy the boot manager files to the system drive by typing **xcopy C:\bootmgr d:**.

18. Restore the read-only, system, and hidden attributes to the boot manager files on both drives by typing the following commands:

     ❑   **attrib +r +h +s c:\bootmgr**

     ❑   **attrib +r +h +s d:\bootmgr**

     ❑   **attrib +r +h +s d:\boot**

19. Make a copy of the boot files on drive C by typing **xcopy d:\boot c:\boot\ /cherky**. Be sure to type a space between the backslash (\) and slash (/). If you have an Extensible Firmware Interface (EFI) system, also type **xcopy d:\efi c:\efi\ /cherky** to copy additional files.

20. Copy the boot manager files to the C drive by typing **xcopy x:\bootmgr c:**. If you have an EFI system, also type **xcopy x:\bootmgr.efi c:** to copy additional files.

21. Close the Command Prompt window by typing **exit**.

22. Return to the main installation screen by clicking Close.

23. Remove the installation media, and then restart the computer.

24. If the computer has a TPM, you will need to initialize it, as described in the "Initializing a TPM for First Use" section earlier in this chapter.

Configuring and Enabling BitLocker Drive Encryption for a TPM

After you've partitioned the computer's hard drive for BitLocker Drive Encryption (if necessary), the next step to configure your computer to use BitLocker Drive Encryption is to enable the feature on the operating system.

1. Log on to the computer as an administrator.

2. Click Start, click Control Panel, click Security, and then click BitLocker Drive Encryption.

3. For the system volume, click Turn On BitLocker. This starts the Turn On BitLocker Drive Encryption wizard, shown in Figure 11-2.

Figure 11-2   The Turn On BitLocker Drive Encryption wizard

4. Read the welcome message, and then click Next.

5. On the Save The Recovery Key As A Password page, shown in Figure 11-3, the BitLocker Drive Encryption wizard provides options for you to display, print, or save the 48-digit recovery password.

> **Tip**   You will need the recovery password to unlock the secured data on the volume if BitLocker Drive Encryption enters a locked state. This recovery password is unique to this particular BitLocker encryption. You cannot use it to recover encrypted data from any other BitLocker encryption session.

Figure 11-3   The Save The Recovery Key As A Password page

6. Click Print The Password to print the password. Be sure to store the printed password in a secure location.

7. Click Save The Password. In the Save BitLocker Drive Encryption Password As dialog box, type a file name for the password, and then click Save. The password is saved by default in the Documents folder in your user profile.

8. Click Next. The Save The Recovery Key On A USB Device page is displayed, as shown in Figure 11-4. If you want to save the recovery password to a USB memory device, insert the device and select the corresponding drive in the list provided, and then click Save Key.

Figure 11-4   The Save The Recovery Key On A USB Device page

9. Click Next. The Save The Recovery Key To A Folder page is displayed. If you want to save the recovery password to a folder on another computer or a network share, click Save, and then use the Browse For Folder dialog box to specify the save location.

10. Click Next. If you are on a TPM-equipped computer, you will see the Create A PIN For Added Security page. You have the option of creating a PIN for added security. If desired, enter and confirm a PIN, and then click Set PIN. The PIN will then be required to start the computer. Click Next.

11. On the Create A Startup Key For Added Security page, displayed in Figure 11-5, you have the option of creating a startup key. When using a startup key, keep the following in mind:

    ❑ On a TPM-equipped computer, creating a startup key is optional. If you want to require a startup key to start up the computer, insert a USB memory device and select the corresponding drive in the list provided, and then click Save Key.

    ❑ On a non-TPM-equipped computer, creating a startup key is required. Insert a USB memory device and select the corresponding drive in the list provided, and then click Save Key.

> **Note**   The startup key is different from the recovery key. If you create a startup key, this key will then be required to start the computer. The recovery key is required to unlock the computer if BitLocker enters recovery mode, as would happen if BitLocker suspects that the computer has been tampered with while offline.

Figure 11-5   The Create A Startup Key For Added Security page

12. Click Next. On the Encrypt The Selected Disk Volume page, shown in Figure 11-6, click Encrypt to encrypt the selected disk volume. An Encryption In Progress status bar is

displayed. You can monitor the ongoing completion status of the disk volume encryption by moving the pointer over the BitLocker Drive Encryption icon on the toolbar at the bottom of your screen. Volume encryption takes approximately one minute per gigabyte (GB) to complete.

Figure 11-6   The Encrypt The Selected Disk Volume page

When the encryption process is complete, you will have encrypted the entire volume and created a recovery key unique to this volume. If you created a PIN or startup key, you will be required to use the PIN or startup key to start the computer. Otherwise, you will see no change to the computer unless the TPM changes or cannot be accessed, or if someone tries to modify the disk while the operating system is offline. In this case, the computer will enter recovery mode, and you will need to enter the recovery key to unlock the computer.

Recovering Data Protected by BitLocker Drive Encryption

If you've configured BitLocker Drive Encryption and the computer enters recovery mode, you will need to unlock the computer. To unlock the computer by using a startup or recovery key stored on a USB memory drive, follow these steps:

1. Turn on your computer. The computer starts the BitLocker Drive Encryption Recovery console.

2. When you are prompted, insert the portable USB memory drive that contains the startup or recovery key, and then press Enter.

3. The computer will unlock and restart automatically. You will not need to enter the recovery key manually.

To unlock the computer by typing your recovery key, follow these steps:

1. Turn on your computer. The computer starts the BitLocker Drive Encryption Recovery console.

2. Type the recovery password, and then press Enter.

3. The computer will unlock and restart automatically.

> **Tip** In some situations, the computer might become locked. For example, the computer might become locked if you tried to enter the recovery key but were unsuccessful. You can press Esc twice to exit the recovery prompt and turn off your computer. The computer might also become locked if an error related to the TPM occurs or if a boot file is modified. In this case, the computer halts very early in the boot process, before the operating system starts. At this point, the locked computer cannot accept standard keyboard numbers, so you must use the function keys to enter the recovery key password. In this context, the function keys F1 through F9 represent the digits 1 through 9, and the F10 function key represents 0.

Chapter 12
Networking Your Computer

In our increasingly connected world, networking and communications are critically important. Microsoft Windows Vista ensures that you can connect to a network wherever you are and from any device by giving you greater and more flexible options for accessing networks and managing network infrastructure. Not only does Windows Vista enhance support for standard networks, but it also fully supports the next generation of networks, whether you are using wired or wireless technologies.

Note This book was written using the Windows Vista Beta to provide an early introduction to the operating system. More so than any other area of Windows Vista, the security features discussed in this book are subject to change. Some of the features might not be included in the final product, and some of the features might be changed substantially.

Introducing TCP/IP Networking for Windows Vista

The networking components in Windows Vista have been extensively reworked. In this section, you'll look at the changes to these components and how they are used to improve reliability while reducing transfer times. You'll learn about:

- The next generation of networking components.
- The dual stack and the IP management enhancements.

Getting to Know the Next Generation TCP/IP Stack

Whether they are using wired or wireless technology, most networks use TCP/IP. TCP/IP is a protocol suite consisting of Transmission Control Protocol (TCP) and Internet Protocol (IP). TCP is a connection-oriented protocol designed for reliable end-to-end communications. IP is an internetworking protocol that is used to route packets of data over a network. Two versions of IP are in use:

- **IP version 4 (IPv4)**   IPv4 is the primary version of IP used today on networks, including the Internet. IPv4 has 32-bit addresses.

- **IP version 6 (IPv6)**   IPv6 is the next-generation version of IP. IPv6 has 128-bit addresses.

While many computers use only IPv4, IPv6 is increasingly being used, and eventually IPv4 may be phased out in favor of IPv6. Why? IPv4 allows only 2^{32} unique addresses to be used. While 4,294,967,296 unique addresses might seem like a huge amount, it really isn't when you look at the number of computing devices in our connected world. This is why we need IPv6, with its virtually unlimited address space, and why computers running Windows Vista have both IPv4 and IPv6 configured by default.

Windows Vista includes many other changes to the core networking components as well. Windows Vista provides a new implementation of the TCP/IP protocol stack known as the Next Generation TCP/IP stack. This stack is a complete redesign of TCP/IP functionality for both IPv4 and IPv6. The Next Generation TCP/IP stack supports:

- **Receive Window Auto Tuning**   Optimizes TCP transfers for the host receiving data by automatically managing the size of the memory buffer (the receive windows) to use for storing incoming data based on the current network conditions.

- **Compound TCP (CTCP)**   Optimizes TCP transfers for the sending host by aggressively increasing the amount of data sent in a connection while ensuring that other TCP connections are not impacted.

- **Neighbor Unreachability Detection**   Determines when neighboring nodes, including routers, are no longer reachable and reports the condition.

- **Automatic Dead Gateway Retry**   Ensures that an unreachable gateway is tried again periodically to determine whether it has become available.

- **Automatic Black Hole Router Detection**   Prevents TCP connections from terminating due to intermediate routers silently discarding large TCP segments, retransmissions, or error messages.

- **Routing Compartments**   Prevents unwanted forwarding of traffic between interfaces by associating an interface or a set of interfaces with a login session that has its own routing tables.

- **Network Diagnostics Framework**   Provides an extensible architecture that helps users recover from and troubleshoot problems with network connections.

- **TCP Extended Statistics**   Helps determine whether a performance bottleneck for a connection is the sending application, the receiving application, or the network.

- **Windows Filtering Platform**   Provides application programming interfaces (APIs) for extending the TCP/IP filtering architecture so that it can support additional features.

To optimize throughput in high-loss environments, the Next Generation TCP/IP stack supports industry standard Requests For Comments (RFCs) 2582, 2883, 3517, and 4138. These changes allow the Next Generation TCP/IP stack to:

- Modify how the TCP fast recovery algorithm is used. The new algorithm provides faster throughput by changing the way that a sender can increase its sending rate when multiple segments in a window of data are lost and the sender receives an acknowledgement stating that only part of the data has been successfully received. The old algorithm worked well for single lost segments, but it did not perform well when multiple lost segments were involved.

- Extend the use of the Selective Acknowledgement (SACK) option for TCP. This option now allows a receiver to indicate up to four noncontiguous blocks of received data and to acknowledge duplicate packets. The sender can then determine when it has retransmitted a segment unnecessarily and adjust its behavior to prevent future retransmissions.

- Introduce a conservative SACK-based loss recovery algorithm for TCP. This new algorithm makes it possible to use SACK information to perform loss recovery when TCP senders receive duplicate acknowledgements and to recover more effectively and quickly when multiple segments are not received at the destination.

- Detect spurious retransmission time-outs (RTOs) with TCP. This provides correction for sudden, temporary increases in RTOs and prevents unnecessary retransmission of segments.

Learning About the Dual Stack and the IP Management Enhancements

As mentioned earlier, computers running Windows Vista have both IPv4 and IPv6 configured by default. This is a major change from earlier versions of Microsoft Windows, in which only IPv4 is used by default.

Windows Vista supports IPv4 and IPv6 by using the dual-layer Next Generation TCP/IP stack. This stack features an implementation of IP in which IPv4 and IPv6 share common transport and framing layers. Because Windows Vista enables IPv4 and IPv6 by default, there is no need to install a separate component to obtain IPv6 support.

To make IPv6 more dynamic, Windows Vista includes a number of enhancements. These enhancements include support for:

- **Symmetric network address translators (NATs)** A symmetric NAT maps the internal (private) address and port number to different external (public) addresses and ports, depending on the external destination address. This new behavior allows an IPv6 feature called Teredo to act as the go-between for a larger set of Internet-connected host computers.

- **IP Security in IPv6**   Windows Vista supports IP Security for IPv6 traffic in the same way it supports IPv4 traffic. As a result, IPv6 can use Internet Key Exchange (IKE) and data encryption in the same way as IPv4. This ensures IPv6 traffic can be as secured as IPv4 traffic. When you configure an IP filter as part of an IP filter list in the IP Security Policies snap-in, you can now specify IPv6 addresses and address prefixes in IP Address or Subnet when specifying a specific source or destination IP address.

- **IPv6 over Point-to-Point Protocol (PPPv6)**   PPPv6 allows native IPv6 traffic to be sent over PPP-based connections. This means that remote access clients can connect with an IPv6-based Internet service provider (ISP) through dial-up or PPP over Ethernet (PPPoE)–based connections.

- **Multicast Listener Discovery version 2 (MLDv2)**   IPv6 routers use MLDv2 to identify the presence of multicast listeners and to provide support for source-specific multicast traffic. MLDv2 is equivalent to Internet Group Management Protocol version 3 (IGMPv3) for IPv4. (Multicast listeners are nodes that are configured to receive multicast packets.)

- **Link-Local Multicast Name Resolution (LLMNR)**   LLMNR allows IPv6 hosts on a single subnet without a DNS server to resolve each other's names. This feature is useful for single-subnet home networks and ad hoc wireless networks.

- **Random Interface IDs**   Random Interface IDs prevent address scanning of IPv6 addresses based on the known company IDs of network adapter manufacturers. By default, Windows Vista generates Random Interface IDs for nontemporary autoconfigured IPv6 addresses, including public and local link addresses.

- **Dynamic Host Configuration Protocol version 6 (DHCPv6)**   Windows Vista includes a DHCPv6-capable DHCP client. This client can use stateful address autoconfiguration with a DHCPv6 server. Or, the client can use stateless address autoconfiguration when a DHCPv6 server is not present.

From the experts
Configuring IPv4 and IPv6 settings

In Windows Vista, you can manually configure both IPv4 and IPv6 settings through a set of dialog boxes accessible from the Network Connections console. Click Start, and then click Control Panel. In Control Panel, under the Network And Internet heading, click View Network Status And Tasks. In the left pane in Network Center, click Manage Network Connections. Right-click a connection and then select Properties. In the connection's Properties dialog box, double-click Internet Protocol Version 6 (TCP/IPv6) or Internet Protocol Version 4 (TCP/IPv4) as appropriate.

You configure IPv4 settings through the Properties dialog box of the Internet Protocol version 4 (TCP/IPv4) component and through commands in the Netsh Interface IPv4 context. You can disable IPv4 for connections by clearing the check box next to the Internet Protocol version 4 (TCP/IPv4) component from the properties of a connection.

You configure IPv6 settings through the Properties dialog box of the Internet Protocol version 6 (TCP/IPv6) component and through commands in the Netsh Interface IPv6 context. You can disable IPv6 for connections by clearing the check box next to the Internet Protocol version 6 (TCP/IPv6) component from the properties of a connection. For more information about configuring IPv4 and IPv6, refer to the *Microsoft Windows Vista Administrator's Pocket Consultant* (Microsoft Press, 2006).

William Stanek
Author, MVP, and series editor for the Microsoft Press Administrator's Pocket Consultants

Mapping Your Networking Capabilities and Infrastructure

Windows Vista provides a whole new way to navigate and manage the networking features of your computer. In this section, you'll learn about these features, including Network Center, Network List, Network Map, and Network Connections.

Using Network Center

When you want to work with the networking features of your computer, you'll start with Network Center. You can access Network Center by following these steps:

1. Click Start, and then click Control Panel.

2. In Control Panel, under the Network And Internet heading, click View Network Status And Tasks.

This displays Network Center, as shown in Figure 12-1.

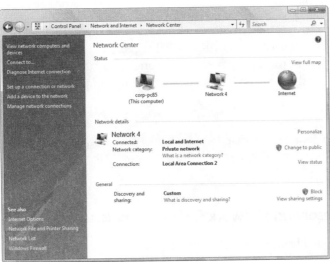

Figure 12-1   Network Center shows that you are connected to a network that in turn has connectivity to the Internet.

Once you've accessed Network Center, you can use it to manage your general network settings and network status. When you are connected to a network, Network Center provides an overview of your networking configuration and allows you to determine your network status and view or change settings.

The three main areas in Network Center are:

- **Status**   Provides a visual overview of the network infrastructure. The map depicts whether you are connected to a network and whether you can access the Internet on that network. Clicking View Full Map displays an expanded Network Map, as described in the "Using Network Map" section later in this chapter.

- **Network Details**   Provides details about the network to which the computer is currently connected. These details include the connections being used and whether the network has Internet access. Using the links provided, you can manage the connections in use and the networks to which those connections are linked, as described in the "Viewing and Managing Your Networks" section later in this chapter.

- **General**   Provides a summary of the computer's firewall, detection, and sharing settings. Depending on the configuration, several options are provided, including Block, Allow, and View Sharing Settings. You'll learn how to manage general settings in the next section, "Managing General Networking Settings."

The sections that follow discuss using Network Center to manage settings, diagnose and repair connectivity issues, and manage your network status.

Managing General Networking Settings

In Network Center, the settings in the General panel allow you to block or allow connections to your computer. If you click Block, the computer's firewall blocks all access to the network. While access is blocked, you will be unable to access other computers on the network or on the Internet, and other computers will be unable to access your computer.

To unblock the computer, you need to click Allow. Clicking Allow sets the computer's firewall to its normal configuration. In this configuration, you can access other computers on the network or on the Internet, and other computers can access your computer, if allowed by the firewall configuration.

> **Tip**   To configure Windows Firewall from Network Center, click View Sharing Settings. This link opens the Windows Firewall dialog box, which you can use to manage the Windows Firewall configuration.

Diagnosing and Resolving Network Connectivity Issues

When you are disconnected from a network, Network Center displays a modified view, as shown in Figure 12-2. Based on this view of your network configuration, you know at a glance that you are not connected to a network or the Internet.

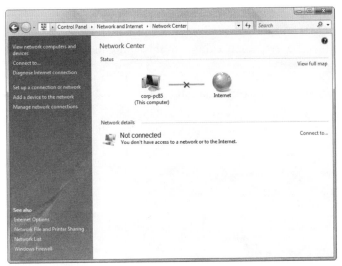

Figure 12-2   Network Center shows that you are not connected to a network or the Internet.

To resolve this problem, you should check the network cable that connects to your computer as well as any wireless adapters. If your network cable or wireless adapters are properly connected, you can click Diagnose Internet Connection in the left pane to start the new Windows Networks Diagnostics Tool. This tool uses the Network Diagnostics Framework to help you recover from and troubleshoot problems with network connections.

The Windows Networks Diagnostics Tool offers step-by-step advice on resolving your network connectivity problem. For example, in Figure 12-3, the tool advises that you should connect a network cable to the computer's network adapter. When you plug in the cable and then click the diagnostics box, the tool will validate the repair. If a problem is detected, the tool continues troubleshooting the connection. Otherwise, you'll see a prompt confirming that the problem has been repaired.

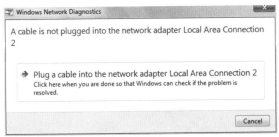

Figure 12-3   The Windows Networks Diagnostics Tool offers step-by-step advice.

Viewing and Managing Your Networks

In Network Center, you can browse computers and devices on the network by clicking Browse The Network in the left pane. While browsing the network, you use Network view. In a domain, options on the Network view toolbar allow you to search Active Directory, connect to a network, or return to Network Center. In a workgroup, options on the Network view toolbar allow you to connect to a network or return to Network Center. If you double-click a computer while browsing, you'll be able to see devices associated with the computer, such as printers.

In Network Center, you can create network connections by clicking Connect To in the left pane and then clicking Create A New Connection in the Connect To A Network dialog box. This opens the Connect To A Network Wizard, shown in Figure 12-4. You can use this wizard to add a network, create a virtual private network (VPN) connection or create a dial-up connection.

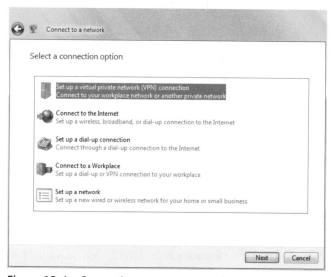

Figure 12-4   Connecting to a new network

When you connect to a network in a new location, a network profile is created. Windows can save settings in this location and automatically use these settings the next time you connect to this network. Sometimes, you can connect to one network in multiple ways. For example, you might be able to connect to a network by plugging in a cable, by using a wireless connection, or both. Or your computer might have multiple network adapters and those adapters might be connected to different networks or to the same network. You can determine the devices and connections associated with the current network by following these steps:

1. Click Start, and then click Control Panel.

2. In Control Panel, under the Network And Internet heading, click View Network Status And Tasks.

3. If you have a valid connection to the network, click Personalize under Network Details.

4. The Personalize Settings dialog box, shown in Figure 12-5, provides details about the network to which you are currently connected.

Figure 12-5   The Personalize Settings dialog box

5. The Network text box shows the name of the profile associated with the network. You can change the profile name by typing a new name.

6. The Category text box shows the category of the network to which you are connected as either private or public. You can switch the category from private to public or vice versa by clicking Switch Category.

7. The Connections In Use list shows the connections being used to connect to the current network.

8. You can manage connections by selecting them and then clicking one of these buttons:

    ■ **Disconnect**   Allows you to disconnect a wireless connection from a network. This button is available only when you are using a wireless connection.

    ■ **Properties**   Displays the connection's Status dialog box, which you use to get details about the TCP/IP configuration and to manage the TCP/IP configuration.

    ■ **Diagnose**   Starts the Windows Networks Diagnostics Tool for troubleshooting.

9. Click OK to close the Status dialog box.

Using Network List

Network List displays a list of all the networks you've accessed from the computer. Managed and unmanaged networks are listed separately, as shown in Figure 12-6. You can access Network List by following these steps:

1. Click Start, and then click Control Panel.

2. In Control Panel, under the Network And Internet heading, click View Network Status And Tasks.

3. In Network Center, click Network List under See Also in the left pane.

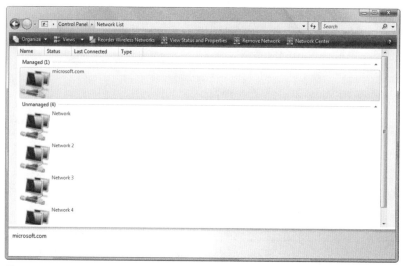

Figure 12-6   Using Network List

Network List has several different views. You can access these views by clicking the Views button and then selecting the desired view. The view you'll use most often is the Details view.

Using the Details view of the Network List, you can quickly determine the following information:

- **Name**   The name of the profile associated with the network.

- **Status**   The status of your connection to the network as either connected (and active) or disconnected (and inactive).

- **Last Connected**   The data and time you last connected to the network.

- **Type**   The type of network, such as managed or unmanaged.

The Network List toolbar allows you to work with networks in several different ways. The option buttons are used as follows:

- **Reorder Wireless Networks**   Click Reorder Wireless Networks to set the preference order for using wireless networks. To change the order, drag a network entry up or down the list. You can also add or remote network profiles.

- **View Status And Properties**   Click View Status And Properties to display a Status dialog box for a selected network. As discussed in the "Viewing and Managing Your Networks" section of this chapter, you can then manage the network's profile name and connection configuration.

- **Remove Network**   Click Remove Network to remove and delete the profile associated with the network. When prompted, confirm that you want to delete this information by clicking OK.

Note   You can return to Network Center by clicking the Network Center button on the toolbar. Right-clicking a network entry displays a shortcut menu with Properties, Delete, and Rename options.

Using Network Map

Network Map uses the neighbor detection functionality built into the Next Generation TCP/IP stack to display an expanded view of your network. As Figure 12-7 shows, the expanded Network Map view includes your computer, the computers near your computer, and the devices near your computer. You can access Network Map by following these steps:

1. Click Start, and then click Control Panel.

2. In Control Panel, under the Network And Internet heading, click View Network Status And Tasks.

3. In Network Center, under Network Map, click View Full Map.

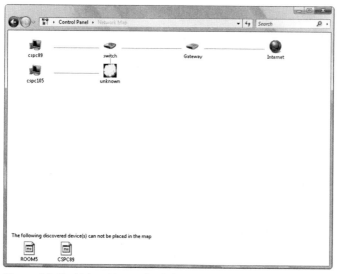

Figure 12-7   Using Network Map

If you have questions about your network infrastructure and have permission to browse the network, you can use Network Map to get a better understanding of how you are connected to the network and what devices are near you.

Note   Sometimes Network Map will detect devices or computers near you but will not be able to place the devices on the map. If this happens, you'll see a list of discovered but not mapped devices in the lower portion of the Network Map window.

Viewing and Managing Network Connections

Network Connections displays a list of all network connections configured for use on the computer, as shown in Figure 12-8. You can quickly obtain a list of open network connections by completing the following steps:

1. Click Start, and then click Control Panel.

2. In Control Panel, under the Network And Internet heading, click View Network Status And Tasks.

3. In the left pane in Network Center, click Manage Network Connections.

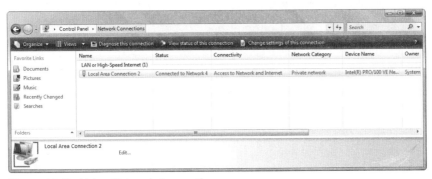

Figure 12-8 Using Network Connections

Network Connections has several different views. You can access these views by clicking the Views button and then selecting the desired view. The view you'll use most often is the Details view.

Using the Details view of Network Connections, you can quickly determine the following information:

- **Name** The name of the network connection.
- **Type** The type of connection, such as LAN or High-Speed Internet.
- **Status** The status of the connection, such as Connected or Disabled.
- **Device Name** The manufacturer and type of network adapter.
- **Phone # Or Host Address** The phone number associated with a dial-up connection or the host address associated with a remote access connection.
- **Owner** The owner of the connection, such as System.

If you select a connection, the Network Connection toolbar allows you to work with connections in several different ways. The option buttons are used as follows:

- **Diagnose This Connection** Starts the Windows Networks Diagnostics Tool for troubleshooting.

■ **View Status Of This Connection**   Displays the connection's Status dialog box, which can be used to get details about the TCP/IP configuration and to manage the TCP/IP configuration.

■ **Change Settings Of This Connection**   Displays the connection's Properties dialog box, which can be used to manage the TCP/IP configuration.

> **Tip**   If you right-click a connection, a shortcut menu will provide an expanded set of options.

Introducing Wireless Networking for Windows Vista

The wireless components in Windows Vista have been extensively reworked. In this section, you'll look at the changes to these components and how they are used to improve flexibility and security. You'll learn about:

■ Wireless networking changes.

■ New ways of connecting to wireless networks.

■ Fast roaming and auto configuration.

Exploring Wireless Networking Changes

Wireless connections in earlier versions of Windows are designed to emulate Ethernet connections and can be extended only when using additional Extensible Authentication Protocol (EAP) types for IEEE 802.1X authentication. Wireless connections in Windows Vista use a software infrastructure for 802.11 wireless connections called the Native Wireless Fidelity (Wi-Fi) architecture.

Native Wi-Fi architecture has many benefits. It allows:

■ Windows Vista to represent wireless (IEEE 802.11) as a media type separate from Ethernet (IEEE 802.3). This increases flexibility by allowing hardware vendors to support advanced features specific to IEEE 802.11 networks, such as larger frame sizes than Ethernet.

■ Windows Vista to include the authentication, authorization, and management components necessary for 802.11 connections. This streamlines the development of miniport drivers that expose a native 802.11 interface and makes it easier for hardware vendors to develop wireless network adapter drivers.

■ Hardware vendors to extend the built-in wireless client for additional wireless services and custom capabilities. This allows vendors to create extensible components and also makes it possible for vendors to provide customized configuration dialog boxes and wizards.

You can configure wireless networking by using the Wireless Network Setup Wizard. This wizard retrieves the security capabilities of the wireless network adapter and recommends the strongest security setting that is supported by the wireless network adapter as the default configuration. For example, if a wireless network adapter supports both Wired Equivalent Privacy (WEP) and Wi-Fi Protected Access (WPA), the Wireless Network Setup Wizard will configure settings for WPA by default.

Learning New Ways to Connect to Wireless Networks

Wireless clients can connect to three different types of networks:

- **Secure**   Secure wireless networks transmit passwords and data securely. Typically, they use some form of encryption, and the stronger the encryption, the more protection offered.

- **Unsecured**   Unsecured wireless networks do not transmit passwords or data securely. While they may require a password to establish a connection, they typically transmit all data without encryption or protection.

- **Hidden**   Hidden wireless networks do not advertise their network names and can be either secured or unsecured. You can connect to a hidden network only if you know its network name.

Windows Vista works with hidden and unsecured networks in different ways than earlier versions of Windows. Because of the many changes, keep the following information in mind:

- Wireless access points used by hidden wireless networks can be configured to use non-broadcast Service Set Identifiers (SSIDs). In this configuration, the wireless access points either do not send Beacon frames, which announce their network names, or they send Beacon frames with an SSID set to NULL. Although earlier versions of Windows do not allow you to mark a preferred wireless network as hidden, Windows Vista allows you to indicate that a preferred wireless network is hidden by configuring it as a non-broadcast network.

- Wireless access points used by unsecured networks are at high risk of being compromised. To help improve awareness about unsecured networks, Windows Vista displays a prompt when you connect to an unsecured wireless network and allows you to confirm or cancel the connection attempt.

When connecting to wireless networks, if preferred wireless networks are not found or if connections to detected preferred wireless networks are not successful, the wireless client in earlier versions of Windows prompts you to connect to any detected wireless network. Wireless clients running earlier versions of Windows cannot be configured to prompt you to connect only to specific wireless networks or to never prompt you to connect to specific wireless networks.

Group Policy settings in Windows Vista allow administrators to configure lists of allowed and denied wireless network names. With an *allow* list, administrators can specify by name the set of wireless networks to which wireless clients are allowed to connect, thereby limiting wireless connections to a specific set of wireless networks. With a *deny* list, administrators can specify by name the set of wireless networks to which wireless clients are not allowed to connect and in this way prevent connections to known unsecured wireless networks as well as to any other wireless networks that might be available but should not be used.

Using Fast Roaming and Auto Configuration with Wireless Connections

Through Group Policy settings, administrators can also configure fast roaming and automatic connections on preferred wireless networks. With fast roaming, wireless clients can more quickly roam from one wireless access point to another by using preauthentication and Pairwise Master Key (PMK) caching. With automatic connections, wireless clients can establish connections automatically when preferred networks are detected. If you don't want to use automatic connections, you can specify that manual connections should be used instead.

Wireless Auto Configuration is a service that dynamically selects the wireless network to which the computer will automatically connect, based either on your preferences or on default settings. This includes automatically selecting and connecting to a more preferred wireless network when it becomes available.

Wireless Auto Configuration in Windows Vista helps to protect computers running Windows Vista from attackers. As with earlier versions of Windows, a computer running Windows Vista uses a randomly named wireless network if no preferred network is available and periodically scans for a preferred network to become available. Unlike earlier versions of Windows, Windows Vista prevents a wireless connection to a wireless network matching the random wireless network name. Further, because Windows Vista attempts to connect preferred networks in the order specified, you can connect to a hidden network before a nonhidden network if the hidden network is higher in the preferred network list.

Wireless connections also support integration with Network Access Protection (NAP) when using 802.1X authentication and Single Sign-On profiles. Using Network Access Protection and 802.1X authentication, administrators can prevent wireless clients that do not comply with system health requirements from gaining unlimited access to a private network. With Single Sign-On profiles, administrators can ensure that only an appropriate user or device is allowed on the protected network and that their data is secure when establishing the connection as well as once the connection is established.

When a Single Sign-On profile is configured, 802.1X authentication is used prior to the computer logon to the domain and users are prompted for credential information only if needed. This ensures that the wireless connection is established prior to the computer domain logon, which enables scenarios that require network connectivity prior to user logon such Group Policy updates, wireless client domain joins, and execution of logon scripts.

Mapping Your Wireless Networking Capabilities and Infrastructure

The same features that can be used to work with wired connections can be used to work with wireless connections. This means that everything you've learned about Network Center, Network List, Network Map, and Network Connections can be used to help you work with wireless connections. Because Windows Vista represents wireless (IEEE 802.11) as a media type separate from Ethernet (IEEE 802.3), there are a few differences that should be noted. These differences are explored in the sections that follow.

Listing and Connecting to Available Wireless Networks

These days, most laptops and portable computers have wireless network adapters, and so do some workstations. No matter where you are, you can get a list of available wireless networks in your area and connect to one by using your wireless network adapter.

To view and connect to an available wireless network, follow these steps:

1. Click Start, and then click Connect To.

2. A list of the wireless networks currently available is displayed.

3. Select a network, and then click Connect.

The network list is available only if your computer has a wireless network adapter installed, the adapter is turned on, and there are no policy settings blocking your computer from browsing for available wireless networks. If you don't see the network to which you want to connect, click the I Don't See The Networks I Am Looking For link. On the Select A Connection Option page, select the Show All Connection Options check box. Select the type of connection that you are trying to use, and then follow the prompts to configure the connection.

Tip   Some networks are protected with a network security key. To connect to one of these networks, you must obtain the key from your network administrator or the service provider.

Connecting to Public Wireless Networks

When connecting to public networks, you might be asked to set up an account and save files to your computer. Before you do this, however, make sure that you understand which files, if any, are saved to your computer and what type of information the network provider collects from your computer. Read the service provider's privacy statement carefully, and keep in mind that even if the service provider requires you to create an account, that doesn't mean that the connection you are using is secure.

Caution   You should be wary of working on company-sensitive information or accessing password-protected areas of your business network while you are connected to a public network. If you connect to a network that is not secure, anyone with the right tools can intercept the data being transmitted from your computer, and they would see any user names and passwords you use, the Web sites you visit, the documents you work on, and the messages you send.

You can view and connect to a public wireless network in the same way as you can connect to an available wireless network:

1. Click Start, and then click Connect To.

2. A list of the wireless networks currently available is displayed.

3. Select a network, and then click Connect.

When you connect to a wireless network that supports Wireless Provisioning Service (WPS) technology, you are prompted to download provisioning files that will allow your computer to connect to the network. While these files are generally safe to download, you should verify that the Web site from which the files will be downloaded is one that you expected based on your location or one that you trust to provide you with the information. If you choose to download provisioning files, you download the files from the provider and then store them on your computer for as long as you want to use the wireless network. The files do not contain any personal information about you or your computer. Instead, they provide details on the network configuration and on how you can access the network. If you choose not to download the files, you will not be able to connect to the wireless network.

When the provisioning files are downloaded, the Wireless Network Registration Wizard requests additional information from you. At this point, you might have to enter your credit card information to provide payment or you might simply have to acknowledge the service provider's usage policy. Follow the instructions in the Wireless Network Registration Wizard to provide the appropriate information to the network provider.

After you have signed up with a wireless network that supports WPS, the provisioning files stored on your computer can be updated automatically. If you choose this option, your computer will connect to the wireless network provider's computers and update the information stored on your computer according to the schedule set by the wireless network provider. Typically, the provider schedules an update once a week or once a month. The update process will occur only while you are already connected to the Internet and will not interfere with your use of your Internet connection. If you choose not to update the provisioning files automatically, the files will be updated the next time you connect to the wireless network. Updating the files is required to ensure that your computer has the correct information for the network.

Disconnecting a Wireless Connection

When you no longer need a wireless connection, you should disconnect the connection. To disconnect a wireless connection to the current network, follow these steps:

1. Click Start, and then click Control Panel.

2. In Control Panel, under the Network And Internet heading, click View Network Status And Tasks.

3. If you have a valid connection to the network, click Personalize under Network Details. The Status dialog box appears.

4. The Connections In Use list show the connections you are using. Click the wireless connection, and then click Disconnect.

To disconnect an open wireless connection when your computer has multiple active connections, follow these steps:

1. Click Start, and then click Control Panel.

2. In Control Panel, under the Network And Internet heading, click View Network Status And Tasks.

3. In the left pane in Network Center, click Open Connections.

4. Right-click the wireless connection, and then select Disable.

Chapter 13

Securing Your Network Connection

Whenever you connect to the Internet, your computer is at increased risk. To mitigate that risk, Microsoft Windows Vista includes many new and updated features that make it easier for you to secure your computer when the computer is connected to the Internet. As discussed in Chapter 4, "Using Internet Explorer 7," Microsoft Internet Explorer 7 operates in a protected mode that isolates it from other applications and prevents add-ons from writing content in any location other than temporary Internet file folders without explicit user consent. Isolating Internet Explorer from other applications and restricting write locations prevents many types of malicious software (malware) from exploiting the computer.

To protect your computer from other types of malicious software and attacks, Windows Vista includes Windows Security Center, Windows Firewall, and Windows Defender. Windows Security Center helps protect your computer by giving you a central location for checking and managing essential security settings. Windows Firewall helps prevent hackers and malicious software from gaining access to your computer. Windows Defender helps protect your computer from spyware and other types of malicious programs.

Note This book was written using the Windows Vista Beta to provide an early introduction to the operating system. More so than any other area of Windows Vista, the security features discussed in this book are subject to change. Some of the features might not be included in the final product, and some of the features might be changed substantially.

Introducing Windows Security Center

Windows Security Center provides a one-stop destination for managing essential security features. To access Windows Security Center, click Start, and then click Control Panel. In Control Panel, click Security, and then click Security Center.

The way Windows Security Center works depends on whether your computer is configured for use as a member of a domain or as a stand-alone computer in a workgroup. In a domain, administrators rather than individual users manage the computer's security settings, and Windows Security Center doesn't report the current status of security features. In a workgroup, individual users can manage the security settings, and Windows Security Center reports the current status of security features, as shown in Figure 13-1.

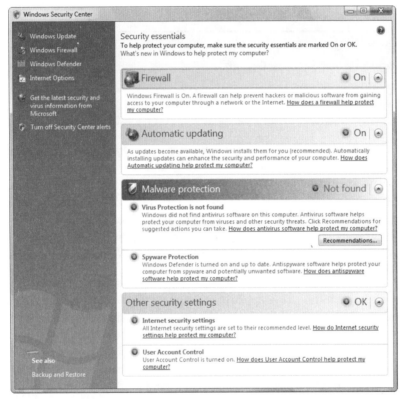

Figure 13-1   Using Windows Security Center

In workgroup configurations, Windows Security Center tracks security features using separate options panels that you can click to expand and to view additional details. The features tracked are:

- **Firewall**   Shows the status of the computer's firewall. A firewall protects a computer by preventing unauthorized users from connecting over a network or from the Internet. If the firewall is off or in an unknown state, a red button is displayed next to the features that are turned off and you'll see a Recommendations button when you expand the Firewall panel. Click the Recommendations button to display the Firewall Recommendations dialog box shown in Figure 13-2. You can click Turn On Windows Firewall to enable Windows Firewall. Or you can select I Have A Firewall Solution That I'll Monitor Myself.

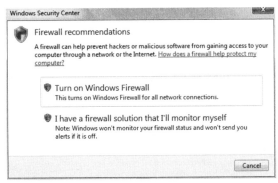

Figure 13-2   Getting firewall recommendations

■ **Automatic Updating**   Shows the status of automatic updating. Automatic updates help keep a computer up to date by examining the computer's current state and determining whether there are updates from Microsoft that need to be applied. If automatic updating is not configured, you'll see a Turn On Now button when you expand the Automatic Updating panel. Click the Turn On Now button to turn on Windows Update, and use the default (recommended) mode, in which updates for the operating system are downloaded and installed automatically. See Chapter 14, "Supporting Windows Vista," for more information about Windows Update.

■ **Malware Protection**   Shows the overall status of your computer's malicious software protection, which includes both antivirus and antispyware software. When working with these components, keep the following in mind:

❑ Windows Vista does not include antivirus software. You'll need to use a third-party solution. If antivirus software is not found or is in an unknown state, you'll see a Not Found warning. Click the Recommendations button to display the Antivirus Recommendations dialog box shown in Figure 13-3. To clear the warning, you click I Have An Antivirus Program That I'll Monitor Myself.

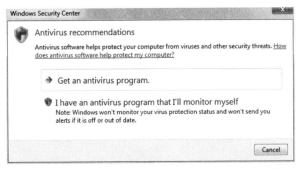

Figure 13-3   Getting antivirus recommendations

❑ Windows Defender is included in Windows Vista to provide antispyware protection. If Windows Defender is turned off, you'll see a Not Found warning. Click the Recommendations button to display the Antispyware Recommendations dialog box shown in Figure 13-4. You can click Turn On Spyware Scanning For Windows Defender to turn on Windows Defender. Or you can select the I Have An Antispyware Program That I'll Monitor Myself.

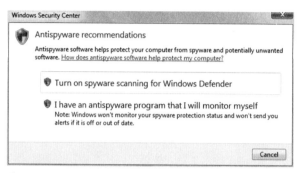

Figure 13-4   Getting antispyware recommendations

- **Other Security Settings**   Shows the overall status of Internet security settings and User Account Control. You'll see a warning if Internet security settings are set below their recommended levels or if user accounts are configured in a way that increases risk. The recommendations offered depend on the settings that put the computer at risk.

In both domain and workgroup configurations, the left panel of Windows Security Center provides the following links:

- **Windows Update**   Opens the Windows Update utility in Control Panel. This window shows the date of the most recent check for updates, the date on which the updates were last installed, and the current update configuration. You can also use this window to check for updates.

- **Windows Defender**   Opens Windows Defender if this feature is turned on. This window lists whether Windows Defender has detected any harmful or unwanted software, the date of the last scan, the scan's schedule, the spyware signatures version, and whether you have turned on real-time protection. If Windows Defender is turned off, you'll see a warning prompt. You'll need to click Turn On And Open Windows Defender to access Windows Defender.

- **Windows Firewall**   Opens the Windows Firewall dialog box. This dialog box allows you to turn on or off the firewall and to set firewall options.

- **Internet Options**   Opens the Internet Properties dialog box with the Security tab selected so that you can set security options for the Internet, local intranet, trusted sites, and restricted sites.

- **Get The Latest Security And Virus Information From Microsoft**   Opens Internet Explorer and accesses the Security Update page on the Microsoft Web site, where you can read about the latest security threats and can download security tools that protect your computer against malicious software.

Getting to Know Windows Firewall

Windows Vista includes two versions of its firewall:

- **Windows Firewall** The basic version of Windows Firewall is similar to the version in Microsoft Windows XP Service Pack 2 (SP2) and Microsoft Windows Server 2003 Service Pack 1 (SP1). Windows Firewall is a stateful firewall that helps protect the computer against network-based attacks and other security threats. Using the basic firewall, you can define allowed types of network traffic and specify programs that are allowed to access the network.

- **Windows Firewall With Advanced Security** The advanced version of Windows Firewall features a new management console and supports both incoming and outgoing traffic. This allows you to define separate incoming and outgoing rules for specific programs or ports. Additionally, you can configure connection security, which requires authentication.

Using Windows Firewall

Windows Firewall is installed and enabled by default for all dial-up, network, IEEE 1394 (FireWire), and wireless connections on a computer. Windows Firewall protects the computer by preventing unauthorized users and programs from gaining access. It does this by blocking incoming network connections, except for specifically allowed programs, services, and ports.

> **Note** Windows Firewall does not control outgoing connections. Only Windows Firewall With Advanced Security controls outgoing connections. Because of this, Windows Firewall allows any program running on your computer to connect to the network.

To access Windows Firewall, click Start, and then click Control Panel. In Control Panel, click Security, and then click Windows Firewall. As Figure 13-5 shows, Windows Firewall has three main configurations tabs:

- **General** Configures general firewall settings, including whether the firewall is turned on and whether all programs are blocked when connected to public networks in less secure locations.

- **Exceptions** Specifies programs and services that are allowed to access the network, such as Remote Assistance and File and Printer Sharing.

- **Advanced** Configures protected connections, security logging, and allowed types of control messages.

The sections that follow discuss the options on these tabs. In most cases, you will be able to configure Windows Firewall options only when you are logged on as a local computer administrator. When a computer is a member of a domain, additional Group Policy restrictions might be in place, preventing any user from changing Windows Firewall settings locally.

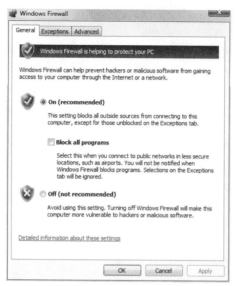

Figure 13-5   The Windows Firewall dialog box

Enabling and Using Windows Firewall

Unless you have installed a third-party firewall, you'll usually want Windows Firewall to be turned on. When you connect to a public network in less secure locations or want to isolate the computer, you might also want to block incoming connections to all programs (even those listed as exceptions).

You can turn on Windows Firewall and optionally block all programs by following these steps:

1. Click Start, and then click Control Panel.

2. In Control Panel, click Security, and then click Windows Firewall.

3. On the General tab, select On (Recommended).

4. If you want to isolate the computer by blocking incoming connections to all programs, select the Block All Programs check box.

5. Click OK.

Configuring Firewall Exceptions

By default, Windows Firewall blocks incoming network connections, except for specifically allowed programs, services, and ports. The only program or service granted permission to make an incoming connection by default is Remote Assistance. If you want to allow additional programs or services to establish connections to the computer, you can configure these programs or services as exceptions by following these steps:

1. Click Start, and then click Control Panel.

2. In Control Panel, click Security, and then click Windows Firewall.

3. On the Exceptions tab, shown in Figure 13-6, common programs and services for which exceptions are needed can be easily allowed or disallowed. Selecting one of these options allows the program and typically opens a related port.

Figure 13-6   Configuring exceptions in the Windows Firewall dialog box

4. If you don't see the specific program that you want to allow, click Add Program, and then use the Add A Program dialog box to select the program to allow.

5. If you need to allow a specific TCP or User Datagram Protocol (UDP) port to be used for incoming connections, click Add Port, and then use the Add A Port dialog box to specify the port to allow.

As part of its standard configuration, Windows Firewall notifies you when it blocks a program. In Windows Vista, you can turn notification off by clearing the Tell Me When Windows Firewall Blocks A Program check box on the Exceptions tab. You can block incoming connections for all programs, even those listed as exceptions, by selecting the Block All Programs check box on the General tab. Blocking all connections to the computer enhances security, and this is particularly important when you are using a mobile PC on a public network.

Configuring Protected Connections

All connections used by a computer running Windows Vista are protected with Windows Firewall automatically. In some cases, you might not want a connection to use Windows Firewall. In this case, you could turn off Windows Firewall only for that connection by following these steps:

1. Click Start, and then click Control Panel.

2. In Control Panel, click Security, and then click Windows Firewall.

3. On the Advanced tab, under Network Connections, clear the check box for the connection that shouldn't use Windows Firewall.

4. Click OK.

Configuring Security Logging

You can track incoming connections to a computer by enabling security logging. When logging is enabled, the security log is created as a standard text file and stored in the %System-Root%\ folder as pfirewall.log.

To enable security logging, follow these steps:

1. Click Start, and then click Control Panel.

2. In Control Panel, click Security, and then click Windows Firewall.

3. On the Advanced tab, click Settings under Security Logging.

4. In the Log Settings dialog box, shown in Figure 13-7, select the Log Successful Connections check box, and then click OK.

Figure 13-7   Enabling security logging

Configuring Allowed Types of Control Messages

Internet Control Message Protocol (ICMP) allows computers connecting to your computer to share error and status messages. Some of these control messages are used for routine troubleshooting. For example, if you enable Allow Incoming Echo Request messages, someone on another computer can ping your computer. However, many control messages can be abused or used to reveal vulnerabilities. Because of this, you should use control messages only when there is a specific requirement to do so, such as when a program running on the computer requires the control message.

To configure allowed types of control messages, follow these steps:

1. Click Start, and then click Control Panel.

2. In Control Panel, click Security, and then click Windows Firewall.

3. On the Advanced tab, click Settings under ICMP.

4. In the ICMP Settings dialog box, shown in Figure 13-8, select the allowed types of control messages, and then click OK.

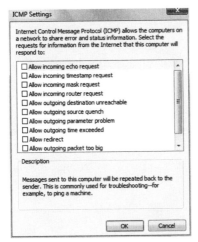

Figure 13-8 Configuring allowed types of control messages

Using Windows Firewall With Advanced Security

Windows Firewall With Advanced Security is a new feature in Windows Vista. It extends and enhances the Windows Firewall basic protection features.

Getting to Know Windows Firewall With Advanced Security

Windows Firewall and Windows Firewall With Advanced Security are integrated. If you change a basic setting in Windows Firewall, the setting you've configured is reflected in Windows Firewall With Advanced Security. You cannot, however, use Windows Firewall to configure any of the enhanced settings in Windows Firewall With Advanced Security.

Windows Firewall With Advanced Security extends the features found in Windows Firewall, allows you to manage some features previously configurable only through Group Policy, and provides many entirely new features. Using Windows Firewall With Advanced Security, you can:

■ Configure separate domain, private network, and public network profiles for the firewall.

■ Block or allow inbound connections.

■ Block or allow outbound connections.

■ Use both firewall filtering and Internet Protocol Security (IPSec) protection settings.

■ Precisely control the users and computers to which rules are applied.

Using the Windows Firewall With Advanced Security snap-in instead of the preconfigured management console found on the Administrative Tools menu, administrators can configure settings for the new Windows Firewall on remote computers, which is something you cannot do with Windows Firewall without using a remote desktop connection. For command-line configuration, you can use the commands in the **netsh advfirewall** context to configure all basic and advanced settings. This context is not available for computers running Windows XP with SP2 or Windows Server 2003 with SP1.

For Group Policy–based configuration of Windows Firewall With Advanced Security, you can use the policy settings under Computer Configuration\Windows Settings\Security Settings\ Windows Firewall With Advanced Security. Windows Firewall With Advanced Security will apply Group Policy settings configured under Computer Configuration\Administrative Templates\Network\Windows Firewall. Computers running Windows XP with SP2 or Windows Server 2003 with SP1 will ignore the Group Policy settings for Windows Firewall With Advanced Security.

From the experts

The single biggest Windows Firewall improvement: Full Group Policy support

In my opinion, the biggest improvement to Windows Firewall in Windows Vista is the least exciting: full Group Policy configurability. Finally, enterprises can take advantage of all Windows Firewall features to protect their thousands of client computers without training the entire staff on how to use a firewall.

With Group Policy, enterprises are able to configure rules for approved applications and even block outgoing communications from unapproved applications. Configuring even the most fine-grained firewall rule will be easy—for example, enterprises can configure an rule that allows management tools to communicate only with a set of IP addresses used for the management server, greatly reducing the potential exposure. When mobile clients leave the enterprise network, the Group Policy settings can further restrict the Windows Firewall security to completely disable features (such as File and Printer Sharing) that might be used on the internal network but, if used, would expose the computer to attack on public networks.

If a feature can't be managed, enterprises can't use it effectively. Now, Windows Firewall is perfect for the enterprise.

Tony Northrup
Author, MCSE, and MVP–For more information, see http://www.northrup.org.

Starting and Using Windows Firewall With Advanced Security

As shown in Figure 13-9, you can manage Windows Firewall With Advanced Security through a special management console that can be accessed by clicking Start, pointing to All Programs,

Administrative Tools, and then clicking Windows Firewall With Advanced Security. If the
Administrative Tools menu isn't accessible, you can access the console by clicking Start and
then clicking Control Panel. In Control Panel, click System And Maintenance, click Administrative Tools, and then click Windows Firewall With Advanced Security.

> **Tip** You will be able to manage Windows Firewall With Advanced Security only when you
> have appropriate permissions. In a workgroup, you will need to be logged on as a local com-
> puter administrator or run the program as an administrator. In a domain, your user account
> must be a member of the Administrators or Network Operators group, or you must be able to
> run the program with the credentials of a user account that is a member of either group. To run
> Windows Firewall With Advanced Security as an administrator, right-click the menu item or
> shortcut, and then select Run As Administrator.

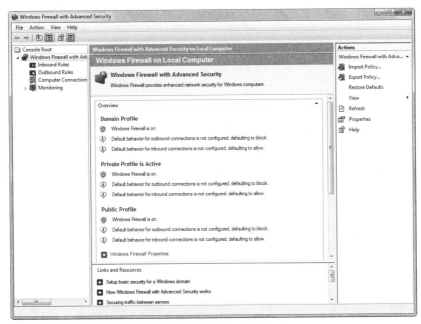

Figure 13-9 Windows Firewall With Advanced Security

Windows Firewall With Advanced Security has the following nodes:

- **Inbound Rules** Lists the set of defined rules for incoming traffic. Inbound rules either
  explicitly allow or explicitly block incoming traffic that matches the criteria of the rule.
  Inbound rules include the basic inbound rules configurable in Windows Firewall, an
  extended list of rules configurable only through Windows Firewall With Advanced
  Security, and any inbound rules that you've defined.

- **Outbound Rules** Lists the set of defined rules for outgoing traffic. Outbound rules
  either explicitly allow or explicitly block outgoing traffic that matches the criteria of the
  rule. Outbound rules are configurable only through Windows Firewall With Advanced
  Security. If you've defined additional outbound rules, these are listed as well.

- **Computer Connection Security**   Lists the set of rules that you've defined for protected traffic, according to the authentication rule type, requirements, and method used.

- **Monitoring**   Displays information about current firewall rules, connection security rules, and security associations.

When you select the Windows Firewall With Advanced Security node in the console tree, the following panes are displayed:

- **Overview**   Displays the current state of the firewall for the domain, private, and public profiles, including which profile is active.

- **Getting Started**   Provides basic information about the functions of the firewall and provides links to nodes in the console tree.

- **Links and Resources**   Provides links to additional information about common procedures and topics for the firewall.

Configuring Windows Firewall With Advanced Security involves:

- Setting firewall profile properties as appropriate.

- Setting any necessary inbound rules.

- Setting any necessary outbound rules.

- Defining any necessary computer connection security rules.

Each of these tasks is discussed in the sections that follow.

Setting Firewall Profile Properties

Windows Firewall With Advanced Security uses separate profiles to define the firewall configuration based on the environment in which the computer is located. Unlike previous versions of Windows, Windows Vista defines three types of profiles:

- **Domain**   You use the Domain profile when a computer is a member of a domain and is attached to its corporate domain.

- **Private**   You use the private profile when a computer is not connected to its corporate domain and is instead connected to a different private network. For example, when you use your laptop on another company's network, the computer uses the Private profile.

- **Public**   You use the Public profile when a computer is not connected to its corporate domain or another private network. For example, when you use your laptop at a coffee shop, the computer uses the Public profile if you connect to a public access point.

Each profile has separate settings, as follows:

- **Firewall states**   Specify whether the firewall is on and how connections are handled.

- **Behavior settings** Specify who is allowed to configure settings, notification about blocking, and response types.

- **Logging settings** Specify whether logging is used.

- **IPSec settings** Specify the settings used by IPSec to establish secured connections.

Setting a Profile's Firewall State Firewall state settings specify whether the firewall is on and how it handles connections. You can configure the firewall state for a profile by following these steps:

1. Open Windows Firewall With Advanced Security.

2. Select the Windows Firewall With Advanced Security node.

3. On the Overview panel, click Windows Firewall Properties.

4. In the Windows Firewall With Advanced Security On Local Computer dialog box, select the Domain Profile, Private Profile, or Public Profile tab as appropriate, as shown in Figure 13-10.

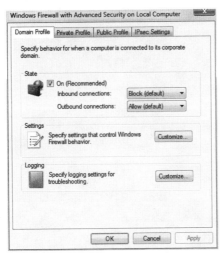

Figure 13-10 Setting the firewall state

5. To enable the firewall state for the profile, select the On (Recommended) check box.

6. To configure the global default setting for inbound connections, click the Inbound Connections list, and then:

   ❑ Select Block (Default) to block all programs not specifically listed as Inbound Allowed rules.

   ❑ Select Block All Connections to block all programs including those specifically listed as Inbound Allowed rules.

   ❑ Select Allow to allow all programs to connect to the computer. This setting is not recommended in most instances.

7. To configure the global default setting for outbound connections, click the Outbound Connections list, and then:

   ❑ Select Block to block all programs not specifically listed as Outbound Allowed rules.

   ❑ Select Allow (Default) to allow all programs to access the network.

8. Click OK.

Setting a Profile's Behavior   Behavior settings specify notification about blocking, response types, and who is allowed to configure settings. You can configure the firewall behavior settings for the Domain, Private, or Public profile by following these steps:

1. Open Windows Firewall With Advanced Security.

2. Select the Windows Firewall With Advanced Security node.

3. On the Overview panel, click Windows Firewall Properties.

4. In the Windows Firewall With Advanced Security On Local Computer dialog box, select the Domain Profile, Private Profile, or Public Profile tab as appropriate.

5. Click Customize in the Settings section.

6. Use the options provided in the Customize Settings dialog box, shown in Figure 13-11, to configure the firewall behavior.

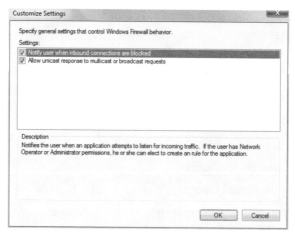

Figure 13-11   Setting the firewall behavior

Setting a Profile's Logging Options   Logging settings specify whether logging is used. You can configure logging for the Domain, Private, or Public profile by following these steps:

1. Open Windows Firewall With Advanced Security.

2. Select the Windows Firewall With Advanced Security node.

3. On the Overview panel, click Windows Firewall Properties.

4. In the Windows Firewall With Advanced Security On Local Computer dialog box, select the Domain Profile, Private Profile, or Public Profile tab as appropriate.

5. Click Customize in the Logging section.

6. In the Customize Logging Options dialog box, shown in Figure 13-12, select the Log Successful Connections check box, and then click OK.

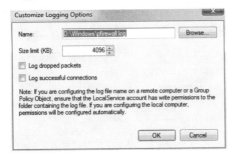

Figure 13-12   Setting the logging options

Setting a Profile's IPSec Options   IPSec settings specify settings used by IPSec to establish secured connections. You can configure IPSec options for a profile by following these steps:

1. Open Windows Firewall With Advanced Security.

2. Select the Windows Firewall With Advanced Security node.

3. On the Overview panel, click Windows Firewall Properties.

4. In the Windows Firewall With Advanced Security On Local Computer dialog box, select the IPSec Settings tab.

5. Click Customize in the Internet Protocol Security (IPsec) section.

6. In the Customize IPsec Settings dialog box, shown in Figure 13-13, use the options provided to set integrity, privacy, and authentication options for IPSec, and then click OK.

Figure 13-13   Setting IPSec options

Setting Inbound Rules

The default configuration for all firewall profiles is to block all inbound connections to a computer unless there are specific inbound rules that allow incoming connections. In the Windows Firewall With Advanced Security console, you can view currently defined inbound rules by selecting the Inbound Rules node, as shown in Figure 13-14.

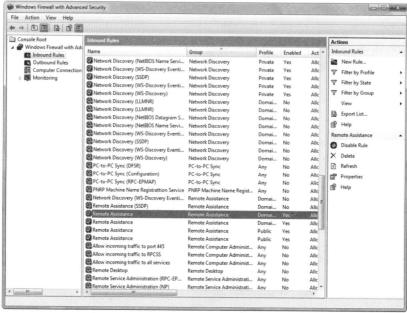

Figure 13-14   Viewing the currently defined inbound rules

Defined inbound rules are not necessarily enabled. In fact, only a select few inbound rules are enabled by default, and these inbound rules are for Remote Assistance. Windows Firewall With Advanced Security has one inbound rule for the TCP ports used by Remote Assistance and one rule for the User Datagram Protocol (UDP) ports used by Remote Assistance. There are two separate inbound rules because of the way Windows Firewall With Advanced Security allows you to precisely control the scope and use of an rule.

With inbound rules, you can:

■ Set an inbound rule for all programs or a specific program.

■ Set an action to allow all inbound connections, to allow only secure inbound connections, or to block all inbound connections.

■ Specify computers and users that are allowed connections based on the rule, and allow an rule to override block rules.

■ Assign the rule to be used with all protocols and port numbers, a specific protocol on any port number, or a specific protocol type and port number.

■ Set the scope so that the rule applies to all local IP addresses, specific local IP addresses, all remote IP addresses, or specific remote IP addresses.

To configure a currently defined inbound rule, follow these steps:

1. Open Windows Firewall With Advanced Security.

2. Select the Inbound Rules node.

3. Double-click the inbound rule that you want to configure.

4. In the Properties dialog box, shown in Figure 13-15, you can configure settings on the following tabs:

   ■ **General** Enables the rule, sets the rule's name, and the rule's action (allow, allow secured, or block).

   ■ **Users And Computers** If the rule's action is to allow secured connections, you can set the computer or user accounts or groups that are authorized to make secure connections.

   ■ **Protocols and Ports** Sets the rule's IP protocol, source and destination TCP or UDP ports, and Internet Control Message Protocol (ICMP) or ICMPv6 settings.

   ■ **Programs And Services** Sets the programs and services to which the rule applies.

   ■ **Scope** Sets the rule's permitted source and destination addresses.

   ■ **Advanced** Sets the profiles, types of interfaces, and services to which the rule applies.

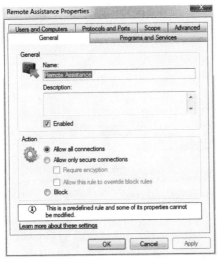

Figure 13-15 Configuring inbound rules

5. If you want to enable the inbound rule, select the Enabled check box on the General tab, and then click OK.

To define a new inbound rule, follow these steps:

1.   Open Windows Firewall With Advanced Security.

2.   Select the Inbound Rules node.

3.   In the Actions panel, click New Rule to start the New Inbound Rule Wizard.

4.   Follow the prompts to define the inbound rule. Click Finish to close the wizard.

5.   If you want the inbound rule to be enabled, right-click it in the console list, and then select Enable Rule.

Setting Outbound Rules

The default configuration for all firewall profiles is to allow all outbound connections unless there is a specific outbound rule. In the Windows Firewall With Advanced Security console, you can view currently defined outbound rules by selecting the Outbound Rules node, as shown in Figure 13-16.

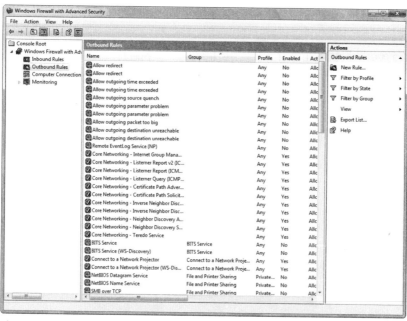

Figure 13-16   Viewing the currently defined outbound rules

Defined outbound rules are not necessarily enabled. In fact, only one outbound rule is enabled by default, and this outbound rule allows Internet Group Management Protocol (IGMP) to be used if you've otherwise blocked outbound connections.

Outbound rules can be configured in almost the same way as inbound rules. With outbound rules, you can:

■   Set an outbound rule for all programs or a specific program.

- Set an action to allow all outbound connections, to allow only secure outbound connections, or to block all outbound connections. You cannot allow an rule to override a block rule, however.

- Specify computers that are allowed connections based on the rule. You cannot configure authorized user rules, however.

- Assign the rule to be used with all protocols and port numbers, a specific protocol on any port number, or a specific protocol type and port number.

- Set the scope so that the rule applies to all local IP addresses, specific local IP addresses, all remote IP addresses, or specific remote IP addresses.

To configure a currently defined outbound rule, follow these steps:

1. Open Windows Firewall With Advanced Security.

2. Select the Outbound Rules node.

3. Double-click the outbound rule that you want to configure.

4. In the Properties dialog box, you can configure settings on the following tabs:

    - **General**   Enables the rule and sets the rule's name, and the rule's action (allow, allow secured, or block).

    - **Computers**   If the rule's action is to allow secured connections, you can set the computer accounts that are authorized to make secure connections.

    - **Protocols and Ports**   Sets the rule's IP protocol, source and destination TCP or UDP ports, and ICMP or ICMPv6 settings.

    - **Programs And Services**   Sets the programs and services to which the rule applies.

    - **Scope**   Sets the rule's permitted source and destination addresses.

    - **Advanced**   Sets the profiles, types of interfaces, and services to which the rule applies.

5. If you want the outbound rule to be enabled, select the Enabled check box on the General tab, and then click OK.

To define a new outbound rule, follow these steps:

1. Open Windows Firewall With Advanced Security.

2. Select the Outbound Rules node.

3. Under Actions, click New Rule to start the New Outbound Rule Wizard.

4. Follow the prompts to define the outbound rule. Click Finish to close the wizard.

5. If you want the outbound rule to be enabled, right-click it in the console list, and then select Enable Rule.

Defining Computer Connection Security Rules

Internet Protocol Security (IPSec) provides a set of rules for securing IP traffic. In Windows XP and Windows Server 2003, you configure Windows Firewall and IPSec separately. Because both firewall filter settings and IPSec rules can block or allow incoming traffic, it is possible to create contradictory or overlapping firewall filters and IPSec rules. Windows Firewall With Advanced Security provides a single, simplified interface for managing both firewall filters and IPSec rules by using the graphical user interface (GUI) console and the command line.

Windows Firewall With Advanced Security uses authentication rules to define IPSec policies. No authentication rules are defined by default. To create a new authentication rule, follow these steps:

1. In Windows Firewall With Advanced Security, select the Computer Connection Security node.

2. Right-click the Computer Connection Security node in the console tree, and then click New Rule. This starts the New Connection Security Rule Wizard.

3. On the Rule Type page, shown in Figure 13-17, you can specify the type of authentication rule to create. The options are as follows:

    - **Isolation** Used to isolate computers by restricting connections based on domain membership or health status. You must specify when you want authentication to occur (for example, for incoming or outgoing traffic), whether you want to require or only request secure connections, the authentication method for protected traffic, and a name for the rule. Isolating computers based on their health status uses the Network Access Protection (NAP) policy, as discussed in the "Getting Started with Network Access Protection" section in Chapter 10.

    - **Authentication Rule** Used to specify computers that do not have to authenticate or secure traffic according to their IP addresses. You must specify the exempt computers and a name for the rule.

    - **Server To Server** Used to designate that authenticated connections should be used between specific computers, typically servers. You must specify the set of endpoints that will use authenticated connections by IP address, when you want authentication to occur, the authentication method for protected traffic, and a name for the rule.

    - **Tunnel** Used to specify authenticated connections that are tunneled, typically used when sending packets across the Internet between two secure gateway computers. You must specify the tunnel endpoints by IP address, the authentication method, and a name for the rule.

    - **Custom** Used to create a rule that does not specify a defined authentication behavior. You can select this option when you want to configure a rule manually. You must specify a name for the rule.

4. After you've configured the rule, click Finish to create and enable the rule.

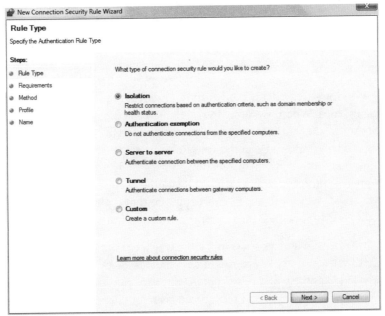

Figure 13-17   The Rule Type page

To disable a rule, right-click the rule, and then select Disable Rule. To configure properties for the rule, right-click the name of the rule, and then click Properties. In the Properties dialog box for a rule, you can configure settings on the following tabs:

- **General**   Used to set the rule's name and description and to enable the rule.
- **Computers**   Used to specify the computers, by IP address, for which authenticated connections are used.
- **Authentication**   Used to specify when you want authentication for connections to occur, such as for incoming or outgoing traffic; whether you want to require or only request authentication; and the authentication method to use.
- **Advanced**   Used to set the profiles and types of interfaces to which the rule applies and the IPSec tunneling behavior.

Introducing Windows Defender

All versions of Windows Vista include Windows Defender. Windows Defender is an antispyware program that protects your computer from harmful and unwanted software. Like all antispyware software, Windows Defender is best used with antivirus software. Together, an antispyware program and an antivirus program can protect your computer from most types of malicious software.

Getting to Know Windows Defender

Similar to antivirus software, Windows Defender has two operating modes:

- Real-time protection
- Scanning

By default, Windows Defender is configured to use real-time protection and to supplement this with daily scans. When operating in real-time protection mode, Windows Defender runs in the background and works to detect spyware that is trying to install itself. When operating in scanning mode, Windows Defender tries to locate spyware that has secretly installed itself on your computer. Both real-time protection and scanning are absolutely essential to ensure that a computer is protected from spyware. Real-time protection can safeguard the computer from known spyware. Scanning can detect spyware that is already installed on the computer or that might have slipped past the real-time protection feature.

Windows Defender recognizes spyware by the way it tries to install itself, the files it tries to create or modify, the registry keys it modifies or creates, or any combination of these items collectively referred to as the spyware's *signature*. Spyware can sometimes slip by real-time protection if the spyware's signature isn't recognized, as might happen if the spyware was recently released or recently modified to bypass detection.

Like antivirus software, Windows Defender uses definition files to maintain up-to-date information about spyware signatures. Microsoft creates new signatures for Windows Defender to counter new spyware and malicious software programs and makes these new signatures available for download. Windows Defender includes an automatic update feature that checks for updates periodically, and you can manually check for updates as well.

One of the key components in Windows Defender is Software Explorer. As described in the "Navigating Your Computer's Startup, Running, and Network-Connected Programs" section in Chapter 6, Software Explorer tracks the status of all programs currently running on the computer. You can use Software Explorer to terminate a program, to block incoming connections to a program, and to disable or remove a program. Windows Defender uses Software Explorer to help detect the activities of malicious programs.

Starting and Using Windows Defender

To access Windows Defender, click Start, and then click Control Panel. In Control Panel, click Security, and then click Windows Defender. If Windows Defender is turned off, you'll see a warning prompt instead. Click Turn On And Open Windows Defender to enable Windows Defender.

The Windows Defender home page provides an overview of the current status. You'll see three color-coded statuses:

- **Green (Normal)**   If Windows Defender's definitions are up-to-date and there is no known unwanted or harmful software installed on the computer, you'll see a green (normal) status indicator similar to the one shown in Figure 13-18.

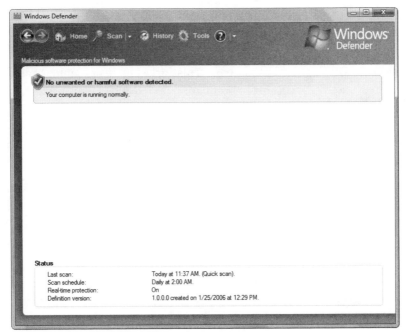

Figure 13-18 Viewing status in Windows Defender

■ **Orange (Warning)** If the Windows Defender definitions are out of date and there is no known unwanted or harmful software installed on the computer, you'll see an orange (warning) status indicator telling you that the Windows Defender definitions need to be updated. You'll be able to retrieve updates over the Internet from the Microsoft Web site and install them automatically by clicking the Check For Update button provided as part of the warning.

■ **Red (Danger)** If the security of your computer is possibly compromised or there is known unwanted or harmful software installed on the computer, you'll see a red (danger) status indicator telling you to take action to protect your computer. You'll be able to start a scan or to quarantine discovered spyware by using the options provided.

The toolbar at the top of the window provides access to the main features in Windows Defender. From left to right, the toolbar has these buttons:

■ **Forward/Back** The Forward and Back buttons on the far left of the toolbar allow you to navigate locations you've already visited. Similar to when you are browsing the Web, the locations you've visited are stored in a history, and you can browse the history by using the Forward and Back buttons.

■ **Home** Displays the Windows Defender home page, shown in Figure 13-18.

■ **Scan** Starts a quick scan of your computer and displays the Scanning Your Computer page, which shows the progress of the scan.

- **Scan Options**   Displays an options list that allows you to specify the type of scan as Quick Scan, Full Scan, or Custom Scan. See the "Scanning the Computer for Spyware" section later in this chapter for more information.

- **History**   Displays the History page. This page contains a summary of all Windows Defender activity according to programs detected and actions taken. Quick access links are provided for Allowed Items and Quarantined Items.

- **Tools**   Displays the All Settings And Tools page. This page allows you to configure general settings, display quarantined items, access Software Explorer, view allowed items, and more.

- **Windows Defender Help**   Displays help documentation for Windows Defender.

- **Windows Defender Help Options**   Displays an options list that allows you to display additional help items, such as the Windows Help And Support Index.

The Status section in the lower portion of the Home page provides details about the general status of Windows Defender:

- **Last Scan**   Shows the date and time of the last scan and the type of scan, such as Quick Scan or Full Scan.

- **Scan Schedule**   Shows the schedule for automatic scans, such as Daily at 2:00 AM.

- **Real-time Protection**   Shows the status of real-time protection, such as On.

- **Definition Version**   Shows the version, time, and date of the most recent definitions file.

When you work with Windows Defender, the main actions you'll want to perform include:

- Configuring general settings.

- Scanning the computer for spyware.

- Checking for updates.

- Viewing or restoring quarantined items.

- Viewing or changing software programs that you allow.

- Turning Windows Defender off or on.

Configuring General Settings

General settings allow you to choose how you want Windows Defender to run. You can configure general settings by following these steps:

1. Open Windows Defender.

2. Click Tools, and then click Options.

3. On the Options page, shown in Figure 13-19, the following options sections are provided:

      - **Automatic Scanning**   Used to manage automatic scanning and automatic updating options. To have Windows Defender scan automatically, you must select the Automatically Scan My Computer (Recommended) check box and then set the scan frequency, time of day, and type of scan. If you want Windows Defender to check for updates before scanning, select Check For Updated Definitions Before Scanning.

      - **Default Actions**   Used to set the default action to take based on the alert level of a detected spyware program. Spyware with a high alert level is considered to be the most dangerous and to have the highest probability of doing damage to a computer. Spyware with a medium alert level is considered to be moderately dangerous and to have a moderate probability of doing damage to a computer or performing nuisance/malicious actions. Spyware with a low alert level is considered a low danger and is primarily a nuisance. If you enable Apply Actions On Detected Items After Scanning under Automatic Scanning, Windows Defender performs the recommended action after completing an automatic scan. Items marked Ignore are ignored. Items marked Remove are removed and quarantined. Items marked Signature Default are handled according to the default setting in the signature associated with the spyware. In most cases, Signature Default means that high and moderate alert items are removed.

      - **Real-Time Protection Options**   Used to turn on real-time protection. Real-time protection uses a number of security agents to determine which areas of the operating system and which components receive real-time protection. Each of these security agents can be enabled or disabled individually using the check boxes provided. If you want to receive alerts related to real-time protection, you can enable the notification options provided.

      - **Advanced Options**   Used to configure advanced techniques for detecting spyware. These options allow you to scan inside archives to detect suspicious files. Enabling these options is particularly important for detecting new spyware, hidden spyware, and software performing possibly malicious actions.

      - **Administrator Options**   Used to specify whether Windows Defender is turned on or off. If you clear the Use Windows Defender check box, Windows Defender won't provide protection against spyware. Also used to specify whether normal users can perform scans and remove potentially unwanted software. By default, users who do not have administrator rights can perform scans and remove potentially unwanted software. This is the recommended configuration.

4. Click Save to save any changes you've made to the configuration.

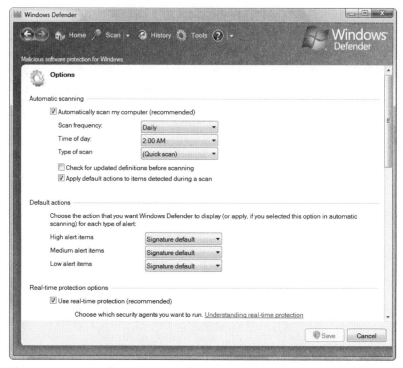

Figure 13-19   Configuring general settings in Windows Defender

Scanning the Computer for Spyware

Windows Defender can be used to perform quick scans, full scans, and custom scans. Quick scans and full scans are easy to initiate:

- For a quick scan, Windows Defender checks areas of memory, the registry, and the file system known to be used by spyware for any unwanted or potentially harmful software. You can start a quick scan by clicking the Scan button on the toolbar.

- For a full scan, Windows Defender performs a thorough check of all areas of memory, the registry, and the file system for any unwanted or potentially harmful software. You can start a full scan by clicking the Scan Options button on the toolbar and selecting Full Scan.

Windows Defender shows the progress of the scan by reporting:

- The start time of the scan.

- The total amount of time spent scanning the computer so far (the elapsed time).

- The location or item currently being examined.

- The total number of files scanned.

When the scan is complete, Windows Defender provides scan statistics, as shown in Figure 13-20.

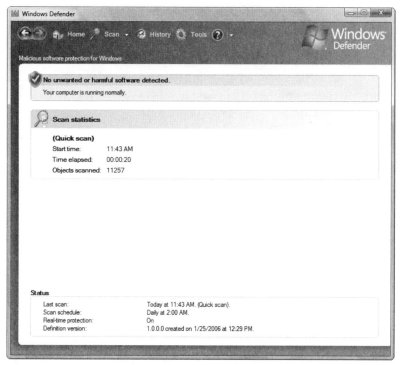

Figure 13-20   Performing a scan using Windows Defender

For a custom scan, Windows Defender checks selected areas of the file system for any unwanted or potentially harmful software. You start a custom scan by following these steps:

1.   Open Windows Defender.

2.   Click the Scan Options button, and then select Custom Scan.

3.   On the Select Scan Options page, click Select.

4.   Select the drives and folders to scan, as shown in Figure 13-21, and then click OK.

5.   In Windows Defender, click Scan Now to start the scan.

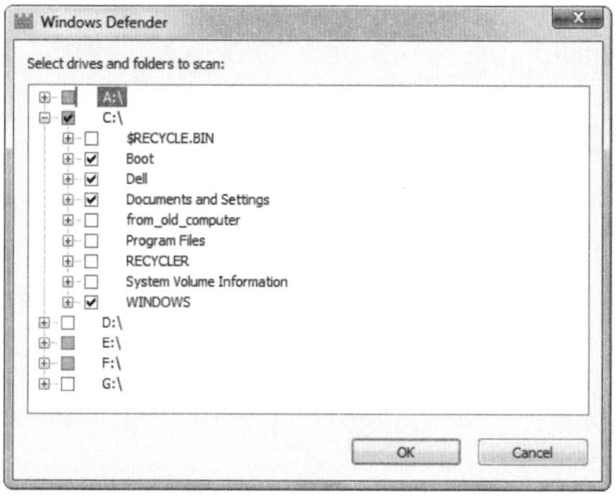

Figure 13-21   Selecting the drives and folders to scan

Checking for Updates

Out-of-date spyware definitions can put your computer at risk. By default, Windows Defender automatically checks for updated spyware definitions prior to performing an automatic scan. If the computer has access to the Internet or an update server, Windows Defender updates the spyware definitions. If the computer doesn't have access to the Internet or an update server, Windows Defender cannot update the spyware definitions.

You can manually update spyware definitions at any time by following these steps:

1. Click Start, and then click Control Panel.

2. In Control Panel, click Security, and then click Check For New Definitions under Windows Defender.

 Tip   In Windows Defender, you can also check for updates by clicking the Windows Defender Help Options button, selecting About Windows Defender, and then clicking Check For Updates.

Viewing or Restoring Quarantined Items

Quarantined items are items that have been disabled and moved to a protected location on the computer because Windows Defender suspects that they are harmful or potentially unwanted software. You can access and work with quarantined items by completing the steps:

1. Open Windows Defender.

2. Click Tools, and then click Quarantined Items.

3. If you click a quarantined item, you can remove or restore the item.

    ❑ Select Remove to permanently remove the item from the computer.

    ❑ Select Restore to restore the item to its original location so that it can be used and mark it as an allowed item. See the next section, "Viewing or Changing Software Programs That You Allow," for more information.

4. If you want to remove all quarantined items, click Remove All.

Viewing or Changing Software Programs That You Allow

Sometimes, you'll install programs that perform actions that Windows Defender considers to be potentially harmful or malicious. In this case, Windows Defender will either quarantine the program automatically, such as for a high threat item, or alert you about the program, such as for a moderate threat item. If you are sure that a quarantined program is safe, you can restore it, and Windows Defender will mark the program as an allowed item. Or if you receive a warning about a program that you know to be safe, you can mark the item as allowed.

You can view or change currently allowed items by following these steps:

1. Open Windows Defender.
2. Click Tools, and then click Allowed Items.

    On the Allowed Items page, allowed items are listed by name with an alert level and a recommendation for how the program should be handled.

3. You can remove an item from the Allowed Items list by clicking it and then selecting Remove.

Turning Windows Defender Off or On

You can turn Windows Defender off or on by following these steps:

1. Open Windows Defender.
2. Click Tools, and then click Options.
3. Scroll down to the bottom of the Options page.
4. You can now:

    ❑ Clear the Use Windows Defender check box to disable and turn off Windows Defender.

    ❑ Select the Use Windows Defender check box to enable and turn on Windows Defender.

5. Click Save.

Part IV
Supporting and Deploying Windows Vista

In this part of the book, you'll learn about supporting and deploying Microsoft Windows Vista. Chapter 14, "Supporting Windows Vista," introduces new tools and techniques for maintaining and managing Windows Vista. Chapter 15, "Deploying Windows Vista," examines features and techniques for deploying Windows Vista in an enterprise.

Chapter 14
Supporting Windows Vista

Supporting Microsoft Windows Vista is significantly different from supporting earlier versions of Microsoft Windows. The many new and enhanced features in Windows Vista fundamentally change the way common support tasks are performed and also provide entirely new ways of performing management and maintenance tasks. This chapter looks at what's changed in terms of support and how these changes impact support staff and administrators. You'll learn about:

- Centrally managing computer configuration.

- Diagnosing and resolving problems.

- Updating computers running Windows Vista.

- Improving system stability and recovery.

- Using the new and enhanced management tools.

Note This book was written using the Windows Vista Beta to provide an early introduction to the operating system. More so than any other area of Windows Vista, the security features discussed in this book are subject to change. Some of the features might not be included in the final product, and some of the features might be changed substantially.

Centrally Managing Computer Configuration

To help reduce the total cost of ownership (TCO), Windows Vista is more configurable than its predecessors, and more of its configuration settings can be managed by using Group Policy. Because Group Policy can be managed locally and on an enterprise-wide basis, this makes it easier to centrally manage computer configurations.

Introducing the Group Policy Management Console

Windows Vista is the first version of Windows to include the Group Policy Management Console (GPMC), which provides an extended management interface for working with Group Policy. Previously, GPMC was available only as a separate download and was not included with the operating system.

Figure 14-1 shows the Group Policy Management Console. You can access GPMC by clicking Group Policy Management on the Administrative Tools menu. Before you can use GPMC, you must log on to the computer using a domain user account.

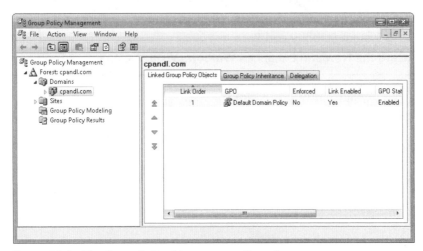

Figure 14-1 The Group Policy Management Console

Tip If the Administrative Tools menu isn't available on the All Programs menu or the Start menu, you can display it by using the Task Bar And Start Menu Properties dialog box. Right-click an open area of the taskbar, and select Properties. In the Task Bar And Start Menu Properties dialog box, click the Start Menu tab, and then click the Customize button. In the Customize Start Menu dialog box, scroll down through the list of options until you find System Administrative Tools, and then select Display On The All Programs Menu And The Start Menu option. Click OK twice.

Using GPMC, you can access Group Policy information throughout the enterprise. If you log on to a computer using a domain user account, you can use GPMC to manage Group Policy in multiple Active Directory forests and domains. You add forests and domains that you want to manage by name. You can then manage the additional forests and domains as you do the local forest or domain. GPMC also allows you to import and export Group Policy settings and to back up and restore Group Policy settings.

Introducing Important Group Policy Changes

All versions of Windows since Windows 2000 support Group Policy. Group Policy settings on a local computer are stored in a Local Group Policy Object (LGPO). Unlike earlier versions of

Windows in which there was only one local GPO, Windows Vista can be configured to support multiple local GPOs, enabling administrators to specify different policies for different users on a single computer. In a shared-use environment, such as a library or a school, this feature improves security and manageability.

Group Policy settings for sites, domains, and organizational units are stored in Active Directory Group Policy Objects (GPOs). Active Directory Group Policy settings can be loosely divided into two classes: registry-based settings and non-registry-based settings. Any time you make a change to a registry-based policy setting, the change is made in the GPO and applied to a related value in the registry. Any time you make a change to a non-registry-based policy setting, the change is made only in the GPO.

In Active Directory Group Policy, Administrative Templates are used to store registry-based policy settings. While earlier versions of Windows that support Group Policy use ADM files with a proprietary markup language to store registry-based policy settings, Windows Vista uses a standards-based Extensible Markup Language (XML) file format called ADMX. Unlike ADM files, which are stored in the GPO to which they relate, ADMX files are not stored with the GPOs with which they are associated by default. Instead, ADMX files are stored in a central location that the administrator creates. The ADMX files are accessible by anyone with permissions to create or edit GPOs. Central storage of ADMX files makes them easier to work with and manage.

> **Note** A complete discussion of GPMC, GPOs, and ADMX is beyond the scope of this book. For more information, refer to the *Microsoft Windows Vista Administrator's Pocket Consultant* (Microsoft Press, 2006).

Diagnosing and Resolving Problems

Built-in diagnostics are your front line of defense for ensuring that computers run smoothly. If you can detect potential problems before they occur or current problems as they occur, you can limit downtime and help to maximize productivity. Earlier versions of Windows included some diagnostics features, but for the most part, those features were not automated or designed to self-correct problems.

Windows Vista introduces an extensive diagnostics architecture that is both automated and self-correcting. Because of this new architecture, Windows Vista can detect many types of hardware, memory, and network problems and either resolve them automatically or help users through the process of resolving them. Windows Vista supplements the diagnostics components with problem reporting and assistance features. In this section, you'll learn about the following features:

- Hardware diagnostics
- Performance diagnostics

- Memory diagnostics
- Network diagnostics
- Problem reporting
- User Assistance
- Remote Assistance

Ask the experts

Making the business case for Windows Vista

If you're an IT manager looking for ways to make a good business case to upper management for moving your desktops to Vista, you might be feeling a bit hard pressed. Sure, the new deployment tools are great, but only if your business needs to deploy Vista. And while the new Aero Glass GUI is definitely more than just eye-candy, you might need to upgrade your desktop systems to get the hardware that supports it. How can you make a convincing case then for upgrading or migrating to Vista?

Diagnostics could be the key. With its new built-in diagnostics capabilities, Vista is more reliable than ever and is less likely to crash or hang or lose application data than any previous version of Windows. And system crashes or data loss mean lost productivity to your business, so these new reliability features can improve your bottom line. Vista also has advanced self-healing capabilities to help your system maintain its health and an increased level of artificial intelligence that can help you troubleshoot when things go wrong. Therefore, over time, moving to Vista should save your business money and your staff and help desk from frustration—despite the up-front cost and effort of doing a desktop upgrade or migration.

Mitch Tulloch
Author and MVP—For more information, see http://www.mtit.com.

Introducing Built-In Diagnostics

Windows Vista has multiple enhancements for diagnosing and resolving problems. To proactively and automatically identify potential problems, Windows Vista includes built-in diagnostics that can automatically detect and diagnose common support problems. In Active Directory domains, administrators can configure built-in diagnostics by using Group Policy settings.

The Windows Vista built-in diagnostics can automatically identify and help users resolve the following problems:

- Hardware error conditions

- Failing disks

- Degraded performance

- Failure to shut down properly

- Memory problems

- Problems related to installing drivers and applications

- Problems related to using drivers and applications

In most cases, the built-in diagnostics prompt users to make them aware of any problems as they occur and then help to guide users through resolving the problem.

Understanding Hardware, Performance, and Memory Diagnostics

Hardware, memory, and performance diagnostics are the heart of the Windows Vista self-correcting architecture. *Hardware diagnostics* can detect error conditions and either repair the problem automatically or guide the user through a recovery process. With potential disk failures, hardware diagnostics guide users through the backup procedure to minimize downtime and data loss.

Performance problems addressed by built-in diagnostics include slow application startup, slow boot, and network-related delays. If a computer is experiencing degraded performance, *performance diagnostics* can detect the problem and tune performance automatically. For advanced performance issues, Windows Vista provides an improved Performance console that offers more detailed information and additional performance counters that can help administrators more quickly identify performance issues.

Memory problems addressed by built-in diagnostics include both memory leaks and failing memory. *Memory diagnostics* work with the new Microsoft Online Crash Analysis tool to detect system crashes possibly caused by failing memory and then prompt the user to schedule a memory test the next time the computer is restarted. Three different types of memory testing can be performed.

If you suspect that a computer has a memory problem that is not being automatically detected, you can run *Windows Memory Diagnostics* manually by completing the following steps:

1. Click Start, point to All Programs, and then click Accessories.

2. Right-click Command Prompt, and then select Run As Administrator.

3. At the command prompt, type **mdsched.exe**.

4. As shown in Figure 14-2, you can choose to restart the computer and run the tool immediately or schedule the tool to run at the next restart.

5. If you choose to run the tool at the next restart, Windows Memory Diagnostics runs automatically after the computer restart, allowing you to choose the type of testing to perform.

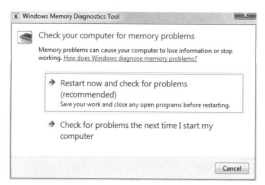

Figure 14-2   The Windows Memory Diagnostics Tool

Understanding Network Diagnostics

As discussed in Chapter 12, "Networking Your Computer," Windows Vista includes a separate architecture for diagnosing and resolving networking issues called the *Network Diagnostics Framework*. The related *Windows Networks Diagnostics Tool* offers step-by-step advice on resolving network connectivity problems.

If you suspect that a computer has a networking or connectivity problem, you can open the Windows Networks Diagnostics Tool by following these steps:

1. Click Start, and then click Control Panel.

2. In Control Panel, under the Network And Internet heading, click View Network Status And Tasks.

3. If there is a known problem or you suspect a problem, click Diagnose Internet Connection in the left pane to begin diagnosing it.

Introducing Problem Reporting and Assistance

The built-in diagnostics track each instance of a program or driver failing to install or becoming nonresponsive and displays a "Check For Solutions" balloon message as these instances occur. If you click the balloon, Windows Vista opens the Problem Reports And Solutions dialog box, shown in Figure 14-3, allowing you to check on the Internet for solutions to selected problems. You can view a list of current problems at any time by following these steps:

1. Click Start, and then click Control Panel.

2. In Control Panel, click System And Maintenance and then click Problem Reports And Solutions.

3. In the Problem Reports And Solutions dialog box, click See Problems To Check in the left pane.

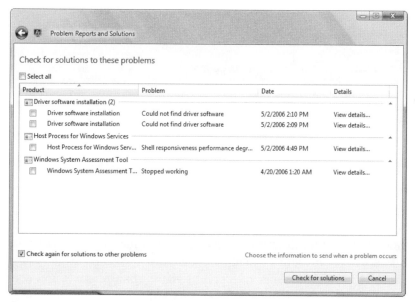

Figure 14-3   The Problem Reports And Solutions dialog box

In addition to the built-in diagnostics features, users can get additional help and support with:

- **User Assistance**   The Windows Vista version of help files, User Assistance provides answers to questions about the operating system and can be extended with custom content that provides answers to questions about the organization's network and custom applications.

- **Remote Assistance**   Originally included in Microsoft Windows XP, Remote Assistance enables Help Desk staff to resolve problems by remotely viewing and controlling a computer's desktop.

You access User Assistance documentation through Windows Help And Support. Click Start, and then select Help And Support. You can then use the Windows Help And Support console, shown in Figure 14-4, to look for answers to any questions you might have about Windows Vista. Any custom content created by your organization can be made available for searching as extensions to the standard User Assistance documentation.

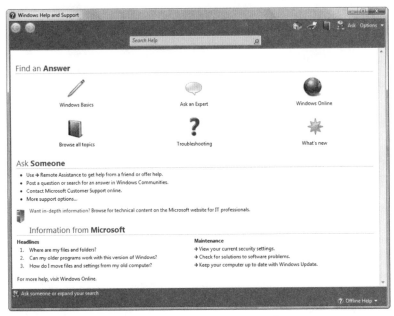

Figure 14-4   The Windows Help And Support console

In Windows Vista, Remote Assistance has been enhanced so that it is faster, uses less bandwidth, and can function through Network Address Translation (NAT) firewalls. Remote Assistance also now has built-in diagnostic tools that Help Desk staff can run using a single click. Remote Assistance has been modified in other important ways as well. To allow for escalation and easier troubleshooting, two different support staff can connect to a remote computer simultaneously. When troubleshooting requires restarting the computer, Remote Assistance sessions are reestablished automatically after the computer being diagnosed restarts.

When you are working with the Windows Help And Support console, you can get help using Remote Assistance at any time by following these steps:

1. Click the Help And Support Home button on the toolbar, and then click Remote Assistance under Ask Someone.

2. In the Remote Assistance Wizard, shown in Figure 14-5, click Invite Someone You Trust To Help You, and then click Use E-Mail To Send An Invitation.

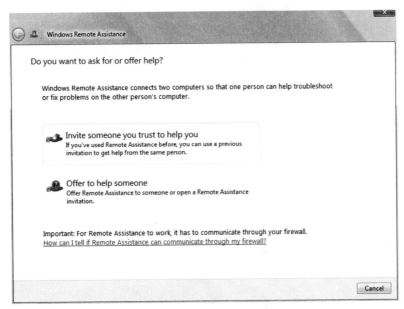

Figure 14-5   The Remote Assistance Wizard

> **Tip**   If the computer isn't configured to use Remote Assistance, follow the prompt and click the Click Here To Open System Properties link. On the Remote tab of the System Properties dialog box, select the Remote Assistance Invitations Can Be Sent From This Computer check box and then click OK. Afterward, repeat Step 2 in the Remote Assistance Wizard.

3. When prompted, enter and confirm a secure password for connecting to the computer. This password is used by the person you are inviting and is valid only for the Remote Assistance session.

4. When you click Next, Windows Vista starts your default mail program and creates an e-mail message with the invitation. In the To field, type the e-mail address of the person you are inviting, and then click Send.

By default, computers running Windows Vista are configured so that Remote Assistance is not enabled. As a result, Windows Vista computers cannot receive or send Remote Assistance invitations by default.

To view or change Remote Assistance settings, follow these steps:

1. Click Start, and then click Control Panel.

2. In Control Panel, click System And Maintenance.

3. On the System And Maintenance page, click Allow Remote Access under System.

4.   You can use the System Properties dialog box, shown in Figure 14-6, to configure Remote Assistance.

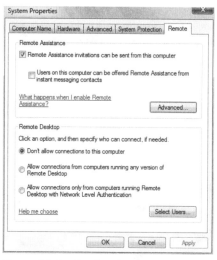

Figure 14-6   Configuring Remote Assistance

Updating Windows Vista Computers: What's Changed

Maintaining Windows Vista is a critically important area of support. If the operating system is not properly maintained and updated with appropriate security patches, updates, hot fixes, and service packs, the operating system will not function as expected and your computer will be more vulnerable to attack. Like both Windows 2000 and Windows XP, Windows Vista includes a feature for automatically updating the operating system. Unlike the default update feature in Windows 2000 and Windows XP, the update feature in Windows Vista, called Windows Update, has been enhanced in many ways and has been extended to cover the operating system, programs that ship with the operating system such as Microsoft Internet Explorer, and hardware device drivers.

Introducing Windows Update Improvements

Windows Vista significantly streamlines the update process by:

- Requiring computers to be restarted less frequently.
- Simplifying the process of deploying updates.
- Using bandwidth more efficiently.
- Providing separate tracking for both successful and unsuccessful updates.

Windows Vista reduces the number of restarts required after updates by allowing installation of a new version of an updated file even if the old file is currently in use by an application or a system component. Windows Vista simply marks the in-use file for update and then automatically replaces the file the next time the application is started. With some applications and components, Windows Vista can save the application's data, close the application, update the file, and then restart the application. As a result, the update process has less impact on users.

Windows Update can act as a Windows Server Update Services (WSUS) client as well. WSUS is a new version of Software Update Services (SUS). Administrators can use WSUS to manage automatic updates on an enterprise-wide basis. WSUS allows administrators to more easily review new updates that are available and then deploy any updates that are needed by using designated update servers. Not only does this allow central management of the update process, it also simplifies the process of deploying updates, saving time and reducing the costs associated with maintaining the operating system.

Windows Update runs as a separate, stand-alone application. Regardless of whether updates are provided by an internal update server or obtained directly from Microsoft, Windows Update provides a single interface for managing the update process and working with updates. This means that users do not have to learn how to use two separate tools, and Windows Update can now take advantage of its configuration environment to reduce the bandwidth required to maintain updates.

Using Background Intelligent Transfer Service (BITS), Windows Update can now obtain updates from trusted peers across a local area network (LAN) as well as from an update server or from Microsoft directly. Once a peer has a copy of an update, other computers on the local network can automatically detect this and download the update directly from the peer, meaning that a required update might need to be transferred across the wide area network (WAN) only once instead of dozens or hundreds of times.

Additionally, Windows Vista has a new download manager for updates. The download manager's history log provides separate tracking for both successful and unsuccessful updates, making it easier to determine when there are update problems that need to be resolved.

Configuring Windows Update

Windows Vista organizes updates into two broad categories:

- **Security and standard updates**   Includes critical updates, security updates, update rollups, and service packs for the operating system and programs that ship with the operating system.

- **Drivers and other optional updates**   Includes updates to drivers that are provided with the operating system and recommended updates.

By default, Windows Vista is configured to automatically install security and standard updates only. New updates are installed daily at 3:00 A.M. As with earlier versions of Windows, you can modify this configuration to:

- Change the frequency and the time that new updates install.

- Download updates and let the user choose whether to install them.

- Check for updates but let the user choose whether to download and install them.

- Never check for updates.

You can also install drivers and other optional updates.

To configure how Windows Update works, follow these steps:

1. Click Start, and then click Control Panel.

2. In Control Panel, click System And Maintenance.

3. On the System And Maintenance page, click Windows Update.

4. In the left panel, click Change Settings. This displays the Settings page, shown in Figure 14-7.

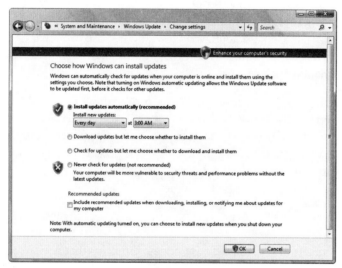

Figure 14-7   Configuring Windows Update

5. Specify whether and how updates should occur. In the recommended configuration, Install Updates Automatically is selected.

6. If you've enabled updates and want to also install drivers and optional updates, select the Include Recommended Updates check box.

7. Click OK.

Checking for Updates

Windows Vista provides more information about how Windows Update is being used than earlier versions of Windows. You can quickly:

- Determine the last time the computer or a user checked for updates.

- Determine the last time updates were installed.

- Manually check for updates.

To determine Windows Update usage or manually check for updates, follow these steps:

1. Click Start, and then click Control Panel.

2. In Control Panel, click System And Maintenance.

3. On the System And Maintenance page, click Windows Update. As shown in Figure 14-8, statistics are provided regarding the most recent check for updates, the last time updates were installed, and the current update configuration.

4. If you want to manually check for updates, click the Check For Updates button.

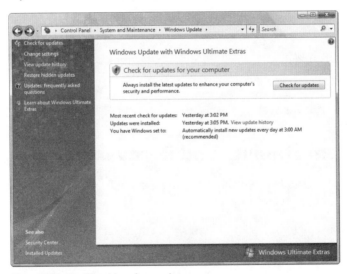

Figure 14-8   Checking for updates

Viewing Update History and Installed Updates

As mentioned earlier, the Windows Update download manager provides separate tracking for both successful and unsuccessful updates by using an update history log. This log can be accessed by following these steps:

1. Click Start, and then click Control Panel.

2. In Control Panel, click System And Maintenance.

3. On the System And Maintenance page, click Windows Update.

4. In the left panel, click View Update History. This displays the History page, shown in Figure 14-9.

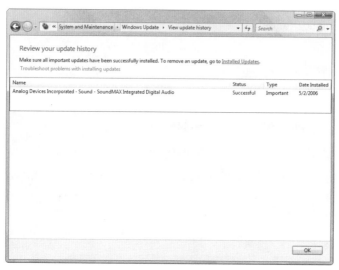

Figure 14-9   Viewing the update history

On the History page, updates listed with a Successful status were downloaded and installed. Updates listed with an Unsuccessful status were downloaded but installation failed. To remove an update while accessing the History page, click Installed Updates. Right-click the update that you don't want, and then select Remove.

Improving System Stability and Recovery

Windows Vista is more stable and reliable than Windows XP. Not only does the operating system include fixes for known crashes and hangs, but it also:

- Prevents many common causes of hangs and crashes.

- Provides for automatic recovery in the case of failure.

- Recovers frozen applications and releases resources automatically.

Preventing Common Causes of Hangs and Crashes

Windows Vista prevents many common causes of hangs and crashes by addressing performance issues and including more reliable drivers. Windows Vista uses memory more efficiently and provides new process scheduling mechanisms that can adjust system performance to better meet the needs of applications and system components. Optimized memory usage ensures that background processes have less performance impact. Improved input/output (I/O) cancellation for device drivers ensures that the operating system can recover gracefully from blocking calls and that there are fewer blocking disk I/O operations. Overall, these improvements provide a more responsive environment, even over Windows XP on the same computer hardware.

With earlier versions of Windows, application crashes and hangs were difficult for developers to troubleshoot because error reporting provided limited or no information. Windows Vista resolves this problem by providing better guidance on what causes unresponsive conditions and ensuring that error reporting has the additional information needed to identify and resolve issues. To reduce downtime and restarts required for application installations and updates, Windows Vista can use the update process to mark in-use files for update and then automatically replace the files the next time the application is started. In some cases, Windows Vista can save the application's data, close the application, update the in-use files, and then restart the application—as is possible with Windows Update.

Recovering Automatically from Failure

Windows Vista includes features to automatically recover from many common types of failures, including failed services and corrupted system files. Unlike earlier versions of Windows, in Windows Vista, every service has a recovery policy, as shown in Figure 14-10. If a service fails, Windows Vista will try to restart it automatically. Windows Vista automatically handles both service and nonservice dependencies as well, and it automatically starts any necessary dependent services and system components prior to attempting to start a failed service.

Figure 14-10   All services have recovery policy.

In earlier versions of Windows, corrupted system files were one of the most common causes of startup failure. Sometimes administrators could successfully replace corrupted files by using the System Repair feature or the Recovery Console. At other times the system could be recovered only by attempting to repair the installation or reinstalling the operating system.

Windows Vista includes the Startup Repair Tool (StR) to automatically fix many common problems and to enable both users and administrators to rapidly diagnose and resolve startup issues. Once started, StR performs diagnostics and attempts to determine the cause of the startup failure by analyzing startup logs and error reports. Then StR attempts to fix the problem automatically. If StR is unable to resolve the problem, it restores the system to the last known working state and then provides diagnostic information and support options to make further troubleshooting easier for the user or administrator.

Similar to the Recovery Console that is used with Windows XP, StR is included on the Windows Vista installation disc and can be preinstalled on computers. By preinstalling StR on computers, you make it available as an option on the Windows Advanced Startup Options menu. If you don't preinstall StR and the system fails to start up, you can still run it from the Windows Vista installation disc. If the system fails to start and you haven't preinstalled StR, follow these steps to launch StR:

1. Insert the Windows Vista installation disc, and then restart the computer.
2. Click View System Recovery Options (Advanced).
3. Type the name and password for an account on the computer.
4. Click Startup Repair in the list of recovery tools.
5. Follow the Startup Repair prompts to recover the system.

Recovering Frozen Applications and Releasing Resources Automatically

Few things are as frustrating as unresponsive applications or running out of memory. In earlier versions of Windows, an application crash or hang is marked as not responding, and it is up to the user to exit and then restart the application. The same is true for conditions that cause the computer to run out of memory. Earlier versions of Windows warned you that you were running low on virtual memory, but they did not take corrective action.

Windows Vista attempts to resolve the issue of unresponsive applications by using Restart Manager. Restart Manager can shut down and restart unresponsive applications automatically. This means that you typically don't have to intervene, log out, or restart the computer to try to resolve issues with frozen applications.

Windows Vista attempts to resolve issues related to running out of virtual memory by providing Resource Exhaustion Detection And Recovery. Resource Exhaustion Detection and Recovery constantly monitors the system-wide virtual memory commit limit automatically and warns you when you are running low on virtual memory. At the same time, it also identifies the processes consuming the largest amount of memory. You can close any or all of these high-resource-consuming applications directly from the Close Programs To Prevent Information Loss dialog box provided. The resource exhaustion warning is also logged in the System event log, where it can be analyzed later by administrators.

Introducing the New and Enhanced Windows Vista Management Tools

Windows Vista includes new and updated tools that make it easier for you to maintain and manage computers throughout the enterprise. This section provides an introduction to key tools, including the following:

- Event Viewer
- Task Scheduler
- Performance rating and monitoring
- The Previous Versions feature
- Backup

Introducing Event Viewer: What's Changed

The event logs are used to track informational, warning, and error messages generated by applications, services, and system components. Earlier versions of Windows store most events in one of three event logs:

- Application
- Security
- System

You access the event logs by using Event Viewer; the event logs themselves are written using the Event Viewer (.evt) file format. If you search through the logs, you can identify many types of problems or potential problems that need your attention. Unfortunately, however, many applications, services, and system components have their own logs. Typically these logs are stored in separate folders and aren't always accessible or in a readable format, which makes it difficult to diagnose and resolve problems.

Windows Vista seeks to resolve problems with logging by requiring all applications, services, and components to use centralized logging and the native Windows Vista event log (.elf) file format. The version of Event Viewer included in Windows Vista supports both .elf and .evt files. As Figure 14-11 shows, centralized logging in Windows Vista is very different from the way logging is handled in earlier versions of Windows.

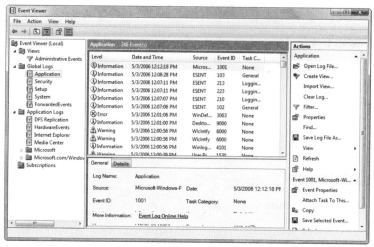

Figure 14-11   The Event Viewer

The best way to master the new Event Viewer is to consider the way logs and events are organized. You have:

- **Individual logs**   Logs for individual applications, services, and system components, referred to as *application logs*, are listed under the Application Logs node by type and vendor. For example, you'll find individual application logs for Internet Explorer and HardwareEvents. If you expand the Application Logs, Microsoft, and Windows nodes, you'll find application logs for every installed service and system component that creates its own event log.

- **Global logs**   Global logs are system-wide logs. You'll find the Application log, a system-wide log for events logged by applications installed on the system; the Security log, a system-wide log for security-related events, such as those related to user rights assignment or logon; and the System log, a system-wide log for events logged by the operating system and its components.

- **Cross-log views**   Cross-log views, as the name implies, provide a view across multiple logs. Event Viewer can run queries that search across multiple logs simultaneously. The results of these cross-log queries can be stored with custom views, which you can define to display events that match specific criteria from selected log files. The Administrative Events view is provided by default to help administrators find warning and error events in the global logs.

When you want to search across all logs on a computer, you'll use cross-log views. You can create a cross-log view by following these steps:

1.   Open Event Viewer by clicking Event Viewer on the Administrative Tools menu or typing **wevtvwr.msc** in a Command Prompt window.

2. Right-click the Views node, and then select Create View to display the Create View dialog box, shown in Figure 14-12.

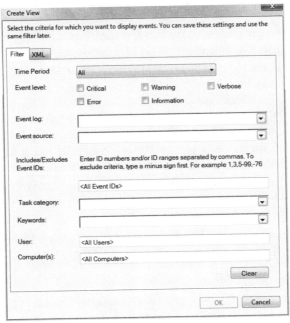

Figure 14-12   Creating a cross-log view

3. Use the Time Period list to select the time period you want to work with when using the view. For example, if you want to the view to always display events for the last 24 hours, select Last 24 Hours as the time period.

4. Use the Event Level check boxes to specify the types of events to search for.

5. Click the Event Log list to display an options entry. Expand the Global Logs and Application Logs nodes, and then specify the event logs that you want to search across. Multiple event logs can be selected by using the check boxes provided.

6. If you are looking for events generated by a specific event source, such as Software Installation or Software Licensing Service, use the Event Source list to specify the event sources to use as part of the search criteria.

7. Provide event task, keyword, user, and event ID details as necessary.

8. If you are looking for events that occurred on a specific date or a range of dates, use the From and To options to set the event dates to use as part of the search criteria.

9. Click OK. Type a name for the view, and then click OK again to begin the search and create the cross-log view, which is accessible under the Views node in Event Viewer.

Introducing Task Scheduler: What's Changed

For automation, Windows Vista includes the new Task Scheduler service. Similar to the Scheduled Task service in Windows XP, the Task Scheduler service allows you schedule tasks to occur at specific times and on specific dates. You can configure recurring tasks, such as daily, weekly, or monthly tasks. For example, you could schedule Disk Cleanup to occur once on Monday at 3:00 P.M. or every Monday at 3:00 P.M. That's about where the similarities end, however, because the Windows Vista Task Scheduler is much smarter than its predecessors.

Not only can you specify whether the task should run when a user is logged on, but you can also start tasks immediately at startup, logon, or both (according to task configuration) if a scheduled run of a task was missed. If a task fails, you can configure Task Scheduler so that it attempts to restart the task automatically. For example, you could configure an automatic restart to occur once every two hours until the task runs successfully. In addition to standard power management features that control whether a task runs when a computer is running on battery, you can also configure whether a task should start only if a network connection is available. Task Scheduler can also wake a computer to run a task and allow it to return to sleep when the task is complete, saving energy while still ensuring that critical tasks run on time.

Figure 14-13 shows the Task Scheduler window. You can access Task Scheduler by clicking Task Scheduler on the Administrator Tools menu. To improve the security of scheduled tasks, each task runs in a separate user session that is based on the user credentials provided when the task was created.

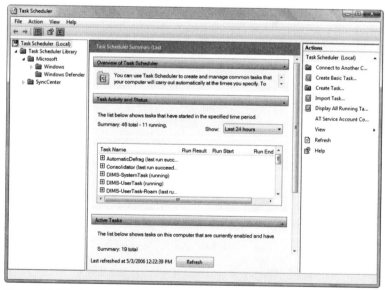

Figure 14-13   Using Task Scheduler

Windows Vista introduces the following concepts:

■ Hidden tasks

- Triggers

- Actions

Most tasks run by the operating system to perform automated maintenance and support are configured as hidden tasks. When you are working with Task Scheduler, you can view hidden tasks by selecting Show Hidden Tasks on the View menu. When you are creating tasks, you can designate them as hidden as well. Because tasks in Windows Vista cannot be directly copied to or used by earlier versions of Windows, you have the option of specifying that a task should be configured for Windows Server 2003, Windows XP, or Windows 2000 when creating a new task. In this way, the task is created so that it is compatible with earlier version of Windows, and you can then copy the task to other computers without worrying about compatibility issues.

You can create a new task by selecting the Task Scheduler node and clicking the Create Task option in the Actions pane. The Create New Task dialog box, shown in Figure 14-14 has five tabs:

- **General**   Use the options on this tab to set the name and description of the task, specify the user account under which the task runs, specify whether the task should be hidden, and specify whether the task should be configured for Windows Vista or for earlier versions of Windows.

- **Triggers**   Use the options on this tab to create and manage triggers that are associated with a task. On the Triggers tab, you click the New button to create a new trigger.

- **Actions**   Use the options on this tab to create and manage actions that are associated with a task. On the Actions tab, you click the New button to create a new action.

- **Conditions**   Use the options on this tab to specify the conditions under which the task should run.

- **Settings**   use the options on this tab to specify additional options that affect the behavior of the task.

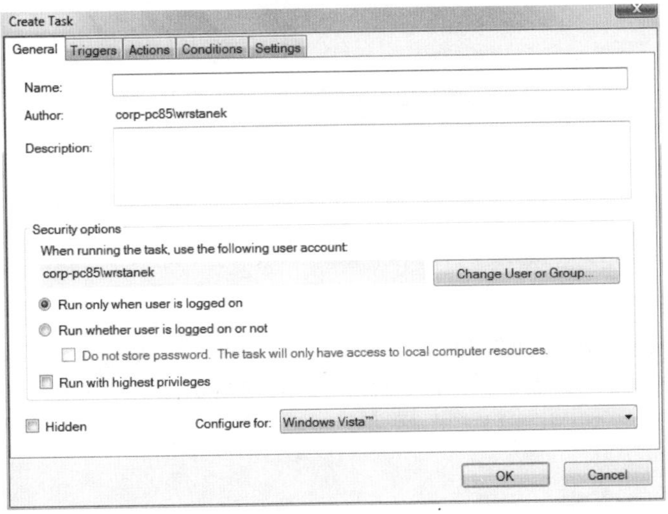

Figure 14-14   Creating a new task

> **Note**   All tasks can have triggers and actions associated with them.

As Figure 14-15 shows, triggers allow you to specify the circumstances under which a task begins and ends. You can begin a task in one of the following ways:

- On a schedule

- At logon

- At startup

- On idle

- On an event

- On registration

- On Terminal Server session connect

- On Terminal Server session disconnect

- On workstation lock

- On workstation unlock

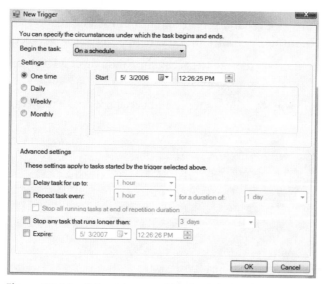

Figure 14-15   Using triggers with scheduled tasks

You can specify multiple triggers as well. Being able to trigger a scheduled task when a specific event occurs is extremely powerful. It allows you to gracefully handle errors and to resolve warning states before bigger problems occur. In this way, you can proactively maintain computers in your organization.

As Figure 14-16 shows, actions allow you to start programs, send e-mail messages, and show messages when a scheduled task runs. You can specify multiple actions if necessary.

Figure 14-16   Associating actions with scheduled tasks

Introducing Performance Rating and Monitoring: What's New and What's Changed

Built-in performance diagnostics make monitoring performance in Windows Vista very different from monitoring performance in earlier versions of Windows. First of all, Windows Vista monitors performance automatically and adjusts system settings as necessary to improve performance. Often, but not always, Windows Vista prompts the user before adjusting computer settings.

Windows Vista tracks performance by assigning a performance rating to a computer. A performance rating is a measure of the computer's overall capability in terms of the following:

- Processor speed
- Total physical memory
- Free hard disk space
- Graphics processor
- Graphics memory

When you first install a computer, it will not have a performance rating, and you might be able to improve performance by allowing Windows Vista to assign a performance rating. To assign a performance rating to a computer or to refresh a computer's rating, follow these steps:

1. Click Start, and then click Control Panel.
2. In Control Panel, click System And Maintenance.
3. On the System And Maintenance page, click Performance Ratings And Tools.

4.   On the Performance Ratings And Tools page, click Rate This Computer or Refresh My Rating Now as appropriate for the state of the computer.

5.   A higher rating usually means that the computer will perform better and faster than a computer with a lower rating. You can learn more about what a rating means by clicking What Does This Number Mean.

Once you've allowed Windows Vista to assign a performance rating to a computer, Windows Vista can do a better job of tracking performance issues. Over time, a list of issues affecting performance will be listed under the Performance Issues heading, as shown in Figure 14-17. Click an issue to see details about addressing the problem.

Because of the built-in diagnostics capabilities, performance monitoring is very different in Windows Vista. For starters, the Performance console has been completely redesigned and renamed the Windows Performance Diagnostic console. You can open the Windows Performance Diagnostic console by clicking Performance on the Administrative Tools menu.

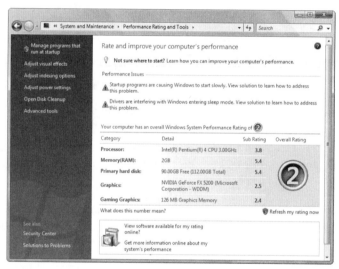

Figure 14-17   Viewing a computer's performance details and rating

The standard Performance console features provided in earlier versions of Windows can be accessed by clicking the Performance Monitor node, as shown in Figure 14-18. Windows Vista enhances the standard features by providing an expanded set of objects and counters for improved performance tracking.

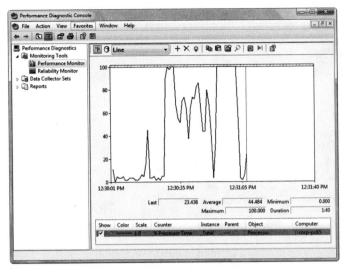

Figure 14-18   Using the Windows Performance Diagnostic console

Windows Vista also introduces Data Collector Sets and Reports. Data Collector Sets allow you to specify sets of performance objects and counters that you want to track. Once you've created a Data Collector Set, you can easily start or stop monitoring of the performance objects and counters included in the set. In a way, this makes Data Collector Sets similar to performance logs. However, Data Collector Sets are much more sophisticated. A single data set can be used to generate multiple performance counters and trace logs. You can also:

- Associate multiple run schedules and stop conditions for monitoring.

- Assign access controls to manage who can access collected data.

- Use data managers to control the size of collected data and reporting.

- Generate reports based on collected data.

The Windows Performance Diagnostic console also includes Reliability Monitor, shown in Figure 14-19. Reliability Monitor tracks changes to the system and compares them to changes in system stability. In this way, you can see a graphical representation of the relationship between changes in the system configuration and changes in system stability. By recording software installation, software removal, application failure, driver failure, and hardware failure as well as key events regarding the configuration of a system, you can see a timeline of changes in both the system and its reliability and then use this information to pinpoint changes that are causing problems with stability. For example, if you see a sudden drop in stability, you can click a data point and then expand the related data set, such as Application Failure, to find the specific event that caused the drop in stability.

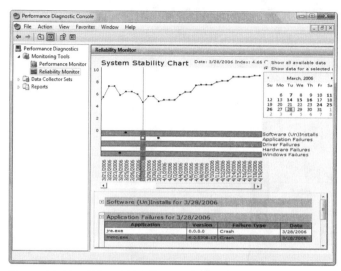

Figure 14-19 Using Reliability Monitor

Introducing the Previous Versions Feature

Previous Versions allows you to restore files that have been inadvertently changed or deleted. You can:

- Make a copy of a previous version.
- Revert a file or folder to any previous version.
- Restore a previous version from a backup (made by using the Backup utility).

With the Previous Versions feature, Windows Vista brings the Shadow Copy feature provided in Microsoft Windows Server 2003 to the client. Computers running Windows Vista automatically make daily copies of files and folders that have changed. You can also create copies of files that have changed by setting a system protection point on the System Protection tab in the System utility. A system protection point is a point-in-time backup that includes any files and folders that have changed.

Although protection points are created daily, only those versions of files that are actually different from the current version are stored as previous versions. Previous Versions is automatically enabled in Windows Vista. You can enable or disable the feature for each available volume by using the System Protection tab in the System Properties dialog box. Because Previous Versions uses the protection points stored on the local computer, it does not require a server to act as a repository for the shadow copies, and administrators are no longer required to manage the Previous Versions configuration.

To view or change the protection settings, click Start, right-click Computer, and then click Properties. In the System window, click System Protection to open the System Properties dialog box. You can then use the options on the System Protection tab, shown in Figure 14-20, to configure how protection points are created and used. If you want protection points to be created for a disk, select the check box for that disk under Available Disks. If you don't want protection points to be created for a disk, clear the check box for that disk under Available Disks.

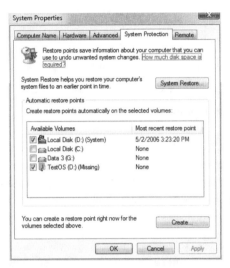

Figure 14-20   Working with System Protection

When you right-click a file or folder for which previous versions are available and then select Properties, you see a Previous Versions tab. If you select this tab, you should see previous versions of the file or folder. You can then use:

- **Open** to open any of the previous versions.
- **Copy** to create a copy of a previous version.
- **Restore** to revert the file or folder to a selected previous version.

Backing Up and Recovering Windows Vista: What's New and What's Changed

Windows Vista includes Previous Versions, Protection Points, and System Restore as part of its comprehensive data protection feature set. Previous Versions and Protection Points work as discussed in the preceding section. System Restore is the system component that creates Protection Points. In addition to being used to create previous versions of files and folders, Protection Points are also used to store the information needed to recover a system to the state it was in prior to a configuration change or an application installation.

> **Note**   System Restore doesn't affect any documents, pictures, or other personal data. It affects only the system configuration.

You can work with System Restore in Windows Vista in much the same way as you work with System Restore in Windows XP. If you want to create a protection point prior to installing an application or making a system configuration change, you can do so by following these steps:

1. Click Start, right-click Computer, and then click Properties.

2. In the left pane of the System window, click System Protection.

3. In the System Properties dialog box, click Create on the System Protection tab.

4. Type a descriptive name for the protection point.

5. Click Create.

To restore a computer to a previous protection point, you use the System Restore utility. You can run this utility by clicking Start, pointing to All Programs, Accessories, System Tools, and then clicking System Restore. The System Restore Wizard starts. Follow the instructions on the subsequent pages, and then click Finish to restore your computer's system to the protection point you selected.

System Restore doesn't create a full backup of a computer and all its data. To create a full backup of a computer, you must use Windows Backup, shown in Figure 14-21. This utility is an enhanced version of the Backup utility included in earlier versions of Windows. You can run this utility by clicking Start, pointing to All Programs, Accessories, System Tools, and then clicking Backup.

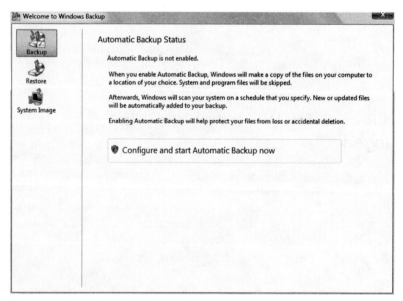

Figure 14-21   Using Windows Backup

Windows Backup is designed to help you automate the backup process. If you enable automatic backups, you can identify the disks, folders, and files you want to back up regularly and then set a schedule for backing up these items to the media you've selected. Windows Backup supports writing to local disks, shared network folders, CD media, and DVD media.

Using Windows Backup, you can restore files using a basic or an advanced restore operation. A basic restore allows you to recover accidentally deleted files or folders. It also allows you to restore all files and folders. An advanced restore allows you to load a backup from another computer and restore files with administrator privilege.

For creating backups of an entire computer, Windows Backup includes System Image. A System Image backup contains everything needed to completely restore a computer. If the computer you've imaged is damaged or stolen, you can restore the computer from an image by using the System Recovery Troubleshooter. Similar to the Startup Repair Tool discussed previously under "Recovering Automatically from Failure," System Recovery Troubleshooter is available as a recovery option when you are attempting to recover a computer.

Chapter 15
Deploying Windows Vista

Making the decision to move to a new operating system isn't easy, and return on investment (ROI) typically is an essential element in this decision. Many businesses delay deploying new operating systems for six months to a year while they perform planning, test application compatibility, and develop deployment scenarios. Other businesses elect to perform small initial deployments while they get their plans and procedures in place for the new operating system. Additionally, in many medium and large enterprises, new operating systems often are rolled out to mobile PC users first, as these users typically get the highest benefits from adopting the next-generation operating system, and then to other users within the organization, as these users get the most benefits when there are well-planned migration and upgrade paths in place.

Unfortunately, if your organization is looking purely at return on investment, you might be missing the mark. Microsoft Windows Vista is not just another upgrade—it is the single largest rollout of the Microsoft Windows operating system since Windows 95. Windows Vista is significantly easier to deploy than its predecessors, primarily because one of Microsoft's key development goals was to make the operating system easier to deploy. A key part of this effort was to streamline the deployment process by making deployment tools easier to use and more versatile. Microsoft took this one step further though by introducing the following features:

- Operating system modularization, providing a selective capability to customize Windows Vista, with separate device driver and language components

- Single-format answer files for unattended setup with scriptable installation

- Windows Preinstallation Environment (Windows PE) for managing computer configuration prior to installation

- System imaging with single-instance storage and a hardware-independent format

Answering the question of why these enhancements are important and how they help reduce deployment costs and complexity is what this chapter is all about. In addition to discussing the Windows Vista deployment enhancements, this chapter describes upgrading and migrating computers, using the User State Migration Tool Version (USMT) 3.0, and running Windows Easy Transfer.

> **Note**   This book was written using the Windows Vista Beta to provide an early introduction to the operating system. More so than any other area of Windows Vista, the features discussed in this book are subject to change. Some of the features might not be included in the final product, and some of the features might be changed substantially.

Introducing Deployment Enhancements for Windows Vista

Many organizations use some form of automation to deploy the Windows operating system, such as disk imaging technology, remote installation, or unattended installation. With disk imaging, administrators typically have to create and maintain separate images for each type of hardware and language used throughout the enterprise. When administrators add new hardware language packs, updates, or drivers, they usually have to create and then test new disk images. Updating disk images every time changes occur is not only time-consuming but also costly. The same is true, but to a lesser extent, for maintaining multiple answer files—multiple answer files are costly to create and maintain, especially when implementations require different types of files and those files use different file formats.

Microsoft used several approaches to reduce deployment complexity and costs. These approaches include using the following features:

- Language-independent modularization
- Hardware-independent disk imaging
- Customizable and extensible preinstallation environments
- Standards-based single-format answer files

How do these features work? Well, let's take a look.

Introducing Modularization and Hardware-Independent Disk Imaging

Microsoft reengineered the basic architectural framework of the Windows operating system so that it uses independent units of programming logic called modules and provides a selective capability to customize Windows Vista by swapping out modules. In this modular architecture, system components, device drivers, and language packs are all created as modules, and so are service packs and updates.

Understanding Modules and Disk Images

The benefits of a modular architecture are far-reaching. Thanks to modularization, when you need to add device drives, language packs, or service packs or make other updates, you can more easily introduce these new components because you are simply adding new modules to the system. When you need to update or remove an existing component, you can do so without impacting the system as a whole—the changes affect only the related module or modules for that component. Because language packs are separate modular components from the operating system itself, you don't need a separate image for each language used in your organization, thereby reducing the total number of disk images large organizations need to maintain.

Microsoft reengineered the basic distribution format of the Windows operating system so that it uses a hardware-independent image-file format. The new imaging format is called *Windows Imaging Format* (WIM), and Windows Vista is distributed using this format. Thanks to WIM, Microsoft can ship a single binary to all of its customers around the world: one binary format for 32-bit architectures and one binary format for 64-bit architectures. WIM allows you to store multiple images in one file and significantly reduces image size by using a combination of compression and single-instance storage. With compression, the total size of the image file is reduced in much the same way as Zip compression reduces the size of files. With single-instance storage, the disk image contains only one physical copy of a file for each instance of that file in the disk image. This substantially reduces the size of the image because there are no duplicate files.

WIM allows administrators to modify and maintain disk images offline, which means that administrators can add or remove optional components and drivers or perform updates without having to create a new image. Administrators can also mount images as folders and work with them in much the same way as any other folder, making it easier to update files within images. For example, you can mount an image and then use Windows Explorer to update or remove files as necessary. The ease with which you can update disk images and the removal of the requirement to have multiple hardware-specific disk images greatly reduces deployment complexity and costs.

> **Tip**   The new image-based operating system setup also makes upgrades easier and more reliable. Thanks to WIM, upgrading to Windows Vista essentially means that Setup performs a clean installation of the operating system followed by a migration of user settings, documents, and applications from the earlier version of Windows.

Creating and Managing Disk Images

At a high level, deploying Windows Vista with imaging requires the following procedures:

1. Creating the configuration to be deployed.
2. Preparing the system for capture.
3. Capturing the image.
4. Maintaining the image as necessary.
5. Applying the image.

Creating the Configuration to Be Deployed   Creating the configuration to be deployed means setting up the operating system, configuring the operating system, installing any necessary applications, and then configuring those applications. Once you do this, you can prepare the system for capture by running the System Preparation command-line tool (SysPrep.exe). SysPrep irrevocably alters the computer and designates it as a master deployment computer by removing the unique identification information from the computer.

By removing the unique identifiers from the computer, SysPrep creates a resulting image that can be installed on multiple computers without creating identification conflicts. However, the computer no longer has identifying information that allows it to be logged on to and used within a domain or workgroup setting. Typically, you must reinstall the operating system.

Capturing the Image   In the Windows Automated Installation Kit (Windows AIK), you'll find a tool called *XImage*. Using the Windows Vista XImage tool, you can capture your image file from Windows PE or with the operating system fully loaded. The best technique for capturing an entire installation, however, is to use Windows PE. When capturing an image with Windows PE, no locked files or folders will be included in your installation image, and as a result, you should experience fewer problems capturing the image.

> **Note**   Although you can capture an image from a running version of Windows, you can capture only files and folders not in use by the operating system. Later, when you are installing from the image, any in-use files must also be listed in the exclusion list of the configuration script. Although excluding these in-use files reduces the errors you see during installation, it doesn't ensure that the image is usable. If essential files were locked during the image capture, the image won't install the operating system properly.

You can capture an image by using XImage with the following syntax:

```
ximage /capture ImageSource ImageDest "ImageDescription"
```

ImageSource is the location of the files to image, *ImageDest* is the name and location of the new image file, and *"ImageDescription"* is a description of the image file, such as

```
ximage /capture C:\Windows D:\WinVistaStandard.wim "Windows Vista Standard"
```

If you don't specify a destination drive, XImage creates the image and stores it in the XImage folder on the system drive. If the image file is too large for your selected media, you can use the /split option to split an existing image file into smaller .swm files, such as for spanning across several CDs. Before you split an image, you must determine the size of the media required for the image and then provide this value as one of the parameters passed to XImage. In the following example, you split a previously created image file into 600-megabyte (MB) .swm files:

```
ximage /split D:\WinVistaStandard.wim 600
```

Maintaining the Image   Once you've created an image file, you can easily maintain the image. To do this, you must install the Windows Imaging File System Filter (WIM FS Filter) driver on your computer by right-clicking the Wimfltr.inf file in the XImage folder and then selecting Install. After installing the filter driver, you can mount image files to folders on your computer. The files in the mounted image can be browsed via the folder by using Windows Explorer or other software. You can perform copy, paste, and editing operations on files in the mounted folder without having to re-create the image.

> **Tip**   Although it is a best practice to mount images to an empty folder, you don't have to mount to empty folders. The contents of non-empty folders are inaccessible, but they are not affected by the mount operation. When you unmount the image, you'll be able to access the existing files on the folder.

Images can be mounted as read-only or read/write. Read-only images cannot be edited; read/write images can be edited.

You can mount an image as read-only by using the following syntax:

```
ximage /mount MountPath ImageFilePath ReferenceNumber
```

MountPath is the location of the mount folder, *ImageFilePath* is the name and location of the .wim file to mount, and *ReferenceNumber* is the reference number of the specific volume in the .wim file to use, such as:

```
ximage /mount C:\Data D:\Images\Data.wim 1
```

You can mount an image as read/write by using the following syntax:

```
ximage /mountrw MountPath ImageFilePath ReferenceNumber
```

MountPath is the location of the mount folder, *ImageFilePath* is the name and location of the .wim file to mount, and *ReferenceNumber* is the reference number of the specific volume in the .wim file, such as:

```
ximage /mountrw C:\Data D:\Images\Data.wim 1
```

Using the mounted folder, you can:

- Open files and folders and view their contents.
- Add files or folders.
- Move the files and folders within an image.
- Edit existing files and folders.
- Delete files and folders.

When you have finished working with an image, you must unmount the image and optionally commit your changes. You use the following syntax to unmount an image and save your changes:

```
ximage /unmount /commit MountPath
```

MountPath is the location of the mount folder, such as:

```
ximage /unmount /commit C:\Data
```

If you mounted an image as read-only, you don't need to use the /commit option. There are no changes to save.

> **Caution**   When working in Windows PE, keep in mind that mounted images cannot persist across restarts. If you have file system changes to be committed as the computer restarts, you will lose the changes. Additionally, Windows PE restarts automatically after 24 hours, so if you leave a changed image mounted and go home, the changes will likely be lost when you return to work the next day. For these reasons, Microsoft recommends that you do not use ximage /unmount /commit from Windows PE.

Applying the Image   When you are ready to apply the image, you can do so using a variety of automatic techniques, such as deployment scripts, or you can apply an image manually. Either way, you must first prepare the target computer by creating and formatting the disk partitions. If you choose to perform these tasks from a script, insert the commands to create and format the disk partitions prior to executing the XImage commands that apply the image. You apply an image by using the following syntax:

```
ximage /apply ImageFilePath ReferenceNumber
```

ImageFilePath is the name and location of the .wim file to apply, and *ReferenceNumber* is the reference number of the specific volume to use in the .wim file, such as:

```
ximage /apply D:\Images\Data.wim 1
```

To have XImage apply and then verify the image, you can add the /verify option, as follows:

```
ximage /apply D:\Images\Data.wim 1 /verify
```

Introducing the Customizable and Extensible Preinstallation Environment

Another new feature in Windows Vista is Windows Preinstallation Environment Version 2.0. Windows PE 2.0 is a bootable startup environment that provides operating system features for installation, recovery, and troubleshooting.

Understanding Windows PE 2.0

When you install Windows Vista, the graphical tools that collect configuration information during the setup phase are running within Windows PE. If Windows Vista fails to start because of a corrupted system file, Windows PE allows you to access and run the Startup Recovery Tool. You can also manually start Windows PE to use built-in or custom trouble-shooting and diagnostic tools.

Windows PE replaces MS-DOS as the preinstallation environment. Windows PE is built from Windows Vista components to provide a versatile and extensible environment. Not only can Windows PE run many Windows Vista applications, it can also detect and enable most hardware devices and communicate across IP networks. Windows PE can run entirely from RAM, allowing you to run Windows PE computers that do not currently have a formatted hard disk or an installed operating system.

Windows PE provides full access to both FAT and NTFS file systems. Before you replace or reformat a hard disk, you can start the computer with Windows PE first and then copy any needed files to another disk or to a shared folder.

Windows PE includes several built-in management tools, including:

- **DiskPart**   A command-line tool for managing disks, partitions, and volumes.
- **Drvload**   A command-line tool for adding device drivers and dynamically loading a driver after Windows PE has started.
- **Net**   A suite of commands that allow you to manage local users, start and stop services, and connect to shared folders.
- **Netcfg**   A network configuration tool that configures network access.

Administrators can create customized Windows PE images with configuration scripts that customize the deployment process. When a new computer is connected to the network, the built-in Preboot Execution Environment (PXE) client connects to a Windows Deployment Service server and downloads the customized Windows PE image across the network. The new computer then loads Windows PE into memory and launches the configuration script.

Working with Windows PE 2.0

Many types of configuration scripts can be used within Windows PE. Configuration scripts can be used to:

- Verify the computer configuration.
- Use Netcfg to configure network access.
- Use Drvload to install a driver and use the hardware without restarting the computer.
- Back up the user data to a shared folder on another computer.

- Run DiskPart to partition and format the computer's hard disk.

- Use NET SHARE to connect to a shared folder containing the Windows Vista Setup files.

- Run the Windows Vista Setup program to install the operating system.

Like Windows Vista, Windows PE can be contained within a WIM file. However, when you store a Windows Vista image in a WIM file, the only way to start Windows Vista is to copy the full image to the computer's hard disk. Windows PE, on the other hand, can start directly from a WIM file without being copied to a hard disk. Because of this, you can create a WIM file that includes Windows PE, store this file on bootable media such as a DVD or USB flash drive, and then start Windows PE directly from that media. The Windows Vista distribution media uses this technique to load Windows PE into RAM when you run Setup.

Administrators can load Windows PE fully into memory as well for troubleshooting and recovery. If you choose to run Windows PE from memory, the Windows PE boot loader:

1. Creates a virtual RAM disk in memory.

2. Copies a compressed version of Windows PE to the RAM disk.

3. Mounts the RAM disk as if it were a disk drive and starts Windows PE.

Loading Windows PE from RAM allows you to remove the Windows PE media after Windows PE has started and then insert different media into the computer's CD/DVD drive. When Windows PE runs from memory, it supports writing temporary files to the virtual RAM disk. This isn't possible, however, when running from read-only media such as a CD.

Windows PE has several limitations. It requires a computer with a VESA-compatible display and a minimum of 256 MB of RAM. During startup, if Windows PE can't detect the video settings, it uses a screen resolution of 640 × 480 pixels. Otherwise, it uses the highest resolution possible. Windows PE supports both IPv4 and IPv6. Although you can access shared folders on other computers from Windows PE, other computers cannot access files or folders on a computer running Windows PE.

Windows PE has other limitations as well. Drive letter assignments aren't persistent between sessions. Windows PE always starts with the default drive letter assignments. Because Windows PE doesn't support the Microsoft .NET Framework or Windows On Windows (WOW), you cannot use .NET applications on any versions of Windows PE, 16-bit applications on 32-bit versions of Windows PE, or 32-bit applications on 64-bit versions of Windows PE. Additionally, as a safeguard to prevent Windows PE from being used as a general-purpose operating system, Windows PE automatically restarts after running for 24 hours.

Introducing Standards-Based Single-Format Answer Files

With standards-based single-format answer files, Windows Vista introduces significant enhancements for remote and unattended installations. Although earlier versions of the Windows operating system use multiple answer file formats and often require the use of several different types of answer files, Windows Vista uses a single Extensible Markup Language (XML)–based answer file format that allows administrators to deploy systems using only a single answer file.

Instead of having to use unattend.txt, winbom.ini, and sysprep.inf for deployments, you have to use only the Windows Vista unattend.xml answer file. Because XML is based on an existing standard, many different tools can be used to create and modify unattend.xml files, including Ximage (discussed earlier in this chapter). This simplification and reliance on an industry standard can help to ensure that unattended installations are less prone to errors and are more manageable.

From the experts
The Solution Accelerator for Business Desktop Deployment

The deployment tools this chapter describes are building blocks that help you build, customize, and service images. The Windows Automated Installation Kit (Windows AIK) provides Windows System Image Manager (Windows SIM) and Ximage, for example. Windows SIM is the tool you use to create unattended setup answer files for Windows Vista. Ximage is the tool you use to capture, apply, and service images offline.

These tools combined with the many other deployment tools that Microsoft provides for Windows Vista are very capable. They are not a complete solution, however. If you were to rely solely on these tools, you'd eventually build a framework of scripts and related files that automates the deployment process. For example, you'd write scripts that gather information about each destination computer. You'd write scripts that automatically save user state and then restore it after applying the image. You'd write scripts that install applications from an application portfolio. You'd build scripts that configure the computer after applying the image. These kinds of scripts are simple. The framework gets complex in zero-touch installation scenarios, though.

To address the need to glue these tools together into a manageable framework, Microsoft provides the Solution Accelerator for Business Desktop Deployment (BDD). BDD is an end-to-end deployment solution based on the tools you read about in this chapter. It supports light-touch *and* zero-touch scenarios. BDD does most of the work for you, allowing you to focus more on important deployment details and less on forcing the tools to work together as a complete solution. Using the Windows Vista deployment tools without the BDD framework just doesn't make sense. For more information about BDD, see *http://www.microsoft.com/technet/desktopdeployment*.

Jerry Honeycutt
Author and MVP–For more information, see http://www.honeycutt.com.

Upgrading Computers and Migrating to New Computers

Deciding whether to perform an in-place upgrade or to migrate to new computers is a key decision when you are deploying Windows Vista—or any new operating system, for that matter. The following sections will help you make this important decision and also introduce the enhanced migration tools included in Windows Vista.

Deciding Whether to Upgrade or to Migrate

Typically, you'll upgrade computers when the underlying hardware meets or exceeds the minimum requirements for physical memory, processing power, and graphics capabilities, and you'll migrate users to new computers when the underlying hardware doesn't meet the minimum requirements. Requirements for memory and graphics are measured in megabytes (MB) and gigabytes (GB); requirements for processors are measured in gigahertz (GHz).

Windows Vista requires a minimum of 512 MB of RAM; a 1.5 GHz Pentium 4, AMD Athlon, or higher processor; and a graphics processor with 64 MB of memory that supports DirectX 9. You'll get better performance if the computer meets or exceeds the recommended requirements of at least 1 GB of RAM; a 3.0 GHz Pentium 4, AMD Athlon, or higher processor; and a graphics processor with 256 MB or more of graphics memory that supports DirectX 9.

Because Windows Vista uses more disk space than its predecessors, the hard disk drive on a computer is also an important consideration. While a base installation of Windows XP uses about 2 GB of disk space, a base installation of Windows Vista uses 4 GB or more of disk space. Various features in Windows Vista, such as protection points that include previous versions of files and folders that have been modified, can quickly increase the size of the installation to 6 GB or more.

Upgrading to Windows Vista is vastly different from upgrading to earlier versions of Windows. When you upgrade a computer to Windows Vista from an earlier version of Windows, Setup essentially performs a clean installation of the operating system followed by a migration of user settings, documents, and applications. This occurs for several reasons, but primarily because Windows Vista uses an entirely new boot environment and also has an entirely new way of storing personal settings and data. These changes are so far-reaching that earlier versions of Windows are now considered to be legacy operating systems.

At startup, computers running Windows Vista enter a preboot environment prior to the loading of the operating system. The preboot environment uses Windows Boot Manager to control the boot experience and to control which boot applications are run. Windows Boot Loader, the standard boot application for Windows Vista, is responsible for accessing entries in the Boot Configuration Data (BCD) store. The BCD store abstracts the underlying firmware, making it easier for Windows Vista to work with new firmware models, and also making it possible for the Startup Repair Tool (StR) to be launched in the preboot environment.

Windows Vista stores user data in the Users folder rather than in the Documents And Settings folder. With the Users folder, each user that logs on to the system has a personal folder, and that personal folder contains additional folders for documents, pictures, music, and so on. If you've upgraded to Windows Vista from an earlier version of Windows, the user's personal folder will also contain shortcuts to the folders and settings used by that earlier version.

Migrating to Windows Vista is also different from migrating to earlier versions of Windows—although not as substantially changed as the new upgrade process. For small migrations, Windows Vista includes Windows Easy Transfer. This migration tool is an enhanced version of the Files And Settings Transfer Wizard included in Windows 2000 and Windows XP. For large migrations, Windows Vista includes version 3.0 of the User State Migration Tool (USMT). This migration tool is an enhanced version of the same tool included in Windows 2000 and Windows XP.

Whether you are performing an upgrade or an actual migration, Windows Vista is designed to make this process as seamless as possible. Users who have their environments configured exactly the way they like them should find that after an in-place upgrade or a migration, the settings are essentially the same. However, Windows Vista:

- Allows administrators to redirect individual personal folders in much the same way as personal folders can be collectively redirected by using Group Policy. If you right-click a user's standard personal folder (Contacts, Documents, Desktop, Links, Favorites, Music, Videos), you can specify an alternative location for that folder on the local computer or on a shared network folder.

- Uses a new shared folder architecture that allows users to mark files or folders as public and assign various levels of access to these files and folders based on user and group accounts. Public files and folders are stored in the Users\Public folder. Windows Vista has Public Desktop, Public Documents, Public Music, Public Pictures, and Public Videos folders. Some applications create additional public folders as well. Some application and user settings are automatically configured as public. For example, the Public Desktop folder might include shortcuts to programs that are accessible to all users on a computer.

 Tip   Through local settings and Group Policy settings, you can modify and restrict the new sharing architecture. On a per-folder basis, you can also configure Windows Vista computers to use classic folder sharing rather than the new sharing architecture. With classic folder sharing, you have the same folder sharing options as with Windows XP.

Introducing the User State Migration Tool

The User State Migration Tool (USMT) version 3.0 combines the best features of USMT version 2.6 and the Files And Settings Transfer Wizard to provide an improved migration framework. Using the latest version of USMT, you can migrate user accounts during large deployments of Windows Vista. USMT captures user accounts and related user state data, including documents, desktop settings, and application settings, from an old computer and helps you move them to a new Windows Vista installation. Because USMT 3.0 includes better procedures for identifying user state data that needs to be migrated and allows for improved automation of the migration process through scripting, USMT 3.0 can help you improve and simplify your migrations.

Getting Started with the User State Migration Tool

USMT is designed to be used by administrators who are performing large-scale automated deployments. If you are upgrading your operating system instead of migrating, you do not need to use USMT. If you are migrating only the user states of a few computers, you do not need to use USMT either and should instead use Windows Easy Transfer.

USMT works by saving user state data to a server and then restoring it to a desktop after installation. You automate the migration by using the two USMT command-line tools:

- **ScanState**   Used to collect user accounts, files, and settings
- **LoadState**   Used to restore user accounts, files, and settings

To migrate user state data, you run ScanState on the source computer to collect user accounts, files, and settings. ScanState creates a data store, called USMT3.MIG, that holds all of the collected information. ScanState does not make any modifications to the source computer–its only job is to collect the necessary information and store that information on a specified server. After you install the new computer, you run LoadState on that computer to restore the user state from the data store.

By default, USMT 3.0 compresses user state data and stores it as image files. This improves performance by reducing network bandwidth usage and storage requirements. When you run LoadState, the entire compressed image is transferred to the destination computer even if you migrate a subset of the data store. USMT then uncompresses all of the files and applies the specified files and settings. Because the compressed store cannot be modified, LoadState does not scan the store, and this reduces the run time for loading state data.

With USMT 3.0, computers running the following operating systems can be source computers:

- Microsoft Windows 2000 Professional with Service Pack 4 (SP4)
- Microsoft Windows XP Home
- Microsoft Windows XP Professional
- Microsoft Windows XP Professional x64 Edition
- Microsoft Windows Vista

Table 15-1 provides an overview of the types of user state data that are and aren't migrated by USMT 3.0. By default, USMT will also migrate settings for some applications, including most Microsoft Office applications and Adobe Acrobat Reader version 5.0 or later. With Microsoft Office Outlook, e-mail settings, contacts, and messages are all migrated. In most cases, you'll want to install all applications on the destination computer before restoring the user state to ensure that migrated application settings are preserved.

Table 15-1   Overview of Migrated and Nonmigrated User State Data

Migrated Data	Nonmigrated Data
Accessibility options	Applications
Command prompt settings	Drivers
Desktop and classic desktop	DLLs
Dial-up connections	Executables
Favorites	Hardware-related settings
Folder options	Passwords
Fonts	Synchronization files
Microsoft Internet Explorer settings	Encrypting File System (EFS) certificates
Microsoft Outlook Express store	
Mouse and keyboard settings	
My Documents folder	
My Music	
My Pictures folder	
My Received Files	
My Videos	
Phone and modem options	
Quick Launch settings	
Regional options	
Screen saver selection	
Sounds settings	
Taskbar settings	

Using the User State Migration Tool

At a high level, working with the User State Migration Tool involves the following steps:

1. Modifying the required migration rule files.

2. Creating and modifying a Config.xml file by using the ScanState /genconfig option.

3. Running ScanState on all source computers by specifying /config:config.xml and specifying the other desired .xml files by using the /i option.

4. Running LoadState on destination computers, specifying the desired .xml files by using the /i option.

You use migration rule (.xml) files to specify what user accounts, files, and settings should be migrated and how those user accounts, files, and settings should migrated. Three default .xml files are provided: MigApp.xml, MigSys.xml, and MigUser.xml. You must edit these files so that they reflect the desired configuration before running ScanState.

> **Tip** When migrating to Windows Vista, you must edit only MigUser.xml and MigApp.xml. By default, when the destination computer is running Windows Vista, USMT 3.0 uses the Component Manifests for Windows Vista to migrate the operating system settings. On computers running Windows Vista, these manifests are a set of .man files located in the %SystemRoot%\installedRepository folder. USMT 3.0 also supports migrating from Windows 2000 to Windows XP. When you migrate to Windows XP, you must edit MigApp.xml, MigSys.xml, and MigUser.xml.

After you modify the migration rule files, you must create a Config.xml file by using the /genconfig option and then modify this file. You can then run ScanState on all source computers by specifying /config:config.xml and the other desired .xml files using the /i option to create the data store on the server. To make sure that EFS certificates are migrated to computers running Windows Vista, you must specify the /copyraw option on the ScanState command line.

After you've created the data store and installed the new computers, you can run LoadState on the new computers and specify the desired .xml files by using the /i option. If you want to migrate the entire store, specify the same set of .xml files that you specified on the ScanState command line. If you want to migrate only a portion of the store, modify the .xml files as necessary and then specify the modified files on the LoadState command line.

> **Note** When running LoadState, you do not have to specify /config:config.xml. You have to specify the Config.xml file only when you've modified Config.xml so that it reflects a subset of the data store.

On Windows Vista, you will need to run ScanState and LoadState in elevated mode from an administrative account to ensure that all user accounts, files, and settings are migrated. If you do not do this, only the logged-on user profile will be included for migration. To run ScanState or LoadState in elevated mode, click Start, point to All Programs, Accessories, right-click Command Prompt, and then click Run As Administrator. Then run ScanState, LoadState, or both by using this command prompt.

In USMT 3.0, options for both ScanState and Load State have changed. Table 15-2 provides a summary of the new and modified options for these commands. To see the full list of options for these commands, type the command name followed by /? at a command prompt, such as **scanstate /?**.

Table 15-2   Command-Line Options for ScanState and LoadState

Command	Option	Description
ScanState	/config	Specifies the Config.xml file to be used in creating the data store.
	/efs:copyraw	Generates EFS certificates (only valid when migrating to Windows Vista).
	/encrypt	Encrypts the data store with the specified key.
	/genconfig[:*StorePath*]	Generates a Config.xml file, but does not create a store. You can specify an optional store path to use when later generating the data store by using /config.
	/nocompress	Disables compression of data (meant only for testing).
	/targetxp	Optimizes ScanState for destination computers running Windows XP. When Windows XP is the destination, USMT 3.0 does not migrate user cookies, network drive settings, or printers.
	/ue	Excludes specific users, domains, or both from the migration. User accounts and domains specified are not migrated.
	/uel	Excludes user accounts based on user logon. Users accounts that have not been logged into within the specified time period are not migrated.
	/ui	Includes specific users, domains, or both from the migration. User accounts and domains specified are migrated.
LoadState	/config	Specifies the Config.xml file that LoadState should use.
	/decrypt	Decrypts the data store with the specified key.
	/md	Modifies old domain names to new domain names during the migration.
	/mu	Modifies old user names to new user names during the migration.
	/nocompress	Specifies that the store is not compressed.
	/ue	Excludes the specified users, domains, or both from the migration.
	/uel	Excludes user accounts that have not been logged into within the specified time period.
	/ui	Migrates the specified users, domains or both.

Introducing Windows Easy Transfer

Windows Easy Transfer is designed to be an easy-to-use migration tool. Similar to the User State Migration Tool, you can use Windows Easy Transfer to migrate files and settings from an old computer to a new computer. Unlike the User State Migration Tool, which is meant for large-scale migrations, Windows Easy Transfer is designed for small-scale migrations. If you are migrating five or fewer computers, Windows Easy Transfer is an ideal choice.

Getting Started with Windows Easy Transfer

Windows Easy Transfer is an administrative-mode application. You can start this application from the System Tools menu. Click Start, point to All Programs, Accessories, System Tools, and then click Windows Easy Transfer.

Using Windows Easy Transfer, you can migrate files and settings for the currently logged on user or for all users on a computer. You can use Windows Easy Transfer to migrate data from computers running the following operating systems:

- Microsoft Windows 2000 Professional with Service Pack 4 (SP4)
- Microsoft Windows XP Home
- Microsoft Windows XP Professional
- Microsoft Windows XP Professional x64 Edition
- Microsoft Windows Vista

Essentially, Windows Easy Transfer migrates the same set of data as USMT 3.0. This means, in most cases, that the types of migrated and nonmigrated data are the same as those listed earlier in Table 15-1. As with USMT 3.0, Windows Easy Transfer will also migrate settings for some applications, including most Microsoft Office applications and Adobe Acrobat Reader version 5.0 or later. With Microsoft Office Outlook, e-mail settings, contacts, and messages are all migrated.

In most cases, you'll want to install all applications on the destination computer before restoring the user state to ensure that migrated application settings are preserved.

Using Windows Easy Transfer

At a high level, working with Windows Easy Transfer involves the following procedures:

1. Starting Windows Easy Transfer and copying the software to your old computer.
2. Selecting and transferring files and settings to the new computer.
3. Completing the migration.

Starting and Copying the Windows Easy Transfer Software

You can start Windows Easy Transfer and migrate settings from a Windows 2000 or Windows XP computer to a Windows Vista computer by completing the following steps:

1. Log on to the computer running Windows Vista to which you plan to transfer files and settings. If you are transferring files and settings for a specific user rather than all users of a computer, you should log on as that user.
2. Click Start, point to All Programs, Accessories, System Tools, and then click Windows Easy Transfer.
3. Read the introductory message, shown in Figure 15-1, and then click Next.

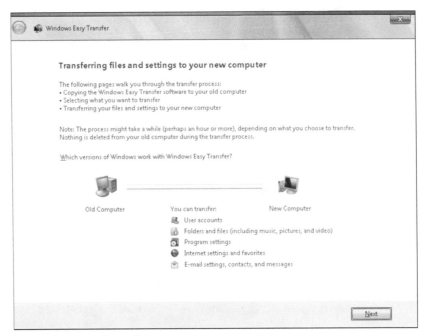

Figure 15-1   Starting Windows Easy Transfer

4.   If you are prompted to close open programs, click Close All to close all open programs.

5.   On the Do You Want To Start A New Transfer Or Continue One In Progress page, click Start A New Transfer.

6.   On the Which Computer Are You Using Now page, click This Is My New Computer.

7.   On the Do You Have A Windows Easy Transfer USB Cable page, do one of the following:

  ❑   Click Yes if you have an easy transfer cable. When prompted, connect the cable between your old and new computers, and then follow the prompts. Skip the rest of the steps.

  ❑   Click No if you don't have an easy transfer cable and then follow the rest of the steps in this procedure.

8.   Computers running Windows 2000 or Windows XP do not have Windows Easy Transfer installed. On the Did You Install Windows Easy Transfer page, click I Need To Install Windows Easy Transfer.

9.   Select the media, drive, or folder as appropriate, and then click Next. Windows Vista immediately copies the Windows Easy Transfer software to the media, drive, or folder you've chosen.

Caution   Don't exit Windows Easy Transfer on the new computer. If you do, you won't be able to connect to the new computer by using a PC-to-PC cable or the network.

10.   Go to the old computer, and follow the procedure outlined in the next section.

Selecting and Transferring Files and Settings

You can select and transfer files and settings to the new computer by completing the following steps:

1. Log on to the old computer as the user whose files and settings you are migrating. If you are migrating all user accounts and their associated files, you should log on using an account with administrator privileges.

2. Insert the media, attach the drive, or connect to the shared folder used in the preceding procedure as appropriate.

3. If Windows Easy Transfer doesn't start automatically, open the MigWiz folder in the media, drive, or shared folder, and then double-click MigWiz.exe.

4. If prompted, close all open programs by clicking the Close All button.

5. On the How Do You Want To Transfer Files And Program Settings To Your New Computer page, specify how you want to transfer files and settings to the new computer by clicking one of the available options. You can transfer files directly by using a network. You can also store the data on a removable storage device or network folder.

6. Follow the prompts to establish a connection or select a save location as appropriate.

7. Once you've connected or selected a save location, you'll be able to select the files and settings to transfer on the What Do You Want To Transfer To Your New Computer page. To transfer files and settings for all users, select Everything – All User Accounts, Files, And Program Settings. To transfer files and settings for the currently logged on user only, select Only My User Accounts, Files, And Program Settings.

8. Click Start Transfer to begin the transfer. Windows Easy Transfer will then inventory all the necessary files. When this operation is complete, you might be prompted to insert a blank, writable CD or DVD, or to plug in a USB flash or tape drive. After you do this, click Next, and then click Close.

9. Complete the migration on the new computer as discussed in the next section.

Finalizing the Migration

You can finalize the migration by completing the following steps:

1. Log on to the computer running Windows Vista to which you plan to transfer files and settings. If you are transferring files and settings for a specific user rather than all users of a computer, you should log on as that user.

2. Click Start, point to All Programs, Accessories, System Tools, and then click Windows Easy Transfer.

3. Read the introductory message, and then click Next.

4. On the Close All Programs page, all open programs must be closed prior to transferring files to the new computer. When prompted, close all open programs by clicking the Close All button, and then click Next.

5. On the Do You Want To Start A New Transfer Or Continue One In Progress page, click Continue A Transfer In Progress.

6. On the Are You Using A Home Network page, specify whether the old computer and new computer are on the same network. Click Yes or No as appropriate and then follow the prompts to complete the migration.

When the transfer is complete, all the selected user accounts, files, and settings should be migrated to the new computer.

Appendix

Installing Windows Vista

Microsoft provides several versions of Windows Vista. Windows Vista can be installed using either interactive or automated setup. This appendix provides an overview of the interactive installation process. For more information about automated setup, see Chapter 15, "Deploying Windows Vista."

Note   This book was written using the Windows Vista Beta to provide an early introduction to the operating system. More so than any other area of Windows Vista, the security features discussed in this book are subject to change. Some of the features might not be included in the final product, and some of the features might be changed substantially.

You can start an interactive installation of Windows Vista using either of the following techniques:

- For a new installation, power on the computer, and insert the Windows Vista distribution media into the computer's CD-ROM or DVD-ROM drive. When prompted, press a key to start the program from the CD or DVD.

- For an upgrade, start the computer and log on using account administrator privileges. Insert the Windows Vista distribution media into the computer's CD-ROM or DVD-ROM drive. The autoloader should start the Windows Vista Setup program automatically. If Setup doesn't start automatically, access the distribution media using Windows Explorer, and then double-click Setup.exe.

Once you've started the Setup program, follow these steps to complete the installation:

1. Click Install Now. Setup starts the installation.

2. If you are connected to a network or the Internet, choose whether to get updates for the installation. If you decide not to get updates, you can update the computer later by using the Windows Update feature.

3. If you aren't using a volume licensed product, enter the product key, and then click Next.

Note   The Automatically Activate Windows When I'm Online check box is selected by default. This option activates Windows when you access the Internet, so you don't have to manually activate the operating system. You can activate the installation manually using the System utility in Control Panel, as discussed later in this section.

4. Read the license terms. If you agree, click I Accept The License Terms (Required To Use Windows), and then click Next.

5. If you are upgrading, you can specify the installation type as either Upgrade or Custom (Advanced). Select Upgrade if you want to upgrade the previously installed operating system to Windows Vista. Otherwise, select Custom (Advanced) to install a clean copy of Windows Vista.

Note   If you install a clean copy of Windows Vista on a computer running an earlier version of Windows, folders and files for the previous installation are moved to a folder named Windows.old and the previous installation will no longer run.

6. Setup asks where you want to install Windows. Select the installation disk from the list, and then click Next. Windows Vista will complete the installation automatically. This process will require several automatic restarts.

7. After Setup finishes, the operating system will be loaded. You can then complete the installation. When prompted, select your country or region and your keyboard layout, and then click Next.

8. On the Choose A User Name And Picture page, you must next create a local machine account. Enter a user name. Type and then confirm a password. Enter an optional password hint, and then choose a picture for the user account. Click Next.

Note   The user account is created as a computer administrator account. Additional local machine accounts can be created later if necessary.

9. On the Type A Computer Name And Choose A Desktop Background page, type a computer name and select a desktop background. Click Next.

10. On the Help Protect Windows Automatically page, select update options. In most cases, you'll want to use the recommended settings to install all available updates and security tools. You can also choose to install updates only or request that Windows ask you later. Click Next.

Caution   The Ask Me Later option disables the update and security features. Typically, this is not the recommended configuration.

11. On the Review Your Time And Date Settings page, make changes as necessary. Click Next.

12. On the You're Ready To Start page, click Start.

When the operating system starts, you can log on using the user account and password you provided previously. The operating system displays the Welcome Center window by default at startup. This tool provides quick access to set up devices, transfer files and settings, add or remove user accounts, and view computer details. If you don't want the Welcome Center window to be displayed the next time you start the computer, clear the Run At Startup check box.

Index

X-Z

About the Author

William R. Stanek (http://www.williamstanek.com/) has over 20 years of hands-on experience with advanced programming and development. He is a leading technology expert, an award-winning author, and a pretty-darn-good instructional trainer. Over the years, his practical advice has helped millions of programmers, developers, and network engineers all over the world. He has written over 25 computer books. Current or forthcoming books include *Microsoft Windows Command-Line Administrator's Pocket Consultant*, *Microsoft Windows Vista Administrator's Pocket Consultant*, *Microsoft Windows Server 2003 Administrator's Pocket Consultant*, Second Edition, and *Windows Server 2003 Inside Out*.

Mr. Stanek has been involved in the commercial Internet community since 1991. His core business and technology experience comes from over 11 years of military service. He has substantial experience in developing server technology, encryption, and Internet solutions. He has written many technical white papers and training courses on a wide variety of topics. He frequently serves as a subject matter expert and consultant.

Mr. Stanek has an MS with distinction in information systems and a BS magna cum laude in computer science. He is proud to have served in the Persian Gulf War as a combat crewmember on an electronic warfare aircraft. He flew on numerous combat missions into Iraq and was awarded nine medals for his wartime service, including one of the United States of America's highest flying honors, the Air Force Distinguished Flying Cross. Currently, he resides in the Pacific Northwest with his wife and children.

About the Experts

Throughout this book, you'll find small chunks of information "From the experts." The following authors generously agreed to contribute to this book's effort to provide early information about a product still in development—that's not an easy task. These three authors are currently coauthoring the *Microsoft Windows Vista Resource Kit*, which is scheduled for publication in 2007. Their contributions to this book are greatly appreciated.

Mitch Tulloch, Most Valuable Professional (MVP), is president of MTIT Enterprises, an IT content development company based in Winnipeg, Canada. Mitch is the author of over a dozen books, including the *Microsoft Encyclopedia of Networking* and the *Microsoft Encyclopedia of Security*. Mitch has written over a hundred articles, is a regular columnist and editorial writer, and contributes articles to several popular Web sites and industry magazines including *NetworkWorld*, *BizTech Magazine*, and *Microsoft Certified Professional Magazine*. For more information about Mitch and his writing activities, see http://www.mtit.com.

Tony Northrup, CISSP, MCSE, and MVP, is a networking consultant and author living in the Boston area. As a consultant, Tony has provided networking guidance to a wide variety of organizations, from Fortune 100 enterprises to nonprofit organizations and small businesses. Tony has authored and coauthored a dozen books on Windows and networking. For more information, see http://www.northrup.org.

Jerry Honeycutt has written more than thirty books, including *Microsoft Windows Desktop Deployment Resource Kit* and *Microsoft Windows Registry Guide, Second Edition*. Jerry is a columnist for Microsoft TechNet, and he is the documentation lead for the Solution Accelerator for Business Desktop Deployment. For more information, see http://www.honeycutt.com.

Prepare for Certification with Self-Paced Training Kits

Official Exam Prep Guides—
Plus Practice Tests

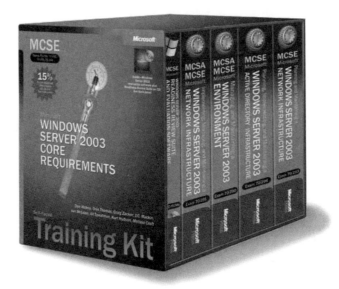

Ace your preparation for the skills measured by the MCP exams—and on the job. With official *Self-Paced Training Kits* from Microsoft, you'll work at your own pace through a system of lessons, hands-on exercises, troubleshooting labs, and review questions. Then test yourself with the Readiness Review Suite on CD, which provides hundreds of challenging questions for in-depth self-assessment and practice.

- **MCSE Self-Paced Training Kit (Exams 70-290, 70-291, 70-293, 70-294): Microsoft® Windows Server™ 2003 Core Requirements.** 4-Volume Boxed Set. ISBN: 0-7356-1953-0. (Individual volumes are available separately.)

- **MCSA/MCSE Self-Paced Training Kit (Exam 70-270): Installing, Configuring, and Administering Microsoft Windows® XP Professional, Second Edition.** ISBN: 0-7356-2152-7.

- **MCSE Self-Paced Training Kit (Exam 70-298): Designing Security for a Microsoft Windows Server 2003 Network.** ISBN: 0-7356-1969-7.

- **MCSA/MCSE Self-Paced Training Kit (Exam 70-350): Implementing Microsoft Internet Security and Acceleration Server 2004.** ISBN: 0-7356-2169-1.

- **MCSA/MCSE Self-Paced Training Kit (Exam 70-284): Implementing and Managing Microsoft Exchange Server 2003.** ISBN: 0-7356-1899-2.

For more information about Microsoft Press® books, visit: **www.microsoft.com/mspress**

For more information about learning tools such as online assessments, e-learning, and certification, visit:
www.microsoft.com/mspress *and* **www.microsoft.com/learning**

Microsoft Windows Server 2003 Resource Kit
The *definitive* resource
for Windows Server 2003!

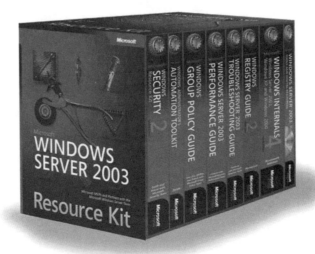

Get the in-depth technical information and tools you need to manage and optimize Microsoft® Windows Server™ 2003—with expert guidance and best practices from Microsoft MVPs, leading industry consultants, and the Microsoft Windows Server team. This official *Resource Kit* delivers seven comprehensive volumes, including:

- **Microsoft Windows® Security Resource Kit, Second Edition**
- **Microsoft Windows Administrator's Automation Toolkit**
- **Microsoft Windows Group Policy Guide**
- **Microsoft Windows Server 2003 Performance Guide**
- **Microsoft Windows Server 2003 Troubleshooting Guide**
- **Microsoft Windows Registry Guide, Second Edition**
- **Microsoft Windows Internals, Fourth Edition**

You'll find 300+ timesaving tools and scripts, an eBook of the entire *Resource Kit*, plus five bonus eBooks. It's everything you need to help maximize system performance and reliability—and help reduce ownership and support costs.

Microsoft Windows Server 2003 Resource Kit
Microsoft MVPs and Partners with the Microsoft Windows Server Team
ISBN: 0-7356-2232-9

For more information about Microsoft Press® books, visit: **www.microsoft.com/mspress**

For more information about learning tools such as online assessments, e-learning, and certification, visit: **www.microsoft.com/learning**

Additional Windows (R2) Resources for Administrators

Published and Forthcoming Titles from Microsoft Press

Microsoft® Windows Server™ 2003 Administrator's Pocket Consultant, Second Edition

William R. Stanek • ISBN 0-7356-2245-0

Here's the practical, pocket-sized reference for IT professionals supporting Microsoft Windows Server 2003—fully updated for Service Pack 1 and Release 2. Designed for quick referencing, this portable guide covers all the essentials for performing everyday system administration tasks. Topics include managing workstations and servers, using Active Directory® directory service, creating and administering user and group accounts, managing files and directories, performing data security and auditing tasks, handling data back-up and recovery, and administering networks using TCP/IP, WINS, and DNS, and more.

MCSE Self-Paced Training Kit (Exams 70-290, 70-291, 70-293, 70-294): Microsoft Windows Server 2003 Core Requirements, Second Edition

Holme, Thomas, Mackin, McLean, Zacker, Spealman, Hudson, and Craft • ISBN 0-7356-2290-6

The Microsoft Certified Systems Engineer (MCSE) credential is the premier certification for professionals who analyze the business requirements and design and implement the infrastructure for business solutions based on the Microsoft Windows Server 2003 platform and Microsoft Windows Server System—now updated for Windows Server 2003 Service Pack 1 and R2. This all-in-one set provides in-depth preparation for the four required networking system exams. Work at your own pace through the lessons, hands-on exercises, troubleshooting labs, and review questions. You get expert exam tips plus a full review section covering all objectives and sub-objectives in each study guide. Then use the Microsoft Practice Tests on the CD to challenge yourself with more than 1500 questions for self-assessment and practice!

Microsoft Windows® Small Business Server 2003 R2 Administrator's Companion

Charlie Russel, Sharon Crawford, and Jason Gerend • ISBN 0-7356-2280-9

Get your small-business network, messaging, and collaboration systems up and running quickly with the essential guide to administering Windows Small Business Server 2003 R2. This reference details the features, capabilities, and technologies for both the standard and premium editions—including Microsoft Windows Server 2003 R2, Exchange Server 2003 with Service Pack 1, Windows SharePoint® Services, SQL Server™ 2005 Workgroup

Edition, and Internet Information Services. Discover how to install, upgrade, or migrate to Windows Small Business Server 2003 R2; plan and implement your network, Internet access, and security services; customize Microsoft Exchange Server for your e-mail needs; and administer user rights, shares, permissions, and Group Policy.

Microsoft Windows Small Business Server 2003 R2 Administrator's Companion

Charlie Russel, Sharon Crawford, and Jason Gerend • ISBN 0-7356-2280-9

Here's the ideal one-volume guide for the IT professional administering Windows Server 2003. Now fully updated for Windows Server 2003 Service Pack 1 and R2, this *Administrator's Companion* offers up-to-date information on core system administration topics for Microsoft Windows, including Active Directory services, security, scripting, disaster planning and recovery, and interoperability with UNIX. It also includes all-new sections on Service Pack 1 security updates and new features for R2. Featuring easy-to-use procedures and handy work-arounds, this book provides ready answers for on-the-job results.

MCSA/MCSE Self-Paced Training Kit (Exam 70-290): Managing and Maintaining a Microsoft Windows Server 2003 Environment, Second Edition

Dan Holme and Orin Thomas • ISBN 0-7356-2289-2

MCSA/MCSE Self-Paced Training Kit (Exam 70-291): Implementing, Managing, and Maintaining a Microsoft Windows Server 2003 Network Infrastructure, Second Edition

J.C. Mackin and Ian McLean • ISBN 0-7356-2288-4

MCSE Self-Paced Training Kit (Exam 70-293): Planning and Maintaining a Microsoft Windows Server 2003 Network Infrastructure, Second Edition

Craig Zacker • ISBN 0-7356-2287-6

MCSE Self-Paced Training Kit (Exam 70-294): Planning, Implementing, and Maintaining a Microsoft Windows Server 2003 Active Directory® Infrastructure, Second Ed.

Jill Spealman, Kurt Hudson, and Melissa Craft • ISBN 0-7356-2286-8

For more information about Microsoft Press® books and other learning products,
visit: **www.microsoft.com/mspress** and **www.microsoft.com/learning**

Additional SQL Server Resources for Administrators

Published and Forthcoming Titles from Microsoft Press

Microsoft® SQL Server™ 2005 Reporting Services *Step by Step*
Hitachi Consulting Services • ISBN 0-7356-2250-7

SQL Server Reporting Services (SRS) is Microsoft's customizable reporting solution for business data analysis. It is one of the key value features of SQL Server 2005: functionality more advanced and much less expensive than its competition. SRS is powerful, so an understanding of how to architect a report, as well as how to install and program SRS, is key to harnessing the full functionality of SQL Server. This procedural tutorial shows how to use the Report Project Wizard, how to think about and access data, and how to build queries. It also walks the reader through the creation of charts and visual layouts to enable maximum visual understanding of the data analysis. Interactivity (enhanced in SQL Server 2005) and security are also covered in detail.

Microsoft SQL Server 2005 Administrator's Pocket Consultant
William R. Stanek • ISBN 0-7356-2107-1

Here's the utterly practical, pocket-sized reference for IT professionals who need to administer, optimize, and maintain SQL Server 2005 in their organizations. This unique guide provides essential details for using SQL Server 2005 to help protect and manage your company's data—whether automating tasks; creating indexes and views; performing backups and recovery; replicating transactions; tuning performance; managing server activity; importing and exporting data; or performing other key tasks. Featuring quick-reference tables, lists, and step-by-step instructions, this handy, one-stop guide provides fast, accurate answers on the spot, whether you're at your desk or in the field!

Microsoft SQL Server 2005 Administrator's Companion
Marci Frohock Garcia, Edward Whalen, and Mitchell Schroeter • ISBN 0-7356-2198-5

Microsoft SQL Server 2005 Administrator's Companion is the comprehensive, in-depth guide that saves time by providing all the technical information you need to deploy, administer, optimize, and support SQL Server 2005. Using a hands-on, example-rich approach, this authoritative, one-volume reference book provides expert advice, product information, detailed solutions, procedures, and real-world troubleshooting tips from experienced SQL Server 2005 professionals. This expert guide shows you how to design high-availability database systems, prepare for installation, install and configure SQL Server 2005, administer services and features, and maintain and troubleshoot your database system. It covers how to configure your system for your I/O system and model and optimize system capacity. The expert authors provide details on how to create and use defaults, constraints, rules, indexes, views, functions, stored procedures, and triggers. This guide shows you how to administer reporting services, analysis services, notification services, and integration services. It also provides a wealth of information on replication and the specifics of snapshot, transactional, and merge replication. Finally, there is expansive coverage of how to manage and tune your SQL Server system, including automating tasks, backup and restoration of databases, and management of users and security.

Microsoft SQL Server 2005 Analysis Services *Step by Step*
Hitachi Consulting Services • ISBN 0-7356-2199-3

One of the key features of SQL Server 2005 is SQL Server Analysis Services—Microsoft's customizable analysis solution for business data modeling and interpretation. Just compare SQL Server Analysis Services to its competition to understand/grasp the great value of its enhanced features. One of the keys to harnessing the full functionality of SQL Server will be leveraging Analysis Services for the powerful tool that it is—including creating a cube, and deploying, customizing, and extending the basic calculations. This step-by-step tutorial discusses how to get started, how to build scalable analytical applications, and how to use and administer advanced features. Interactivity (which is enhanced in SQL Server 2005), data translation, and security are also covered in detail.

Microsoft SQL Server 2005 Express Edition
Step by Step
Jackie Goldstein • ISBN 0-7356-2184-5

Inside Microsoft SQL Server 2005:
The Storage Engine
Kalen Delaney • ISBN 0-7356-2105-5

Inside Microsoft SQL Server 2005:
T-SQL Programming
Itzik Ben-Gan • ISBN 0-7356-2197-7

Inside Microsoft SQL Server 2005:
Query Processing and Optimization
Kalen Delaney • ISBN 0-7356-2196-9

For more information about Microsoft Press® books and other learning products, visit: **www.microsoft.com/mspress** *and* **www.microsoft.com/learning**

What do you think of this book?
We want to hear from you!

Do you have a few minutes to participate in a brief online survey? Microsoft is interested in hearing your feedback about this publication so that we can continually improve our books and learning resources for you.

To participate in our survey, please visit:

www.microsoft.com/learning/booksurvey

And enter this book's ISBN, 0-7356-2284-1. As a thank-you to survey participants in the United States and Canada, each month we'll randomly select five respondents to win one of five $100 gift certificates from a leading online merchant.* At the conclusion of the survey, you can enter the drawing by providing your e-mail address, which will be used for prize notification *only*.

Thanks in advance for your input. Your opinion counts!

Sincerely,

Microsoft Learning

Learn More. Go Further.

To see special offers on Microsoft Learning products for developers, IT professionals, and home and office users, visit: *www.microsoft.com/learning/booksurvey*